P9-DZY-262

The Sex Lives
of Teenagers

The Sex Lives of Teenagers

*Revealing
the Secret World
of Adolescent
Boys and Girls*

LYNN PONTON, M.D.

ALLSTON BRANCH LIBRARY

A DUTTON BOOK

AL BR
HQ27
.P66
2000

Published by the Penguin Group
Penguin Putnam Inc., 375 Hudson Street, New York, New York 10014, U.S.A.
Penguin Books Ltd, 27 Wrights Lane, London W8 5TZ, England
Penguin Books Australia Ltd, Ringwood, Victoria, Australia
Penguin Books Canada Ltd, 10 Alcorn Avenue, Toronto, Ontario, Canada M4V 3B2
Penguin Books (N.Z.) Ltd, 182–190 Wairau Road, Auckland 10, New Zealand

Penguin Books Ltd, Registered Offices: Harmondsworth, Middlesex, England

First published by Dutton, a member of Penguin Putnam Inc.

First Printing, September, 2000
10   9   8   7   6   5   4   3   2

Copyright © Lynn Ponton, 2000
All rights reserved

REGISTERED TRADEMARK — MARCA REGISTRADA

LIBRARY OF CONGRESS CATALOGING-IN-PUBLICATION DATA
Ponton, Lynn E.
    The sex lives of teenagers : revealing the secret world of adolescent boys and girls /
Lynn Ponton.
        p.   cm.
    ISBN 0-525-94561-X (acid-free)
    1. Teenagers—United States—Sexual behavior. 2. Self-esteem in adolescence—United
States. 3. Sex—United States. 4. Homosexuality—United States. I. Title.
HQ27 .P66 2000
306.7'0835—dc21   00-029526

Printed in the United States of America
Set in Times New Roman

Without limiting the rights under copyright reserved above, no part of this publication may be re-
produced, stored in or introduced into a retrieval system, or transmitted, in any form, or by any
means (electronic, mechanical, photocopying, recording, or otherwise), without the prior written
permission of both the copyright owner and the above publisher of this book.

This book is printed on acid-free paper. ∞

To the healthy sexual lives of adolescents

ACKNOWLEDGMENTS

I would like to thank all the teens with whom I have worked over the past twenty-five years. Adolescence is inherently a time of personal struggle, made even more difficult in a culture that sees teenagers in a negative light. My thanks for their passion, energy, and willingness to talk with me about sexual matters. From them, I have learned a great deal.

I am also grateful to my husband, Fred Waldman, and my two daughters, Sarah and Anne Waldman. Their candid reading of the chapters was more than enlightening, it gave this book energy and honesty. Many members of my family were also helpful readers—Elizabeth Ponton, Patricia Barratt, Barbara Loos Chintz, Sally and Suzanne Musho, and Julia Archer.

I would like to thank my friend and assistant, Amy Wilner. Without her, this book would not have been written. Her strong interest in adolescent therapy and her understanding of the writing process supported its birth.

I also owe thanks to my colleagues—first, Jim Lees, for his willingness to critically discuss each chapter in this book, conversations that inspired my courage. Drs. Mary Ann Shafer, Madeline Meyer, Charles

Irwin, Lois Flaherty, Ruth Noel, Marlene Mills, Larry Brown, Ralph Di-Clemente, Gina Wingood, Gilbert Herdt, Joycelyn Elders, John Sadler, Sam Judice, Alan Skolnikoff, and Stella LeFevre; all read and discussed parts of this books with me. Their help was crucial.

Amy Rennert, my agent, helped this book to find a home at Dutton/Penguin. Brian Tart, my editor at Dutton, skillfully guided the manuscript to publication. Both have a deep respect for teenagers, and I hope we work together for years to come. Peter Kramer and Lenore Terr, fellow writers and psychiatrists both, were also helpful in the publishing process.

A special thanks to the teens who read or talked with me about this book: Paul, Michelle, Monica, Nathalie, Kristin, Emily, Jonathan, and, of course, Anne and Sarah. I thank them for helping me find the words.

Finally, the stories here are based on true stories, but I have had to make many changes to protect the identities of the patients and their parents. I have often made symbolically equivalent substitutes for aspects of a patient's or parent's identity and life circumstances; occasionally I have grafted parts of other patients' or parents' identities onto those I have written about. Often dialogue is fictional, and my personal reflections post hoc. If the disguises are penetrable, it is only by the patients and parents themselves. Any readers who believe they recognize any of the patients or parents in this volume will, I am certain, be mistaken.

CONTENTS

The Sex Lives
of Teenagers

INTRODUCTION
Forbidden Fruit

This book grew out of my interest in and work with adolescent risk-taking. In my earlier book, *The Romance of Risk: Why Teenagers Do the Things They Do,* I endorsed the idea that risk-taking is the primary tool that adolescents use to discover and develop their identities. I also noted that risk-taking, by definition, can go in either direction, of success or failure, and showed how adults can play a formative role in helping teens learn how to assess risk and make healthier choices.

Sexuality is an area of life that is fraught not with danger, as so many believe, but with risk—with the potential for positive or negative outcomes, success or failure. This is no more or less true for adolescents than it is for adults. The difference is that most adolescents don't yet have well-developed risk-assessment skills. In addition, sexuality in our culture is, despite cries about how steeped in sex we are, still a highly taboo subject. There is plenty of noise about the topic of teenage sexuality in general, but there is not much actual communication with these teenagers.

If we want adolescents to be healthy, we have to promote their learning to act in their own best interests. To do that, we have to come to grips with the fact that sexuality is a vital aspect of teens' lives. We can wish it were otherwise, but wishing can't make it so. All adolescents have sex lives, whether they are sexually active with others, with themselves, or seemingly not at all. The question is whether they are going to have healthy experiences, at any or every level of sexual activity. If we want young people to develop into healthy adults, this is a key concern. Parents and other adults can help teens to develop the skills and awareness they need to make healthy choices in this area.

Teenagers often intuitively understand that their sexuality and sexual behaviors involve risk. An adolescent's ability to assess risks realistically requires some practice with weighing dangers and benefits. Peers and emotions play strong roles in most adolescent risk-taking. This is never more apparent than when looking at sex. Teenagers need the assistance of adults to better understand how to take on risks and assess the consequences, and with that acquired knowledge, make the best choices. This is a complex process. Most adults struggle with questions about sex. To expect teens to make their way without adult guidance only increases their ignorance, fear, and rate of failure.

It takes tremendous courage and strength to parent adolescents. There is nothing quite as unpredictable and challenging. It also takes courage and strength to confront ourselves in the process. *Am I comfortable having this conversation with my child? Do I have to? Do I have to tell them details of my private life?* For their part, teens ask some of the very same questions: *Do I have to have this conversation with my parents? Do I have to share the details?* And still, they do want to be heard and understood, even if they can't yet have the conversation with their parents.

In this book, the role of sexuality in adolescent development is shown through stories based on real teens and parents. Although I see teens predominantly in the Bay Area, they come from all backgrounds, and I believe that their struggles reflect those of teens throughout the United States. I hope the reader comes to appreciate both the potentially devastating consequences of ongoing silence, and the profound advantages of open dialogue.

Teens are battling to understand sex during a period when teenage sexuality is changing. Teens and parents need to be aware of important trends. Both boys and girls are entering puberty at least two years earlier than previous generations. This means they are ready for sex earlier physically, but not emotionally or cognitively. Not only are teens having their first sexual experiences earlier than previous generations, at an average age now of sixteen, but they are taking greater risks in this area, with consequences that include sexually transmitted diseases, unwanted pregnancy, and pathological relationships, among others. HIV is still penetrating the teen population; half of all new cases occur in people under the age of twenty-five. Sexuality has become increasingly explicit in videos, movies, and music. As part of the continuing evolution of the sexual liberation and women's movements of the 1960s, the 1990s have been a battleground for many sexual issues, including struggles about gender and sexual stereotypes for adolescents. While gender roles are changing dramatically in the workplace, they are being enforced more rigidly in the school yard. We can even see this visually in extreme physical stereotypes: thin, waiflike girls and exaggerated, hypermasculine boys, each struggling to identify their sexuality in a rapidly changing landscape. A third group, the androgynous teens, is also emerging. In working with these teens, I have often faced this question: *When bodies are the primary means of articulating their emerging sexuality, how do teens manage?* To communicate about the complex subject of sexuality, teens and parents need a language as well as practical guidelines.

This is also a period of fierce disagreement about how the subject of sex should be handled. Sexuality in general, and adolescent sexuality in particular, have become part of an intense political struggle with some supporting celibacy, and others advocating a full range of sexual activity for young teens. The media, which uses adolescent sexuality to create excitement and sell products, only adds to the confusion. Many schools and parents have opted out, backing away from the controversy. Americans have never found it easy to talk about sex—from our Puritan roots through the sexual revolution, it remains a controversial and taboo topic. Missing among all the controversy are sensible, down-to-earth discussions about the choices teenagers are really facing.

Parents struggle with the sex lives of their adolescents. I never understood this as well as when I traveled the United States and Canada, speaking on adolescent risk-taking. Over and over again, parents asked these questions: *How much does my teen need to know about my sexual relationship? How can I help my daughter develop a healthy relationship with her body before she becomes sexually active? What am I supposed to do when I find love letters written to my son from another boy? How should I react when I discover my child's boyfriend or girlfriend sleeping in their bedroom?* Often the parents I encounter in my practice have already reacted—and, typically, without success.

I encourage parents to think and talk about their sexual codes and experience to develop a morality without becoming moralistic. Adolescent sexuality can bring both pain and pleasure to young people and to the parents who love and support them. If more people could view adolescent sexuality as a potentially positive experience, rather than sanctioning it as one fraught with danger, young people would have a better chance of developing healthier patterns and making more positive choices.

All explorations of sexuality are personal. Sexual development is not specific to teenagers, but they are often miscast by it, as mere bodies filled with raging hormones. Exploring sexuality is an important part of all phases of life—childhood, adolescence, adulthood, and older age. All generations struggle with the pleasures and burdens of forbidden fruit, and hopefully all readers can learn from these stories.

Forbidden Fruit: Sexuality, Culture, and Teens

The society in which teens are being raised plays an important role in determining what the sex-role pressures are, and how strongly they will be enforced. Many falsely believe that American society is a sexually permissive culture. It is not. Several experts see it as a hybrid of a restrictive and semi-restrictive society, changing across historical periods. Others see it as semi-restrictive. A permissive society would allow the transition of young people into sexual activity in a continuous fashion beginning in childhood. Instead, American teens are faced with taboo, miscommunication, and often direct prohibition that may contradict other messages they receive from the culture at large.

In the United States, the First Amendment and an ongoing societal tradition work against any type of censorship. This applies to all forms of media—film, radio, print, advertising, television, music video, and, most recently, the Internet. Many of these media have a long-standing history of using adolescent sexuality to attract audiences and sell products.

In addition, with a rapidly growing percentage of teens in the population, a larger number of media efforts are being targeted at teens, efforts that are increasingly violent and sexual in nature. It is important to remember that the media can and do promote unhealthy risk-taking of all types of adolescents. An example of this is anorectic teen models being used to sell products and then the risk-taking becomes less dangerous because it is socially and culturally reinforced. Teenage and teenage-like bodies are also used to sell products. Teens in the media can create false sexual images, lives impossible for the teen viewer . . . sexual images that leave them frustrated and desirous. One example of this can be seen in the popular teenage television show, *Dawson's Creek*. Although the show addresses a range of adolescent sexual behaviors, it also enforces strong gender stereotypes for boys and girls. The boys are "masculine" and the girls are "feminine." There is a double standard, the "wild girl" suffers when her sexual history is revealed. Unrealistic body images are also put forward as handsome white young people cavort in J. Crew clothing. The consumer goods are sold, so are the ideals as these kids are assumed to represent all teens. Unfortunately, the marketing of consumer goods has gone hand in hand with the development of adolescence. The word "teenager" emerged in the late 1940s—a sexier, carefree version of youth designed to promote spending.

In the United States, politics have always played a role in sexual matters. During the past year, when the story of President Clinton's sexual relationship with Monica Lewinsky was revealed to the nation, the country showed an interest, and adolescents were no exception. The teens in my office asked some interesting questions, though. *Why isn't it sex just because he doesn't come inside her? What's the big deal about saving the dress (you should see my closet!)? Is an intern like a student? No matter what he says, they had a relationship—right?*

The 1920s saw the beginning of significant change about sexual ideas in the United States, but sexual intercourse was still supposed to be part of or lead to marriage, and homosexuals and unwed teen mothers were viewed as deviants. The 1960s, a period of massive social upheaval, saw vital changes in the arena of all sexual behavior, including that of adolescents. These changes were sparked by civil rights groups, feminists, the emergence of the gay liberation movement in the late 1960s, and youth and college activist groups. Many things changed among them. The age for a teen's first experience with sexual intercourse decreased, dropping steadily from 18 years to 16. Awareness about the use of images of young girls as consumer objects emerged for the first time. In January of 1973, the Supreme Court, in the case of Roe v. Wade, declared unconstitutional any restrictions on abortions in the first trimester. Throughout the 1970s, the gay movement steadily worked to change the way homosexuality and bisexuality were taught in schools and were successful in modifying hostile and often pathological presentations.

These changes did not occur without a struggle. By the late 1970s, there was a growing and increasingly well-organized movement opposed to the gay movement, abortion, and more progressive sex education—the New Right. Liberals and conservatives continue to battle over sexual issues today. The crisis of AIDS and the continuing movement of sexuality into commercial arenas are part of this.

Current conflicts in the adolescent arena include teen confidentiality, the type of sexual education programs (abstinence, range of choice, or none at all), and teen access to birth control—all highly charged topics, not only for parents and teens, but just about everyone else, too.

My Own Path

More than ten years ago, I began working on a government grant that would care for high-risk and HIV-infected youth in San Francisco. This grant, which is still ongoing, was fortunate for the adolescents in the Bay Area.

I was fortunate to have been chosen to be part of that group because I have learned a great deal from others working on the project, but even more importantly, from the teens themselves. I learned a great deal from these kids: I learned that most teens lack important knowledge about not only sexual behaviors, but their own sexuality. I learned that while most teens are participating in a search to discover these things, they are also terrified about what could happen to them or what others might think about them. Misconceptions are everywhere. Often, there is no one to turn to—not parents, not other adults, not even friends. The grant gave me the opportunity to begin to talk with teens about sex, both those I met with through the grant and those I saw in my private practice or at the university where I teach. It opened my eyes about this vital part of teens' lives, and, ultimately, changed how I worked with all of my patients, even the adults.

So in my own experience, there was no great teacher who helped me understand adolescent sexuality. The truth is that all of the theories helped me think about it theoretically, but none of them really helped me understand it. For that, there was only one route to enlightenment—listening to teens themselves. And, as it turned out, their stories only sounded remotely like the theories! Finally, becoming the parent of adolescents has taught me, too, in ways I could never have expected. My own interest also has been spurred on by my psychoanalytic work with adolescents—work which has helped me to better understand the unconscious aspects of adolescent sexuality, specifically, fantasy and dreams.

In attempting to assist teens with their understanding of sexuality, adolescent development and risk-taking provide models. As with risk, teens are going to experiment with their sexuality. For the most part, teens themselves see this experimentation as extremely positive, and say that it helps them define who they are. Experimentation with sexuality involves risk—physical, psychological, social. It also involves risk assessment, a process whereby teens take on challenges and learn how to make healthy choices. I believe that we have let our teenagers down in this area. We may provide condoms, but we don't offer conversations. Yet if we're open, we can hear teenagers tell us that they want to talk about this topic. They offer us this challenge. It is time to listen.

Finally, I want to acknowledge that this book discusses many sexual matters frankly, and the language is often direct. This is not intended to shock or disturb readers. Sex and sexuality are too often packaged as the proverbial tantalizing forbidden fruit, alluring but taboo, compelling but dangerous. The mixed messages, mystery, and misinformation that inevitably accompany such taboo serve to confuse, mislead, and jeopardize. It isn't easy for anyone in our society to be direct about sex. But adolescents have sexual lives, and they need guidance to learn how to assess the risks involved. The more straightforward we can be, the better the chances that those young lives will be healthy ones.

Studs and Sluts
The Dating Game

She feels angry, but also bad. She starts to think she is a pig—or a slut. —Melissa

Guys are supposed to know how to handle this kind of stuff. —Jacob

Parental concern about adolescent dating or courtship begins very early, in many cultures at the time a child is born. For parents in the United States, their worry often coincides with their child's actual involvement or interest in the process. I never understood this as well as I did on the day I attended a roundtable conference called by the head of my daughter's middle school to discuss growing concerns about "social issues" in the sixth-grade class. I was curious about the topic, both as a mother and as a psychiatrist, and I rearranged my morning patient schedule so I could attend. The night before, my eleven-year-old daughter decided that she had to prepare me. She was glad that I was planning to go, but she also wanted to set me straight. I had noticed all week that she and her friends were buzzing about the upcoming meeting. Clearly, this was an area of great interest.

"Mom, listen. The class is getting along really well. There are kids that are 'going together,' but it just means that they're good friends. Debbie [the administrator who had called the meeting] doesn't understand that. She thinks we're actually dating. She told us that we were too young to even be thinking about it. You have to go, Mom, and give her our perspective." I had to smile at the way she had framed "our perspective." She didn't know I had already begun the task.

Several days earlier, when Debbie had called about the parents' meeting, I had asked her: exactly what were the "social issues" in the sixth grade that were generating so much concern? Debbie told me that she had been contacted by several parents—all mothers of boys, she said—upset because their sons were being bothered at home after school by phone calls from the girls in their classes. The girls apparently were quite persistent (". . . wouldn't take no for an answer . . . kept calling back . . ."). The mothers said that not only they, but their sons, too, were upset by the girls' phone calls, which took time away from the boys' studies and basketball, the things they really wanted to do. Several of these mothers had suggested a moratorium, or at least a curfew for phone calls.

Debbie and I had chatted briefly about both the expected social behaviors of sixth graders, and the behavior of this class in particular. She noted that these boys and girls had socialized together from an early age. I mentioned that despite parental concerns, their greater sociability could also be considered a strength. After all, this class had social skills that other classes did not, and they genuinely enjoyed spending time together. Debbie laughed when I said this, but she agreed, and she thought that sharing this perspective might shed a different light on the "troublesome" behavior. I hung up wondering what was so troubling about telephone conversations between boys and girls.

I arrived early the day of the meeting, but in a few minutes the room was filled. Extra chairs had to be provided—three times. Both mothers and fathers had come. Debbie was surprised. The attendance was better than it had been at any of the other roundtables. The discussion began slowly, since many of the parents were still clutching coffeecups and blinking back sleep. Debby tried to stimulate dialogue, first mentioning important general aspects of adolescent development and then shifting the focus to this particular class of sixth graders. As she had with me, she noted that in earlier years, both the boys and the girls had been more social than the typical class, so in many ways their current interest in social activities was a logical next step. I could see that Debbie had decided I shouldn't really have to go out on a limb with this perspective after all.

After she spoke, the conversation warmed up in a hurry. Several mothers of boys reported their concerns about girls telephoning their sons, emphasizing that their sons were upset by the number of calls that they were receiving. They again mentioned that the calls were keeping their sons away from more important activities, their studies and sports among them. The biggest problem, they said, was that their sons didn't know how to get the girls off the telephone. Several made the suggestion of adopting a class-wide curfew for phone calls, and some said they had set private curfews for their sons already. I heard my daughter's voice in my head: "Mom, you have to stand up for us."

Until this point, no mothers of girls had spoken out. I scanned the room searching for their faces, wondering what their response to all this was. I was one of them, and I had to admit that I found myself feeling pretty defensive about the way that the girls' behavior was being discussed, even if the psychiatrist part of me was not surprised. These mothers wanted to protect their sons. The girls' phone calls were threatening in many ways, not only to homework and basketball. Many of the sixth-grade girls were more than a head taller than the boys, were physically developed, and could talk rings around the boys socially. Yet I believed more was going on than that. The expressions used to describe the girls and their behavior were interesting: "out of control," "relentless," "calling back repeatedly," "did not listen to me," even "devious" (because a girl had failed to identify herself when she called). These women were beginning to regard the girls as predatory as they tested out their blossoming social skills on the telephone.

So there I was, feeling both defensive and interested, when the mother of a girl finally spoke. "What I'm worried about is my daughter's eating. She and her friends have stopped eating lunch. Have you noticed this, Debbie?"

The school administrator was clearly as surprised by this question as I was. "Well, uh, that's important, but I am not sure that it is what we've been talking about—"

She was interrupted by a second mother, then a third, both echoing the first one's comments. They were concerned about the food in the school cafeteria. Did it offer choices that their daughters could eat? They mentioned that several of their daughters were experimenting with vegetarianism because they were worried about getting too fat.

At this point Debbie turned to me, gently guiding me by mentioning how fortunate it was for the group to have a parent who happened to be a child and adolescent psychiatrist with some expertise in disordered eating. I followed her lead and told the parents that many girls at eleven or twelve begin to have problems with eating, believing that they are too fat and struggling to fit the image offered by advertisements that portray adolescent girls, but I was still puzzled by the major shift in the conversation. As I spoke, I struggled to put it together. How did the boys' mothers' concerns about frequent phone calls relate to the girls' disturbed body images? The boys' mothers' comments were clearly threatening to the girls' mothers. I had felt it, too. But what had the response been? *Poor girls, preoccupied with their physical appearances, suffering at the hands of the media and social expectations . . .* clearly, in this light, they were no threat to anyone.

I needed to say something more than a doctor's spiel. I shifted from the girls' eating back to the social concerns, reminding the group of Debbie's description of this class as more socially advanced than others, both the boys and the girls. They had always hung out together, having many girl-boy parties before they got to the sixth grade. I asked the other parents if we could think about how we could nurture this unique gift of our children's and help them to continue to develop their already advanced social skills in safe, healthy ways that were fun.

Silence. Then the boys' moms again started talking about the girls' phone calls, and the girls' moms returned to their daughters' eating. No consensus was reached about either of these problems by the time the meeting ended.

The roundtable gave me a lot to think about. Obviously the interests of these mothers were focused in very different places, depending, it seemed, on whether they had a son or a daughter. Although this meeting involved only thirty parents at most, I believed that their concerns are vital to many parents who have children in the sixth or seventh grade. One of the most interesting points was how opinionated the boys' mothers were. Along with the language they used to describe the girls—"out of control," "relentless," "devious"—their attitudes suggested a theme that is consistent with a larger cultural perspective on girls' developing sexuality: that it is frightening and needs to be curtailed, brought back in line. To add to this problem for girls, society's expectations are changing, becoming increasingly confusing, though no less negative. Girls who reveal or act on developing sexual feelings in an outright manner are frequently sanctioned, not only by parents but by other children. Is it such a mystery, then, that some will try to "diet" enough to limit or stop their bodies from developing?

Prior to the 1960s, girls were expected to "hold the line," avoiding sex until they were married, policing boys' sexual feelings as well as their own. With the development and widespread distribution of birth control pills, the 1960s and 1970s promoted an attitude of sexual experimentation for adolescents of both sexes. In the 1990s, three-quarters of all adolescents are sexually active by the age of nineteen, but the "double standard" is flourishing.

Sexually active girls and boys continue to be treated very differently. The girls that I see both in my clinical psychiatric practice and the pediatric clinics are very concerned about what others will think if their sexual activity or even interest is discovered. Their fear of discovery is not limited to their parents and other adults, but encompasses their girlfriends, classmates, and just about everybody else in their lives. They describe feelings of genuine desire as well as social pressure to have sex, sometimes applied by boyfriends, sometimes by other girls, but at the same time they are frightened that they will be condemned. Most boys have a decidedly different attitude. They, too, can be extremely fearful, especially when they are young, but as they become older, these fears often give way to a sense of accomplishment and pride about their sexual activities, and for many there is a shift in focus to the mechanics of sex.

Melissa's Message

During the next few weeks I continued to wonder about the roundtable discussion. How were the girls' telephone calls to the boys really being perceived? I remembered growing up in the fifties and early sixties, when teenage girls were openly told not to call boys. Few did. Today, girls are calling, but how different are the attitudes from the fifties?

This wasn't entirely an academic question. I had already been struggling with it in my work with some girls, most recently Melissa, a sixth grader who was embroiled in a struggle with her classmates to avoid being labeled a "slut." I had worked with her several years earlier for a few sessions after a treasured grandparent had died. Her mother recently brought her back for school problems.

A green-eyed twelve-year-old, Melissa was noisily talking with her mother, Linda, and my assistant when I entered my waiting room to call her in. All three of them were kneeling on the floor, looking at a collection of drawings that Melissa had spread out. Curious, I knelt down on the floor to look at them. Melissa was a fine artist. I had seen other drawings of hers and had always admired them, but I was particularly struck by these. They were all animals, and not the Walt Disney variety, but gross, ugly animals. In one, a pig with a swollen head and a protruding nose with spiky hairs visible in the nostrils had its eyes narrowed, sharp with anger that seemed to leap off the page. She was standing on her hind legs, wearing un-piglike attire, including platform shoes that closely resembled Melissa's own. At the top of the drawing, Melissa had scrawled, "Pignose—A Slut." The other two drawings included a dog and a cow, also wearing platform shoes and given nicknames—"Bitchy" and "Big Tits" respectively—and the word "slut." The dog's genitalia and the cow's mammary glands were drawn in sharp detail.

Melissa was waiting for a response, but the room was very quiet as her mother, my assistant, and I stared at the drawings. Linda seemed shocked, her face now a deep shade of pink. Unsure what to say myself, I suggested to Melissa that we bring the drawings into her session. Her mother seemed relieved. She may have thought that I was going to handle it somehow, but honestly I was still unsure how to proceed after Melissa and I had spread out the drawings on the floor of my office. She broke the silence by sarcastically saying, "They don't exactly fit in with your other art."

"Not exactly," I said. My walls are covered with prints of Monet's water lilies. "But that artist used his imagination a lot, like you. He was nearly blind when he painted them, so he had to rely on his imagination."

"Wish I was blind at my school. It would help. Blind and deaf."

"How would that help?"

"I wouldn't have to hear it if they call me 'Pignose.'" Then, hardening her jaw, she said, "I actually like 'slut' better."

"They call you 'slut'?" I asked.

She looked at me like I was from the Dark Ages and said, "When was the last time you were in high school? They call all the girls sluts, that is, if they're . . . interested."

"Interested in what?"

At this point Melissa looked at me like I was impossibly stupid.

"What do you think? Interested in boys, in sex. If you show *any* interest, and even if you don't, you're labeled. Not the boys, though, they're the 'studs' . . . the *studs,* Dr. Ponton."

At this point Melissa's face was filled with anger, and she began to crumple her drawings. She also began to cry.

"Melissa, let's look at the drawings together before you destroy them," I said.

I picked up the pig and placed it closer to her so that we could examine it together. I didn't like looking at the picture. The enlarged head and nose were both ugly and frightening, but as I examined it, I could see how skillfully she had combined human and animal features—the pig's hooves clearly usable in the plastic platform shoes. Staring at the drawing, I was reminded of art that depicted Minotaurs, those mysterious creatures with a combination of human and animal features. Minotaurs often represented some of the complexity of human sexuality, linking animal instincts and human fantasies.

Still unsure about how to talk to Melissa about this, I mentioned the unique combination of shoes and hooves, indicating that I could see how carefully she had drawn them.

She smiled. "I like them, too, but I don't know exactly why. The ugly head, the nose, even the pig—pignose—that's something the kids at school have put on me. I guess that's the slut part. I hate it like I hate them. But I like the feet. The feet are different—part pig, part girl." She laughed. "I guess the high-heeled platforms are the girl part. Something that a girl might wear, on a date, if she felt sexy and wanted to attract a boy. She would be feeling good about herself in them, but then"—her face darkened—"the others would see her in the shoes, wearing those flashy high-heeled platforms, and they would have to put her down. They would call her 'Pignose' then."

"Pretty sad. Does the girl forget about how good she feels about her platforms, then?"

"Yeah, she forgets. But even more, she's so upset that the whole picture is ruined. She wonders if she should wear the shoes. She feels angry, but also bad. She starts to think she is a pig—or a slut."

"Sounds like it's hard enough to wear the shoes to begin with."

"Yeah, it's not easy."

After talking about her feelings a few minutes longer, Melissa and I picked up her drawings and placed them in a folder. She agreed to save them for further discussion. I could see that she was feeling better. We hadn't solved her problem, but we had worked together to help her identify it.

Like many twelve-year-olds, Melissa was starting to have sexual feelings. They were showing up in several ways—in her drawings, high-heeled platforms, and in phone calls to boys.

Melissa had her own private prohibitions about showing her sexuality—were the shoes too flashy?—but it was hard for her to feel them when she was being called a slut by the boys at school. Instead of paying attention to her own complex feelings, she focused on her anger at the boys, in many ways a safer experience. She wasn't calling herself a slut; they were.

Melissa's mother met with me after my session with her daughter. Linda was practical and wanted some immediate answers to her questions about what was going on with her daughter, but her voice was shaking with emotion and tight lines formed on her face. She was an experienced mother, having raised two sons now in their twenties, but Melissa was her first and only daughter, and she was frightened by what she saw happening to her, and by her own reactions to it.

"Dr. Ponton, I was so upset when the principal called. It was awful. You have no idea what it's like when they call and tell you that your daughter is being called a slut at school. First, I was angry with the boys. You know, *how dare they* . . . But then I started to get these sneaking doubts about Melissa. After all, she does call boys on the telephone. She wears tight T-shirts and those high-heeled platforms. I wondered if she might be contributing to it. Is she leading them on? It's such a horrible question to have to ask about your own daughter. It's so different from what happened with my sons."

"How?" I asked, hoping Linda's answer would help me, but at this point in our discussion I also hoped that it would help Linda reflect on the period when she had parented her sons so successfully, and acquire the courage to face her current situation.

"For starters, no one ever called me to tell me that one of my sons was being called a slut. You know, there isn't even a word for a male slut. It makes *me* feel so vulnerable, the mother of a slut. How would you feel?"

I had thought about Linda's question before she asked it. Only four days had passed since the roundtable. It wasn't so far from "devious" phone calls to slut.

Developmentally appropriate behaviors on the part of the girls are often perceived as sexual. Smiles can be seen as seductive, a certain walk as provocative, a phone call as manipulative. Even the biologically determined appearance of breast buds can be viewed as willfully sexy. An all too common reaction to the developing bodies of adolescent girls is for their peers, both male and female, to call them "sluts." Many girls discuss their fears of being labeled. Some consciously shut off their sexuality; others, like Melissa, show anger; and still others decide to flaunt it. If they are sluts, so be it, they'll act like sluts; in fact, they'll become the slut to end all sluts.

After my sessions with Melissa and Linda, I climbed the two flights of stairs from my office to my home to discover one of my daughters and four other teenage girls sitting around the kitchen table, eating after-school snacks and reviewing their day. I sat down and poured myself a glass of orange juice. They kept talking. In only a few minutes the word slut came up in conversation here, too. It seemed as if the term itself and its implications were as common as water.

"This girl, she calls me a slut, can you believe it? Me? Just for wearing a red tank top? You should have seen what she was wearing!"

Unable to resist joining in this conversation, I asked what "slut" meant for them. I got a couple of responses.

"Not always critical, but mostly so."

"It's a put-down, sexier than bitch, but more negative, too."

"It's okay when your friends use it, but even then you remember it."

"Yeah, it's how they say it."

"You can even know when they're thinking it about you, like, it's in the air, even if they don't tell you."

"How do you feel after someone says it?" I asked.

The girl in the red tank top laughed. "I just tell them to fuck themselves. Then I go right on doing what I'm doing—do it more, in fact." Here she gave a big grin and her friends laughed. Yet the others at the table didn't look as sure of themselves.

One of them said, "You think about it, even if you don't want to. You can't forget it."

Another said, "It changes how you feel about the person who said it. She's right. I don't forget it."

"Can guys be sluts?" I asked.

"They should be. They act like it, but they don't get called it."

"What are they called instead?" I asked. The noisy table suddenly became quiet.

"It isn't the same with guys. A guy who pushes you over the top is called a fucker or a bastard, but it isn't the same as when they call a girl a slut."

"A guy who's like super sexual—full of himself—he's a hottie, maybe a player if he hooks up with everyone, but probably a stud."

Another said, "A stud, yeah, he's a stud all right," and the rest of the table agreed.

"Seems unfair, he's a stud and she's a slut," said the girl who couldn't forget what it was like to be called a slut.

"Who ever said it was fair?" said another.

I left the table carrying more than my glass of orange juice with me, their last words ringing in my ears. "Who ever said it was fair?"

Jacob's Turn

First the parents' meeting, then my hour with Melissa, followed by the conversation with my daughter's friends—studs and sluts. If that was it, where were the studs? They weren't sitting here in my office. The sluts were, though. Girls who are sexually stereotyped often end up in a therapist's office, and my practice was no exception. I have written elsewhere about ten-year-old Mary, who had been called "Busty" and "Cow" by her entire elementary school, including her four older brothers. She had been brought to see me because she was writing essays about death. I worked with her parents, the teachers, and even her brothers to try and stop the name-calling, but Mary and I both knew that it was going to take more than that for her to heal. Painful words like "busty," "slut," and "cow" stay in your memory a long time. "You don't forget," said Mary.

Yet boys are not immune to confusion about their emerging sexuality.

Urged on by concerned parents, Jacob had come to see me after his house had been destroyed by the Loma Prieta earthquake. His computer and most of his childhood toys had crashed, along with part of his life. Fourteen-year-old Jacob was carrying Benji, Cat, and Joe—his surviving toys—in his backpack the first day he came to see me. This six-foot-three teenager with a shadow of a beard and the physique of a twenty-five-year-old man fooled me the first time I saw him in my waiting room. Where was the sobbing child that his mother had described over the telephone? I discovered that child only moments later when he dumped Benji, a worn purple Care Bear; Cat, a tiger with one ear; and a GI Joe with one remaining leg, on my carpet. Jacob then proceeded to cry harder than almost any child I've ever had in my office. "They're the only survivors—the only ones left."

"You're here, too, Jacob."

"The wreckage crew said all my toys were lost, and I wasn't even there. I should have been with them." He then picked up his Care Bear and held it to his chest. "Benji had five brothers and sisters—all gone."

"Jacob, what would you have done if you had been there?"

"Saved 'em, but I guess that's pretty stupid. My dad said I would have gone down with them. He says I was lucky we weren't in the house when the quake hit."

"He's right, but it doesn't stop you from wanting to be there."

"No. I was supposed to be there."

Thirty minutes and four tissues later, this muscular fourteen-year-old gently returned Benji, Cat, and Joe to his backpack—their traveling home, as he called it—dried his tears, and loped out of my office.

Jacob came to see me several more times, and we talked about what he and his family had lost in the earthquake. During these weeks I began to hear comments about Jacob from girls who saw him in my waiting room, either before or after their sessions. He was referred to as "Young David" by a nineteen-year-old college student, and two girls planned to arrive early for their sessions, hoping that they would run into him. One of them nicknamed him "Studman" and left a note for him in my waiting room, which I found and threw away.

Jacob seemed oblivious to this attention. He continued to work steadily in his sessions, now talking about the memorial that he was building to remember his lost toys. One afternoon he brought in a poem he wrote, "Taken Away." He was reading it to me when he suddenly changed the subject. "Dr. Ponton, this substitute teacher at my school, Sylvia, she, uh, asked me out."

I was surprised, and may even have looked it as I met Jacob's trusting brown eyes searching my face. "She did?"

"Yeah, she said I was gorgeous, and she asked me if I want to go out for coffee Friday night."

"What did you say?"

"I didn't say anything. I think she thinks I'm gonna go with her." After he said this, he started grinding his hiking boots into my carpet.

My mind raced suddenly. *How do we talk about this? Fourteen years old, but he looks twenty-five. Maybe the teacher didn't know that he was a freshman, maybe she did.*

"What do you think about it, Jacob?"

"Confusing," and he stared at the floor. Then, looking at his backpack, he started grinning. "She wouldn't ask me out if she knew I carried a GI Joe in my backpack."

"Sounds like you're worried that she's expecting something different from what she might be getting."

"I worry that she's expecting anything."

"Do you think she knows you're fourteen?"

He turned red and looked down again. "Probably not. I didn't tell her, if that's what you're asking. There are lots of student teachers at the school.

Maybe she thinks I'm one of them. God, if she found out I was a fresh-man—"

"What if she did?"

"It would be weird."

"But you are one."

"Yeah, but what if she already knows?" Here he swallowed hard, and his eyes met mine straight on. "Dr. Ponton, this isn't the first time this has happened to me. About a year ago, when I was helping out at Rec Camp, this woman started sending me letters where she described sexual things I could do to her—like sexual stuff. She was the stepmom of one of the kids."

"How'd you handle it?"

"I threw 'em away."

"Did you tell your mom or dad?"

"No. Do you think I should have told 'em? Should I tell them about this teacher?"

"What do you think?"

"I don't want to. Guys are supposed to know how to handle this kind of stuff."

"Do you feel like you can?"

"I'm fourteen."

"That's right. You're fourteen. It's okay to ask for help."

We decided that Jacob should write a letter to give to the substitute teacher, making it very clear how old he was. He and I also agreed that he would talk with his school counselor the next day and obtain his advice. Jacob left the session thanking me, expressing relief that he had figured out how to handle the situation.

Jacob and I had further conversations about women coming on to him. I listened carefully and learned a great deal. Perhaps not surprisingly, a part of Jacob was pleased with the attention.

"It makes me feel great, Dr. Ponton, until I think about what they want to do to me, or worse, what they expect me to do to them."

Much of our conversation was focused on the doing part. Jacob didn't want to look like he was as sexually naive as he actually was. Slowly, an-other theme emerged in our talks—these women didn't even know him, hadn't ever talked to him, and they wanted sex. Well, maybe not intercourse, but something explicitly sexual with Jacob. Why? He wanted to understand.

Why Studs and Sluts?

Both Melissa and Jacob were what might be called "early develop-ers," each physically changing earlier than their classmates. Melissa had started puberty at age eight, already almost four years before I saw her this second time around. Jacob was about two years ahead of most of the boys in his class, having started to change physically at age ten. Al-though both Melissa and Jacob told me that they were proud that they had developed before their friends, they were also confused by it. Fre-quently, they were mistaken for being older. Most of the time they liked this, but it also had its complications. Others assumed not only that they were sexually experienced—after all, their bodies looked like older kids' bodies, and the older kids were sexually active—but that they had sexual expertise. One of the things that the boys screamed at twelve-year-old Melissa was, "You know how to do it!" The stepmother who wrote Jacob the letter when he was thirteen assumed a wealth of knowledge on his part. This was both flattering and scary for him.

At the same time, though, there was an important difference in how Melissa and Jacob were treated. Melissa's early sexual development was seen hostilely—"slut," "pignose"—whereas Jacob's was welcomed. He did not have a group of boys and girls shouting names at him. Overtures directed toward him were private. This, too, was problematic, of course, because he had a hard time bringing it out into the open. If he had not been seeing a psychiatrist for an entirely different reason, I wonder if he would have talked about the issue with anyone. Still, he was not strug-gling with the public humiliation that Melissa was.

"Slut" is defined by *Webster's Dictionary* as "a woman of low charac-ter," with a second definition, that of a female dog. "Stud" is defined as "a male animal, especially horses, kept for breeding." So although each word is defined at least in part in animal terms, reminding us that the dra-matic and explicit changes seen in early sexual development evoke ani-mal images, there is one important difference. Sluts are perceived as inherently worthy of condemnation. Melissa's emerging breasts and hips, and the fact that she liked her body and was developing an interest in boys, brought on a painful censorship—*you are low-class.*

Interestingly, adult perceptions of pubescent "sexiness" often reveal more about the adult than the child. That is, there is always a lot of projection of the adults' own desires and fantasies onto adolescents. In many ways, the slut label is the twentieth-century counterpart for the scarlet letter. It punishes girls for being sexual, for being powerful, or just for being different. Leora Tanenbaum, a feminist who has interviewed many women who were called sluts in their early adolescence, believes the label is one of the major tools used to enforce the double standard—different rules for the sexuality of boys and girls. Girls' sexuality should be hidden. Girls themselves should be passive, and even the appearance of breasts can be seen as too aggressive, requiring public sanction. Another side of the double standard is seen in Jacob's struggle. The letters that Jacob received described sexual things that he, then a thirteen-year-old, could "do" to an adult woman.

Just because Melissa's and Jacob's developing bodies evoked strong feelings in others, they were not necessarily doing anything "devious" to provoke such responses. In fact, both of these young people were in some ways violated by others, though Jacob suffered a much more subtle form.

Both biology and culture are conspiring to speed up the sexual development of children—boys and girls. It has long been recognized that girls are developing almost two years earlier than they did thirty years ago, due to improved nutrition and a decrease in infectious diseases. Girls with the earliest sexual maturation are hit hard and struggle with more dissatisfaction with their appearance and lowered self-esteem. They also suffer from higher rates of depression, anxiety, and eating disorders. Why? It is hard for these girls to accept their changing bodies in a culture that values thin, prepubertal bodies for girls.

Boys, too, are developing two years earlier. Generally assumed to be an advantage in a world where their sexuality is encouraged, early development in boys is beginning to be recognized as a mixed blessing. Boys who mature earlier than their classmates have better self-esteem and are more popular than other boys, but they are also more likely to get involved in dangerous risk-taking activities, including substance and alcohol abuse. Part of the explanation for this may lie in the fact that because they look older, they may be more likely to develop friendships with older peers who initiate them into risky behaviors.

The earlier onset of puberty for all children is putting pressure on teens to act like adults before they are emotionally or cognitively ready. Pressure to take on a strongly defined gender role early is strong in the American culture of the 1990s. This means that boys are pressured to act in typically masculine ways, and girls in typically feminine ways. This closes off choices for boys and girls. For example, girls may lose the opportunity to develop more typically masculine traits such as logic, independence, and healthy aggression, and boys are less able to develop feminine traits such as relatedness, sociability, and empathy.

This trend can be harmful. Studies show that girls who adopt a strong feminine role (with traits of sociability, empathy, and greater passivity) do not feel as good about themselves as girls who are more androgynous and show a combination of male traits (independence, aggression, and assertiveness) and female traits. This process is different for boys. Boys who adopt a strong masculine role are reported to feel better about themselves than boys who are more androgynous. Even at a young age, boys are pressured to relinquish "female" traits. This process only continues in adolescence, but it is not without its price. Boys who are more "masculine," like the early developers, are more likely to be involved in dangerous risk-taking.

My work with Melissa and Jacob and others like them has given me perspective on the roundtable discussion at my daughter's school. In each setting, the same questions and concerns are revealed, questions that help us understand some of the sexual pressures on boys and girls today. At my daughter's school, the boys' mothers were worried about the behavior of the girls—"too many phone calls"—pushing the boys before both the boys and their mothers were ready for relationships. Things were happening too fast. The girls' mothers were concerned about gender issues, too. Their girls weren't eating enough, responding to social pressures to be thin at the time of greatest physical development. It is striking that the pressure to conceptualize different "tracks" for boys and girls was already present at the sixth-grade level. The boys were seen as acting one way, the girls another. The double standard is also present. The girls' advanced sociability and emerging sexual interest were seen as problems. Instead of conversing with their sons about how to handle girls' phone calls, the boys' mothers suggested a school-wide curfew. I left that meeting on the defensive as one of the girls' mothers, but realized only later that I was struggling with how quickly these eleven- and twelve-year-olds were being pushed into gender-based roles. In fifth grade, the boys and girls had called each other frequently and even hung out together, but now the lines were being drawn, the roles narrowed. All of this occurred at a middle school in Northern California that prides itself on being attuned to the development of children.

When Melissa saw me, she was aware that she was feeling good about her body and starting to have sexual feelings, many very positive, revealed in her liking for her high-heeled platforms. She was also already aware that it was not okay to feel or to look the way she did. She also knew that boys and girls were being treated differently. She was a slut. They were studs.

Jacob faced a different issue. He, too, was proud of his body, but when the letters and the pressures started early, too early for him, he struggled. At age thirteen, what did these women want him to do to them?

Each of these young people was being pushed into strong sexual roles before they were ready, both confusing them and closing off opportunities, and in Melissa's situation, causing her much immediate pain and suffering. The questions remain: Why are gender stereotypes being strongly enforced for young people? Why at earlier ages?

The pressure from the media is, I believe, only a part of the story. The double standard so evident in the 1950s has resurfaced in the 1990s. Expecting and enforcing strong gender roles for children and young teens offers a sense of security to adults. If the gender model is there, then parents don't have to talk about it, and they can continue to maintain the strong taboo around discussing sexual matters. Teens follow their parents' lead. Exploring options becomes nearly impossible in such a rigid environment. If adolescents question, they do so in private, hiding their activities and protecting themselves.

Both Jacob and Melissa felt tagged with sexual identities that weren't genuinely their own. Both were early developers, of course, but again, this is not the only factor that makes others—adults and children alike—push sexuality onto teens before they themselves are ready. Early adolescence is rightfully a time of exploration. We do young people a grave disservice when we presume the results of that exploration when it has barely begun.

2

Here Comes Puberty
The Many Meanings of Menstruation

Am I brainwashed about this? —Jenny

I had noticed changes in fourteen-year-old Jenny's body before she told me the dream about having her first period. Within months she was several inches taller, now looking me squarely in the eye when she stood up to leave her therapy sessions. Her tie-dyed T-shirts started to fit a little tighter, and then she changed her style slightly to those with lower necks and higher waists. Her patched jeans were still baggy, but slightly less so around her hips. I also had noticed her developing arm muscles, which certainly made it much easier for her to carry her two backpacks filled with schoolbooks, CDs, gym clothes, herbal teas, granola bars, incense, and often her pet cat, Angel, up the steep hill to my house. Jenny had begun therapy with me several months earlier, just after her parents had finalized a rough divorce. At that time Jenny had carried two backpacks and a string bag to hold all of her dearest possessions—"Never know what you'll need in the middle of a fight between your parents."

Things were better now with Jenny's parents, Sarah and Jonathan. The fighting had lessened, and a regular pattern of custody had been established. The string bag was gone, and Jenny no longer asked me if she could use my dryer for her slightly damp clothes. Our sessions were no longer filled with stories of loud, angry midnight phone calls between her parents, her mother retreating into her bedroom to escape into a marijuana haze, her father offering to share his pot with Jenny, both parents wanting her to be their friend instead of their daughter. Life was back to normal, kind of.

Jenny didn't think life was normal, however. She had sprouted two microscopic pimples on her forehead that she felt all could see, anyone who wasn't blind, that is, an adjective she ascribed to most adults, including her aging doctor. She also suggested I purchase some Clearasil lotion for the bathroom in my waiting room and improve the lighting in there; after all, I did work with teenagers. I thanked her for her helpful suggestions, and then began listening to her describe cyclical changes in her mood.

Jenny told me about a dream she'd had. This wasn't the first dream Jenny had shared with me. She had let me know soon after I first met her that she had looked through Sigmund Freud's book, *The Interpretation of Dreams,* and even more helpful, she had seen several movies in which patients shared their dreams with their doctors. She knew that in order to have a successful analysis—her word for the work that we were doing together—you had to talk about your dreams, and she wasn't going to miss out on this valuable, exciting experience. She began this time by telling me that this dream wasn't particularly exciting. It was "odd, and kinda gross.

"I'm at a pajama party. All my girlfriends are there, too. The other girls are asleep on the floor. I'm sitting on the bed above them, watching them. It's getting late. I fall asleep, and then end up falling out of bed, landing on top of them. I knock over their leftover Cokes. It's a mess. They don't mind, but I'm embarrassed."

"What do you think about it?" I asked.

"About the dream?"

"Mmm-hmm. What do you think it meant?"

"I don't know. Sometimes I think that you can read my mind even though you can't, of course. Can you?" She laughed. "Maybe I'd like you to read my mind so that I wouldn't have to talk about it."

"I can understand that, but it matters most what you think and feel about it." I was unsure if my silence was the best tack to take at this time, but I also wanted her to voice her own ideas first.

After I said that, she blurted out, "I don't have to guess—I know. It's my period. I'm sure."

Girls had talked with me about their periods before, but even the most open of them talked about beginning or having their periods in an almost secretive way, and usually it took some work on my part, or a direct question or two. I wasn't totally surprised that Jenny was different. She had always been direct, approaching difficult subjects about her parents' divorce in a straightforward manner.

"I got my period six days ago. That's how I know—plus the obvious, spilled Coke, falling on top of other girls, being awake later than them— I'm later in real life, too. They've all had their periods for ages already. God, I'm fourteen! I've been waiting for years." She stopped and took a breath. "So, you're the psychiatrist . . ."

"I may be the psychiatrist, but you're doing a good job with this one. Congratulations on your period, by the way." That comment seemed to surprise, and clearly please, her.

"Thanks. I'm happy about it."

"I see that. In the dream, it's a party."

"Yeah, a party where I fall asleep and spill Coke all over the place. Some party."

"Yes, some party, Jenny. But still a reason to celebrate."

Thoughtfully she added, "I haven't told anybody. It happened when I was at my dad's. I wasn't going to tell him, at least not right away. I want to tell my mom, but I'm worried about what she'll do. She and I don't always think alike."

That was an understatement. Jenny and her mother were very different. Sarah was an architect who specialized in designing spaces where women gather. She would arrive at my office wearing gray suits and carrying mini-blueprints that she would work on in the waiting room. She exuded an icy power and was often combative. From Jenny, though, I knew another side to Sarah. I knew that after the divorce she had cried every night for months and locked herself in her bedroom, away from

Jenny, to secretly, or so she thought, smoke marijuana. She had changed this behavior after I had told her that I didn't think it was good for Jenny.

I asked Jenny how she thought her mother would react to her news.

"I don't know. She's a strict feminist. Maybe she'll give me a badge to wear, something all the world can see."

"What would you like her to do?"

"I dunno. It's funny. I dunno, but I'm going to tell her soon."

"What about your dad?"

She screwed up her forehead and looked straight at me and asked, "Would you tell him if you were me?"

I thought about Jenny's question. This just wasn't the typical "How should I tell my father about my period" question that many adolescent girls ask. There was quite a bit more to consider in Jenny's relationship with her father. Jonathan had made Jenny his "best buddy" after his divorce from Sarah. Part of becoming her dad's best buddy had included going on camping trips with him, where they shared the same sleeping bag. Like Sarah, Jonathan smoked marijuana, but he tended to indulge in front of Jenny, and offered his daughter joints on the camping trips.

Jenny and I had talked a great deal about what it was like to have a father who was a buddy, a little too close for comfort. Jenny was able to talk to me directly about the pressure she felt from Jonathan to be his partner, to step in and take on some of her mother's former role. A case such as Jonathan and Jenny's, in which there is no overt sexual contact but rather a "sexualized" relationship between a parent and child, is challenging for a therapist, and the work with Jenny was no exception. I had to evaluate my legal responsibilities and consider whether I had heard of or witnessed any sexual activity between Jenny and her father that constituted abuse and would have mandated reporting. I had not found any evidence of that. What I had seen was a lonely, charming father reaching out to one of the few people to whom he felt close after a bitter divorce—his child. The problem had been that he was reaching out with inappropriate offers to share marijuana and a certain degree of physical intimacy that was frightening to her. With support, Jonathan had been able to step back and adopt a more balanced role with his daughter—no more shared sleeping bags or drugs, but a lot more comfort. How comfortable Jenny would feel about discussing her first period with her father was a real question, though. I waited to hear more.

The Telling

A week later Jenny returned, and the story about how she told and didn't tell her parents poured out.

"Did you get the invitation yet? I can't believe she sent you an invitation—you, my psychiatrist," she said. "It's bad enough that she invites friends, relatives, but my psychiatrist?"

"What's the invitation for?"

"A celebration of my maidenhood. You'll see it. She wants all of the women to come and talk about their first period, like I really want to hear this."

I tried to imagine steely Sarah having this party for her daughter, a "celebration of maidenhood," as Jenny had so sarcastically referred to it. The fact that this phrase was the title of a book on the shelves in my waiting room wasn't lost on me, but I decided to stick to Jenny's mother for the moment. Thinking about Jenny's extreme response, I wondered if Sarah had any idea of her daughter's feelings about this plan of hers.

"So have you told your mother how you feel?" I asked.

"Are you crazy? She wouldn't see it. She's in her own space, women's world and all, the mother of the young maiden—for her it's so wonderful. . . ." Jenny looked disgusted at this point and gestured a gag in case I had missed what she was trying to communicate.

"Jenny, why do you think even the idea of this party bothers you so much?"

She paused for about a minute and then began slowly, "I don't know. I guess I expect her, sometimes even you, to know exactly what I'm feeling. I don't even know what I'm feeling, but I expect you to know."

"You do know that you're upset about it."

"Yeah, I do know that. It's like the rites of spring, celebration of the maiden's puberty, girls with flowers in their hair dancing around some pole. . . . God, it's just so retro and gross."

We both laughed as she described her vision of the ceremony, and then I asked her how she would like to have her period acknowledged by her mother.

She smiled and said, "Well, I was going to say 'not at all,' but I know that's not totally true, either. We haven't been as close since the divorce. We fight a lot about everything. I guess I want her to listen to me, spend time alone with me, maybe go for a bike ride on Mt. Tamalpais like we used to. This party, though—it's like she's taken it over. It's no longer mine. She's made it into something public, a spectacle."

"How do you feel about your period at this point?"

This stumped her for a moment. It was clearly easier to talk about her mother.

"Back to the dream, I guess—it's a mess, but I'm glad that I'm not waiting any longer. I hope you don't mind that I borrowed that book of yours."

"What book?"

"*Menstruation and Psychoanalysis.* It was right next to *Celebration of the Maiden: Reclaiming the Beauty and Power of a Young Girl's First Period,* probably my mother's handbook at the moment."

"What do you think of it?"

"It's kind of hard to read."

We both laughed, and I promised to find some books on menstruation that were easier to get through. Picturing Jenny poring over this academic text touched me. From my practice I know that girls are hungry for knowledge about their periods. It is not easy to obtain. Several have described reading the small-print ads in the Tampax box, searching for information, any information. I kept several books in my waiting room for just that purpose, including the one she'd clearly rejected, which was much less dense than the psychoanalytic volume. I put them out in the waiting room to show girls that such books existed, that menstruation was a subject worth writing and reading about.

As Jenny packed up her backpacks to leave, I asked her what happened when she told her father, the parent she had been living with over the past week.

"Haven't told him. I'm not sure I'm going to." She pulled on the heavy backpack, but at the same time I could sense she wanted my opinion about this. I thought about how difficult it had been for Jenny to work out the double sleeping bags with her father, the closeness that was too close, and I knew from experience that it often wasn't easy for girls to tell their father. Watching her face closely, I supported her choice. "It's not easy for most girls, Jenny. You'll figure it out."

Waiting for the Invitation

After Jenny left the office, I wondered about her choice of books. She had picked one of the most medically defined texts that I had on the subject. I had seen that same reaction from other girls. Clearly there are long-standing cultural taboos that prevent open discussion about menstruation, and they are transmitted to the girls quite early, long before they have their first period. Keeping it academic is one way to make the subject acceptable.

Yet menstruation is a crucial experience for adolescent girls. The lack of response from the culture only further silences the girls and helps to maintain the taboo. Thinking about this, I waited for my invitation.

Meanwhile, I received a message on my answering machine from Jenny's dad. "Hey, Dr. Ponton, I'm pretty embarrassed about having to call you about this, but I'm not speaking to Sarah at this point and I really can't think of anyone to turn to. Uh, um . . . I'm pretty sure Jenny got her period for the first time when she was at my house last week. I wanted to talk with her about it then, but I didn't. Then Sarah sends this invitation to my sister and my mother. She's having a party for Jenny, and she's inviting them, my mother, my sister. Anyway, could you give me a call?"

"I guess you are wondering why I called," said Jonathan when I reached him. "I wonder too, sort of. I don't know what to do. The divorce has been so bad. I can't believe Sarah's gone behind my back again."

"You said you weren't speaking to her lately."

"I'm not. If I called her now, we'd end up screaming, hanging up."

I decided to sidestep the fighting for a moment. "How do you feel about Jenny having her period?"

"I don't . . . I don't know what to feel. . . . How am I supposed to feel?

I guess I think Sarah's got all the answers. She's one step ahead of me al-ways. You know, that women's space of hers, no space for me."

"Most of the fathers that I have worked with are caught off balance by the news of their daughters' first period. It's hard to know how to react. Have you talked with anyone about it?"

"No. Well, I talked to my mother and my sister. I think they might go . . . to this party. Sarah sure knows how to split us."

I was growing exasperated with Jonathan. As with many divorced par-ents, any discussion with him often led back to the conflict with his ex-wife.

"Jonathan, how do you think Jenny feels about it?"

"I don't know. Should I ask?"

"Yeah, I think it would be a good start."

The conversation with Jonathan reminded me of many of those we had had when he and Sarah were in the heat of their custody battle for their daughter. However, what Jonathan was saying was important, and very similar to many other fathers' reactions. What should he say to his daughter? Should he acknowledge the event at all? Wait for her to say something first? He knows this is supposed to be an important milestone, but he's not so sure it's something to celebrate—he's not so sure how he feels about his daughter growing up, "becoming a woman."

The arrival of Jenny's period left Jonathan unsure about what he felt. Added to that, Sarah was having a party, a "celebration," and he was left out, and felt hurt and very angry. I could understand his feelings, but I also wanted him to try to understand his daughter's.

The invitation arrived on the day of Jenny's next session. I opened it and set it out on the desk. She arrived earlier than usual and was eager to talk about it.

"You know how I feel about it—the celebration of the maiden—it's so embarrassing. I can't tell her that. I start, but I can't go on. I choke up."

Jenny had not "choked up," even during a protracted divorce with her parents, so I acknowledged how different this must feel to her.

"It does. I mean, I know I feel guilty about not wanting it. I guess I know she cares about me with this."

"Lots of the time during the divorce it didn't seem that way for you."

"No, it didn't. I mean, my dad is way off base. He thinks she's having it to get back at him, bond the women in the family against him, really. He probably feels pretty left out."

"He is left out—no party, no period."

Jenny laughed loudly and said, "Good deal on both accounts! Well, maybe not."

"Maybe not."

"I know I'm glad I finally got my period. I'm even glad my mom wants to have the party. It's just that I'm not sure I want it, a period party, so yucky."

"How is it yucky?"

"I don't know, it feels yucky—the period, the tampons, it should be secret."

"And your mom wants to shout about it."

"Yeah, tell the world. Am I brainwashed about this or something? I mean, they separate us from the boys, stick us in the room with a red-faced P.E. teacher, and call it 'our little secret,' but then I believe them. I am brainwashed!"

"How would you do it differently?"

"Not make it embarrassing. I guess I would want teachers to talk about it, what it was like for them. It's like a secret order now."

"Do you talk about it with your friends?"

"I used to, about what it would be like. It was kind of exciting when I was nine or ten. Then even that changed."

"How has it changed?"

"I guess the focus now is on, oh, what a pain, asking each other, 'Do you have any Advil? Any tampons?' So we share the pain. . . . Crazy."

"Not so crazy at all, Jenny. The culture is embarrassed about it, so why should you and your friends act differently?"

"You're saying I should have the party."

"If you want to. I'm saying you should look at your feelings about it."

"Okay. I'll talk to her about the party. It's confusing."

Jenny wasn't the only one left feeling confused after that session. Several months before, I had led a workshop at a women's conference on the topic "Meanings of Menstruation." I had worked for months carefully researching the topic, but when I got in the room with twenty other women, I realized that I hadn't explored my own feelings about it. I soon recognized I wasn't alone. The room was filled with women of all ages, from eighteen to seventy, and all acknowledged both limited knowledge and a shared inability to express or even have feelings about their periods. Many of the younger women wanted hard information—"Tell us." Many of the older women could not give it. I remember the tightened face and dogmatic voice of a senior pediatrician in her sixties. "It is only natural that girls feel embarrassed about their periods and want to hide it. It *is* embarrassing. We have all had 'accidents.' We don't want that to happen to them, so we teach them how to avoid it. This is a medical problem. We should not be talking about feelings, even sharing this. It is not meant to be shared. *That* is embarrassing."

As she spoke, I saw the faces of the younger women, initially open, start to close off. I struggled to address it, talking about different people, different attitudes, but I could see that her words had made an impact, and in an area of silence, words like hers would continue to ring loudly.

Several hours after Jenny's session, Sarah called me. She sounded both more confused and less confident than she usually was.

"Dr. Ponton, I don't know where to begin. I suppose you've received the invitation."

"Yes, thank you."

"And I also guess that you and Jenny have been talking about it."

"We have."

"Well, I know I can't ask you what she is sharing with you—confidentially—nor would I want to violate it, that is . . ."

"But you would like to know what Jenny has said about this party."

"Yes. I guess so. She tells me, 'Fine,' but the communication between us hasn't been great since the divorce. Don't misunderstand me, it's getting better. I feel like this party is a good idea, a good message for her to get, but I think she doesn't want it. Is it because of Jonathan? Embarrassment? I just don't understand why not, I guess, and she isn't telling me."

"Why do you think you want to give this party for her, Sarah?"

She answered after a long pause. "I guess partly for her, partly for me. No one ever helped me with stuff. My parents ignored it. My mother didn't talk with me about it for six months after. When she finally spoke, she said the Kotex were in a drawer. I didn't want it to be like that for

Jenny, especially after we've messed up with this divorce. But she's acting so strange about the party, I guess I just don't know. . . ."

"Sarah, your idea about having this party is good. You want Jenny to have a different experience with her period than you had with yours. And you want better communication with her. Have you shared your experience with her yet?"

"No." Then she said sheepishly, "I guess I was waiting for the party."

"That could be a place to start with her. She wants to talk to you about it, too."

A week later, I received a joint letter from Jenny and her mother. The party had been canceled, but I was being asked to send a letter describing my experience for a book that Sarah was now making for Jenny. The book would substitute for the party. A note at the bottom of the letter mentioned that although the book was for Jenny, the contents of the book would be shared with both of her parents, Sarah and Jonathan.

I was still thinking about what I was going to write when Jenny arrived for her session.

"So you got the letter."

I smiled. "Mmm-hmm. Apparently you were able to work it out with your mother. How did it happen?"

She smiled in return. "I dunno. We just started talking and then kept it going. She has a lot to say about periods—women's world, you know."

"It sounds like you had a lot to say to her."

"Yeah, when she listens, I can talk and hear better, too. I told her about the dream about the period, and then she told me she's had lots of period dreams. Dreams she's having her period, then she wakes up and she is actually having it. She calls them 'power dreams.' She's pretty focused on the period-as-power kind of stuff you've said."

"What do you think of that stuff, the period and power?"

"I guess I can feel it, changes in my energy level, like power surges. . . ." Jenny was starting to laugh, and I could see that she was beginning to make fun of it, maybe even enjoy it a little bit. Not long after this discussion she suggested that, like Freud, I should chart the periods of my women patients, only translate them into power surges. Through talking about her girlfriends', her mother's, and eventually even her father's ideas about periods, Jenny slowly laid out her own. She had been looking forward to the arrival of her period. She recounted stories of talking with girlfriends about it, each of them guessing what it would be like. Then once her girlfriends started to get their periods and she didn't, things got harder. She heard about some of their experiences and some of them weren't great. To her surprise, many of her friends didn't tell her when they had their first period, and often she didn't find out until months later. All of this had affected Jenny's formerly eager anticipation of the event—it must not be great if no one was talking about it.

In contrast, her mother's interest in the upcoming event never wavered, but it increasingly began to bother Jenny. Why was her mother so interested, and why was her mother's reaction so different from her girlfriends'? Jenny slowly became both embarrassed and skeptical of Sarah's interest. When her period arrived, Jenny found to her surprise that she did feel good about it. However, in the atmosphere of surrounding silence, Sarah's excitement was hard to take, and the pattern of fighting that had developed between them during the time of the divorce only made it worse. Yet Sarah's and Jenny's attitudes about Jenny's period had some striking similarities. Both of them were excited about it. Jenny saw her mother as "taking over" with her excitement and most obviously with the party. In a world of silence, Jenny wanted to share her experience with someone, but she wanted it to be her milestone and her celebration, not Sarah's. With some assistance from me, they were able to discuss it and plan a way to acknowledge it that pleased them both.

"I'm glad you talked to my mother."

"I'm glad she talked with you."

"So am I. I could tell it wasn't easy for her. Then when she talked about her own mother—Kotex in the drawer, and only talks to her six months later—from that to a family party. It's crazy. It's such a big step for one generation."

I could sense the all-too-familiar Jenny, a kid who could call you on your own stuff pretty easily. She looked at me and asked, "So how's the letter going, Dr. Ponton, teen expert?" And then, shaking her head, "Not too easy, I bet."

"You're right, Jenny. Not easy to talk or write about it."

"You know, I'm going to have a letter in there. It's about my dream.

I'm going to write about how I wish kids could have 'period parties' and not messes."

"Right now it's still a little bit of both."

"A lot of both."

I eventually wrote my letter for Jenny's book. In it I wrote about her dream and some of our work together on it, letting her know that she had helped open me up to some of my feelings about my period.

Left out of this picture was Jonathan. Initially Jenny had wanted to tell him but felt unsure about how to do it. In this, Jenny was no different from girls whose parents were still together. Telling Dad that she was having her first period was not easy, no way around that. Then he had his suspicions confirmed by a phone call from his mother that left him feeling even more left out. After he and I talked, he decided to talk to Jenny. It wasn't easy for him. Jenny told me about their talk and said that Jonathan was so red-faced she thought he was going to have a heart attack, but then she added that she knew how hard it was, and she admired him for trying. In an important way, her father's embarrassment made it easier for Jenny to talk about her own feelings about her period, with both embarrassment and pride.

The Taboo

Taboos associated with menstruation are universal. The word *taboo* comes from the Polynesian word *tupura,* which means menstruation. The ancient attitude toward "tupura" isn't entirely different from our own culture's response to menstruation today.

An examination of how menstruation is portrayed in advertising, an important aspect of popular culture, enlightens us further about our current cultural beliefs and their impact on girls. Consistent with the medicalization of bodily functions, advertising depicts menstruation as a "hygienic crisis" that is best managed by an "effective security system," affording peace of mind—i.e., protection from soiling, odor, and embarrassment. In addition, menstruating women are depicted as functioning at optimal activity level and uncomplaining, which means girls and women who do experience discomfort may believe that their reactions are unusual. In my experience, teenage girls view their periods as much less of a hygienic crisis than the media does. They find especially relevant the advertising that targets the topic of tampons and loss of virginity. These ads deftly address the beginner myth that tampon use will threaten virginity, and then dispels the myth in order to sell multiple types of specialized tampons. The message is clear: stay a virgin and avoid messes: tampons will help you do both.

Without reading the fine print, one might not discover that the advertising across the spectrum of "feminine hygiene products" is still delivering these seemingly anachronistic messages, but this only further underscores how important it is for mothers and other adults to take an active role. Looking for guidance, Jenny and other girls pore over the advertising inserts in the tampon and sanitary pad boxes searching for information in a society that is largely silent on this topic. For many, it becomes a source of secret interest, a hidden fascination that many girls themselves view as suspect. It is difficult to understand: Why is something that is suddenly so relevant to them kept so hidden?

The founder of psychoanalysis, Sigmund Freud, was also fascinated with the topic of menstruation. This is most clearly illustrated by his letters with Wilhelm Fleiss, his friend and colleague, which show their mutual interest in theories of periodicity and twenty-eight-day cycles. At the time he wrote to Fleiss, Freud was attending to and recording the menstrual patterns of the women in his household. Freud, a breaker of taboos in many areas, did not try to shatter taboos about menstruation. Mary Jane Lupton, in her book *Menstruation and Psychoanalysis,* believes that menstruation and menstrual cycles continued to have an impact on Freud's work, suggesting even that the Freudian concept of libido is a metaphor that imitates the menstrual process. Freud and others, while they may have understood this, failed to write about it, and failed to recognize the importance of menstruation because of the strong taboos on the subject.

The widespread effects of stigma and taboo strongly influence teenage girls' reactions to menstruation. Studies show that many girls are extremely positive about the *anticipation* of their menses, far more so than they are about the event once it has actually arrived. What alters their perspective is unknown. When a group of older adolescent girls were asked how they would prepare younger girls for this important event, the girls emphasized the need for emotional support and assurance that menstruation was normal and healthy, not bad, frightening, and embarrassing. They stressed the importance of educating girls about the pragmatic aspects of tampons and hygiene, but underscored that hearing about the subjective experience, "how it actually felt," from women who had gone through it, would have made a tremendous difference, while downplaying the biological aspects and the link between menstruation and self-definition as a woman. The girls stressed the important role of mothers, requesting a long-term, continuous process, beginning well before menarche and continuing long after.

On the important subject of mothers' reactions to daughters' periods, little has been written. This reflects the lack of significance that our culture assigns to the roles of mothers in the lives of adolescent girls, though this is certainly not the perspective of the girls or the mothers themselves. We do know that mothers play the most important part in a girl's educational process about menstruation. Girls tell their mothers, if they share it with anyone. Girls almost never discuss the subject with boys or with their fathers, and they confide considerably less in girlfriends than they do in mothers. One study found that only one quarter of girls tell anyone other than their mothers when they have their first menstrual period. Little sharing of information with friends seems to take place after the initiation of menstruation, although at a later point friends share stories about symptoms and negative attitudes.

Cultural wisdom and research jointly point to the important role of the mother in this vital area, yet many mothers describe themselves as feeling inadequate. They don't want to transmit negative cultural values—and mothers like Sarah are well aware of them—and often don't want to tell their daughters in the manner that they were told. Personalized educational aids are available to help mothers with this process, among them *Celebration of the Maiden,* an inspiring booklet often given with a congratulatory bracelet that helps a young woman claim her womanhood with joy and pride. A more humorous yet equally positive approach is taken by Karen Gravelle and her adolescent niece Jennifer in *The Period Book.* Both of these volumes educate and, at times, entertain daughter and mother simultaneously.

Modern society has nothing that corresponds to a full initiation ceremony for either girls or boys. The focus in modern cultures is on the other end of adolescence, graduation from high school and going to college or beginning work. I believe that younger teens feel betrayed by this lack of attention, even neglect, for their developmental milestones, and have slowly but surely developed their own initiation rites. Among these, the onset of sexual activity is the most obvious. In addition, because puberty is occurring at progressively earlier ages (and this affects girls more than boys as puberty usually occurs two years earlier for girls), younger and younger girls are grappling with a complex part of life, and they very much need adult assistance. Yet our society's inability to talk about it leaves many girls feeling isolated instead.

Many ancient cultures included a ritual ceremony to mark a girl's first period as a sign of fertility. The Native American people called Mesquakies, "Red Earth People," isolated girls who were having their first periods—not as punishment, but because they were seen as very powerful. The isolation used with a girl's first menstruation paralleled the isolation ceremony used with young males at the time of their first vision. In this context, isolation was a societal convention that honored, rather than ignored, these important passages for young people. Isolation was used to help the young people of both sexes understand that they were now entering a time of great power, and they needed to know how to use it. We have no such means for honoring our own young people.

Audiovisual aids, which are used most frequently in school-based educational programs, often take a hygienic approach and do not stress individual, cultural, or emotional meanings. They often "talk down" to the girls in the effort to explain a hidden mystery. Attending high school and watching the "mystery of life" films of today, I am reminded of a cartoon version that I saw in sixth grade, a film that is interwoven with my memories of the Walt Disney version of *Cinderella*. Each used singing cartoon birds in pastel colors and had a not-so-hidden meaning—keep quiet and don't complain. The problems with the educational tools point to the difficulty in uncovering and promoting positive feelings about menstruation. Potentially the introduction of this important topic to both boys and girls offers an opportunity to introduce positive elements and to erase secrecy, a process that has not yet happened.

Both silence and "taboos" dim our understanding of the important subject of menarche. The lack of light on this topic is reflected further in our overall understanding of the entire process of menstruation, not just the first step. Not surprisingly, adolescent girls and adult women have been among the last asked to add their knowledge.

The onset of menstruation can be an exciting time in a girl's life, but it is also a highly sensitive time. A first period is an important sign of approaching womanhood, but since many girls' first periods occur between ages nine and twelve, parents must remember that these girls are still children. Any celebration of a daughter's first period should take into account her desires, too. Jenny's story illustrates this point. Parents and daughters need to communicate with each other about this event. Many mothers are reluctant to share their own menstrual experiences with their daughters, often because they hope that their daughters will have better experiences than they did, and don't want to frighten or overwhelm them with the details of their own stories. Yet many daughters are interested in knowing at least something about the nature of their mothers' experience. So mothers should bear in mind that they may have to be selective about sharing their own experiences. They can simply ask their daughters how much of their stories they want them to share. Daughters, too, can ask their mothers directly about what this time was like for them. You may both feel shy at first, but discussions like this can also bring you closer together during this time of transition. Fathers parenting daughters need to become knowledgeable about menstruation if they are not already. Divorced and alternative families have increased the possibility that Dad will be the only available adult in a girl's life at this special time when it is important to be able to "share the news" and feel that it will be warmly received. Sharing in this event with a daughter contributes to closeness for fathers and mothers alike.

The onset of a girl's first period raises another family issue as well. Because of its power, the onset of menstruation may evoke strong feelings for many people in the life of a girl, among them brothers, sisters, caretakers, friends, and grandparents, but also others more distantly related. Be aware that there may be teasing or other negative communication directed at adolescent girls during this time, and do your best to discourage or prevent it.

Periods aren't easy to talk about, nor are they particularly easy to write about. While I was writing my contribution to Jenny's book, I, too, felt the force of the taboo. Yet, in such an atmosphere of silence, young girls are left searching. It is up to each one of us to help break the history of silence that surrounds this vital period of life.

3

Alarming Arousal
Sexual Fantasies and Masturbation

What would my dad think? —Daniel

What's happening to me? —Heather

The last thing in the world thirteen-year-old Daniel wanted was to talk to a psychiatrist. He let me know that right away. "I don't have to talk if I don't want. They told me that."

For much of this first session with Daniel, we did not talk, and as we sat together, I reflected on what I had been told about him, the path that had led him, however reluctantly, to my office.

Daniel's pediatrician, Dr. Jim Green, had called me several days before and asked me if I had an hour available to work with a young, sad, and silent adolescent boy. I asked Dr. Green what had happened to Daniel to lead to this phone call. "Well, I'm not—he's not talking about it. That's part of the problem."

I couldn't help noticing that Jim, normally a high-energy, conversational guy whom I generally could never get off the phone, was awkwardly *not* talking to me. What would put him at a loss for words? When he started telling me Daniel's grades at school this semester, A's and B's, I decided to interrupt. "Jim, the grades sound fine, but tell me why you're asking him to come see me."

"He won't talk to me, or my male resident, about it. He won't talk to his mother, either."

"I hear that, Jim, but why aren't you talking to me?"

"It's strange, Lynn. You're right. This one has got me tongue-tied. I guess I wonder if I'm doing the right thing even sending him to you, overkill and all."

"Maybe, but first I have to know why you're sending him."

"We, er, his mother found him alone in a room with a vacuum cleaner."

"And . . . ?"

I could hear Jim take a deep breath on the other end of the line.

"We think, I think, he was jacking off with this thing. You probably don't know anything about this, well, maybe you do, you're a psychiatrist, after all, you're supposed to know about masturbation," and then Jim was off and running, speaking the medical language he was far more comfortable with, quoting an article from the *Journal of Urology,* which reported that not only was erotic stimulation by using vacuum cleaners or electric brooms common, but injury from using them in this way was also common. He then proceeded to describe several types of penile trauma that could result before I stopped him.

"So you think he was masturbating with the vacuum cleaner hose?"

"Well, what else would he be doing with a vacuum cleaner in his room? He's a boy, after all."

"Okay, just one more question. Does he want to come see me?"

"I'm not sure we've asked him. Don't you think it would probably be a good idea?"

"Yes."

After a few minutes I asked Daniel if he would mind if I talked some, not a lot, but some.

He said okay, but then pulled his baseball cap down and his sweatshirt up, as if the clothing would protect him from my words. He had pulled his legs and feet up onto the chair, hiding all of his body from me except for his long, skinny legs in blue jeans, a few inches of his face, including his eyes and the top of his Giants baseball cap.

Wanting to begin somewhere, I commented on what I had already observed. For one, Daniel had come alone to my office for his session, without a parent. This wasn't unusual once I had begun to work with a teen, but it was pretty rare for a first visit. I also knew that since he was too young to drive, he had climbed a very steep hill to get to my office; yet when he had walked into the waiting room right on time, he hadn't seemed out of breath. When I complimented him on it, he finally spoke. Actually, he had been waiting outside my office for over an hour. When I asked him why, he said that he'd "wanted to be prepared" and "see how things worked" at my office.

When I asked him what he'd discovered, he let me know that there had been two Federal Express deliveries on the block during the hour, and that three cats—an orange tabby, a gray Siamese, and a Maine coon—had wandered down the path to the backyard entrance to my office.

The sunny stones in my backyard are a refuge for a group of cats I sometimes call the "therapy cats." Many of the teens I see pet them, but none had watched their comings and goings the way that Daniel did. I commented that he was a sharp observer. He again said that he liked to see how things work, and that maybe I did, too, "not like the other doctor."

"What other doctor?"

"The doctor who sent me here, who do you think? The one who thinks I'm doing weird stuff with the vacuum cleaner." Apparently Daniel shared my perception of Jim Green as distinctly uncurious about the topic of masturbation.

"What *was* happening with the vacuum cleaner?"

"Nothing weird, at least you wouldn't think it was weird. A psychiatrist. I can't believe I'm sitting here with a shrink."

"So let me guess, it wasn't your idea to come here, huh?"

After I asked this question, I could see that Daniel was hiding a smile underneath the pulled-up gray sweatshirt. He pulled it down suddenly and flashed a set of perfectly straight teeth. Leaning forward, he said to me, "What I want to know is what you get out of it."

"Out of what?"

"Out of listening to kids with weird stories."

"Are they weird stories?"

My response surprised him. I wasn't sure whether he expected me to agree with him—a weird psychiatrist, after all, would probably agree that kids have weird stories. Although I was still in the dark about what he had or hadn't done with the vacuum cleaner, I knew that Daniel must think his own story was pretty weird, and that if I agreed up-front that the other kids I saw were really strange, maybe his story wouldn't seem so bad. In the moments that followed, I could see that he was struggling with what to do. It seemed to me then as if he decided that he had already told me too much by sharing his ideas about "kids with weird stories," and that he thought he was one.

At this point he twisted his face into a horrible grimace to avoid crying in front of me, and said quietly but clearly, "Pervert," and ran out of the room.

Daniel didn't go far. I discovered him crying, standing next to one of the large rocks outside my office door, staring at a large Siamese cat that was clearly staring back at him. He did not run away when I walked over and sat down near him. I began to talk softly, telling him what I had observed about the cats who spend their days in my backyard. I knew that Daniel was pretty upset and guessed that he wasn't going to be able to say much more that afternoon. Finally breaking his silence, he asked me a question. Did I know the name of the Siamese cat? When I said that I didn't, he told me that he thought that was "pretty stupid." After all, the cat had come here for years, hadn't it? Then he told me that he was going to try and find out what it was. "I think you probably will," I said. "Anyone who can figure out so much from waiting outside my office probably can discover the name of the gray Siamese cat."

Although Daniel was calmer when he left my yard that afternoon, I still had serious doubts about whether he would show up for a second visit. The manner in which he was sent to me, and the discovery that seemed difficult for everyone to talk about, suggested he might not. I also figured that he was feeling pressured by Dr. Green or his parents to see me. Yet I was struck by the fact that he had managed to find my home office, high on a group of steep hills behind the university medical center, on his own, not an easy task, and certainly a risk of a different sort than potentially dangerous masturbation activities. He had arrived early and he had not run away from my office, or me, when he easily could have. Perhaps most important, he seemed to have a genuine interest in how things worked—the daily activities of my office, the lives of the cats who spent their afternoons in my backyard, what I was "getting out of" listening to the lives and secrets of teenagers. Hopefully, he was also interested in the activities of his own mind, and possibly learning more about it would also help us figure out whatever had happened with the vacuum cleaner.

Daniel did show up for our next appointment, again a bit early. This time he had brought along a camera. I discovered him taking photos of the gray Siamese that spent its afternoons sunning in my backyard. When I joined him to find out what he was doing, he informed me that unless I moved some of the rocks, I was going to have a serious problem with water drainage when the spring rains arrived. I thanked him for that information and asked him if he would like to come inside the office.

"Not really," he said. I asked him if he minded talking in the backyard, then. He shrugged but sat down on one of the big rocks. He was no longer wearing the baseball cap, and his full head of red hair cut short enough to be spiky made him appear both younger and older than thirteen at once.

I began by talking about the collection of cats in my backyard, and I asked him why he was taking photos of the Siamese. I could see Daniel struggling with whether to say I was being stupid again, but this time he decided not to.

"I'm going to post a picture of the cat on the light pole at the bottom of your street."

"That's the way you're going to find out the name?"

He smiled. "No, that's how you'll find out the name."

"I will, huh? Is my phone number going to be on the photograph?"

He laughed. "If you want to know stuff, you got to be the one they call, right?"

"I thought you wanted to know the name of the cat, Daniel."

"I do, but I don't live here, you do."

"That's right. You're just visiting."

He laughed when I said that, and answered quickly, "Just a visit to the shrink to find out what was going on with a vacuum cleaner in my bedroom."

Taking a chance, I followed up on his comment. "Are we going to find that out?"

"I already know. I was there, remember? The kid jacking off with the vacuum cleaner, the one whose mother is worried that he's going to lose his dick in some horrible accident. 'No harm done—he did it to himself, anyway!' "

"Are *you* worried about it?"

"Shit, no." He paused and then looked at me straight in the eyes for the first time. "Should I be?"

"Maybe. I don't know yet."

"Somebody's got to know whether I'm going to lose it." At this point Daniel jumped up and took off quickly, walking out onto the street. As he turned to walk down the hill, he shouted back, "You're crazy! Leave me alone!" It was clear to me that even visiting a psychiatrist made him anxious, and he wanted me to know who the crazy one really was.

I followed him out to the front of my house and watched him round the corner at the end of the street. I *was* worried, concerned that he still could hurt himself if he was masturbating with the vacuum cleaner. Then I saw him stop and examine the light pole. Was he searching for a place to put up his poster about the cat? This possibility reassured me. He was probably planning to come back. But I still wanted to talk with his parents—soon. I had waited longer than I usually do with new patients, knowing the reason that he was sent to me would make privacy an important issue for Daniel. We had connected, even if it wasn't easy for Daniel to talk. Now I could make the call.

Several hours later I was talking to Daniel's mother, Madeline. She returned my phone call after eight o'clock, explaining that she had a full-time job as a drug-company representative and had an hour's commute home. Her territory wasn't located in San Francisco, where her son spent his afternoons. Madeline talked quickly, filling me in on the family history. She was used to talking to doctors. After all, she did it every day, all day long, "repping" drugs. Yes, she was glad he was finally talking to someone. Life had been tough for Daniel after they had moved to California from New Jersey almost two years ago. For one, they had left his dad behind. At first, his mother had thought this was a good thing. Daniel's father had remarried, and Daniel didn't like his father's new wife, a feeling she reciprocated. In addition, Madeline had been offered a well-paying job by her company, with opportunities for travel. She told me that Daniel had wanted to move, too. He had said that he would like being on his own. She had wanted to believe him, so mother and son headed west together to start a new life.

At first things had gone pretty well. Daniel had fit in with the small group of fifth graders at his public school. Then he'd joined a middle school class with more than six hundred kids. Madeline knew that he was unhappy there. Most of his grade-school friends had been sent to a different middle school, so Daniel was left alone, with a lot of time on his hands. Madeline then admitted to me that she had known that he spent a lot of time masturbating. There were socks, T-shirts, underwear, and gym shorts bearing crusty evidence in the clothes hamper each week. She had pretended to ignore them. "After all, it is normal for teenage boys to masturbate, isn't it?" she asked a bit more hesitantly, and he was "doing it" in private. Then she'd found a list—"Ten Ways to Have a Good Time." There were only six ways listed, and all were masturbation—"jerk off," "whack off," "beat off," "jack off," "beat the meat," and "special friend." Madeline told me that she had put the list back carefully where she had found it so that Daniel wouldn't know that she had seen it, but then couldn't stop thinking about it. She'd always believed that masturbation was normal, but now she was worried about her son, who didn't seem to have made any friends.

I asked her if she had talked to Daniel about her worries. There was a long silence followed by shallow gasping noises; Madeline was crying.

"I wanted to ask him about it. I even tried. I guess I thought moms can't talk to their sons about this kind of thing. It seems pretty stupid now, considering what has happened."

I noticed that she chose one of her son's favorite words—stupid—and thought about what I knew about Daniel so far. So far no one wanted to talk about what had happened. In fact, other than Daniel, no one seemed to know what had happened. Maybe his vocalized sense of being a "pervert" had been more accurate than I'd realized at the time. Being discovered with a vacuum cleaner certainly made him feel like one. Having to talk with someone about it probably made it worse.

I was still thinking about the discomfort the topic of masturbation caused for people, myself included, when I met with Daniel the next time.

He was smiling when he handed me a Xeroxed poster with a head shot of the gray Siamese cat. The heading on the poster read, "Psychiatrist Wants to Know the Name of Mystery Cat: Will Help Solve Case."

Daniel smiled even more as he watched my face while I read the poster.

"Good job. So how's it going to help solve the case, Daniel?"

He shrugged. "Simple. The cat calms kids down, makes it easy for them to come here, see you, and talk about stuff. It solves your cases."

"So let me see—since the cat is such a help with my life, you think it's important for me to know its name."

"Yeah, I guess."

"I agree with you, Daniel. I think it is important for me to know the cat's name, and to know the names of other important things that may go unnamed."

"I get it," he said, surprising me with his rapid response. "This is a shrink comment. So what's the name for jacking off with a vacuum cleaner hose?"

"That's one way of describing it, if that's what happened," I said.

After a long pause, he finally spoke. "Kind of. I'm not actually sure what happened. I was going to try it . . . well, I did try it. But I got scared in the middle."

"Scared of what?"

"I don't know, scared that I'd 'lose it,' in the vacuum cleaner, scared about my mom, what she'd think. I mean, you should've seen her face when she heard the vacuum going and then opened the door. God, I'll never forget it."

"Have you talked with her about it yet?"

"She sent me here to talk."

"That hasn't made you too happy."

"No, it made it worse, at least at first."

"How does it seem now?"

"Okay, I guess. I didn't think I could talk with anyone about this." He stopped short and then asked directly, "Hey, are you going to tell them? I need to know."

"Tell whom?"

"My mom, Dr. Green."

"What would you like to have happen?"

"Well, have you not tell them, but it doesn't go like that, I bet."

"If you're not hurting yourself, I don't have to talk with them about it."

"So it depends on whether I'm hurting myself, if that's what you call it?"

"Yeah, it depends on that, on whether you're risking your health."

"It's my life, isn't it?"

"Yes—"

"And my dick."

"Yes, it certainly is, but if you're doing something dangerous, I want to help you, and that may mean I have to let your mom know."

Finally reassured that I wasn't just a spy reporting back, Daniel seemed to make a decision to trust me, at least in part. He began slowly.

"So how bad was it?"

"Daniel, it wasn't 'bad.' It was risky, dangerous, if you did what you said you did and put your penis in the vacuum cleaner hose, turning the vacuum on."

"How risky?"

"It's normal to touch your penis, to bring about sexual feelings, to get excited and reach orgasm. But people can really get hurt putting their penises into things like vacuum cleaner hoses."

Then he hesitated, but once he began to talk again, he spoke very quickly. "A bunch of guys at school were talking about wet dreams. They said that's how you know it works. I never had any wet dreams. I thought I'd better test it."

"How'd you come up with the vacuum cleaner idea?"

"One of the guys was joking. He said it—that that's the way you can really tell if it works—jack off with a vacuum cleaner." He laughed. "Some joke." He looked at me, but kept talking, wanting to get through his story before his courage ran out. "When the vacuum cleaner was going, my mom opens the door, I've got this big hard-on. I'm, like, shocked, and I freeze, and then I think, God, it's really gonna get stuck in there, and I freaked." At this point in his story, Daniel looked more than scared, however. I thought that he appeared rather proud. When I mentioned my observation, he agreed.

"Well, uh, I was glad it worked, and it was big, really big, hard, the way the other guys told me about it. They all talk about ten-inch penises."

"And you believe them."

"Yeah. Well . . . maybe not."

"But you did feel like you needed to test yours out."

"I couldn't have sex with it if I didn't know it worked."

"So that's the next step, first a test run, then trying it with sex?" I was trying to get him to look at his plan of action.

"All right, I know I've gotta be able to talk to girls first, and I can't even do that yet, so I'll work on that, too. But at least my dick works."

"Daniel, it is a relief, and I know you want to make sure everything works, but it all seems kind of fast. Is there a way to slow it down a bit?"

After a long pause, he said, "Maybe," and then, "I was in a hurry to tell the guys at school about the vacuum cleaner, that I'd done it. I didn't expect my mother to come in, and when I think I could have lost it, God. What would she say? What would my dad say?"

This was the first time that Daniel had mentioned both of his parents. I asked him about what he thought his father would say. At first he told me that he thought his father would "kill" him for doing such a "stupid" thing. Gradually, he came around to a different possibility. His father would listen and maybe tell Daniel that he was sorry that it hadn't worked out with his new wife, sorry that Daniel lived on the other side of the country, sorry that he hadn't been around to talk with Daniel. At the end of our conversation, Daniel began to cry, and told me how much he missed his father.

We met two more times before I spoke with his mother again. In these sessions I was drawn to his emerging sense of humor about the topics of sex and his own sexuality. More relaxed, he told me riotous stories about the "jack club" at school, his name for the group of buddies that had shared the vacuum cleaner idea with him. Now realizing that their "bright" idea had nearly cost him his penis, he saw them in a somewhat different light, telling me that they needed to "get a life."

He still hung out with them, but he didn't take what they said so seriously. He was highly suspicious about their ten-inch penises, telling me that "if they ever had 'em, they probably lost 'em in a vacuum cleaner."

Leaving these buddies' tales and advice behind, Daniel began what I

saw as a search for his own sexuality. He did not "go out and find a girl
to do it with." Instead, he continued to masturbate, without the aid of any
household appliances, watched some videos, and applied his curious
mind to reading anything he could get his hands on. To his surprise, his
extensive search revealed quite a bit of information about sex and sexuality, but very little about masturbation.

"No wonder kids like me are desperate for information," he told me
one afternoon. "It's like a conspiracy. 'In private' doesn't mean 'not at
all,' or does it?"

I agreed with him that masturbation was a "private matter" about
which, unfortunately, there was not much information available. Daniel
had already discovered one of the places where masturbation shows up
relatively frequently, in "hate comics," cartoons that usually show men,
and sometimes boys, masturbating. In one way, the comics helped Daniel,
letting him know that other guys were doing it, but at thirteen, he already
had an idea that it was more involved than grunting guys and erect phalli.
He was slowly beginning to share with me parts of stories that he told
himself when he was masturbating, stories that I recognized as part of
his fantasy life. The first time he mentioned these "jack-off stories," as
he called them, was after he told me the tale of the vacuum cleaner. His
mother opening the door had not only caused him to freeze, but it had
made him forget his "story." "That one was pushed so far into my brain,
I ain't never gonna remember it," he said. "It's gone forever—all I have
left is the sound of a really loud vacuum and the image of my mother's
face when she walked in." I silently noted how both elements were now
memories stored as larger-than-life—almost like those odd comic books
he'd found, or the stories of ten-inch penises on thirteen-year-old boys.

"I know she had to do it, open that door, that is. She says she knocked,
but I don't know. I didn't hear her. The story I was using was nothing special, just the ten-inch variety. I have this giant penis, and a whole bunch
of people are watching me." Then he looked at me and said, "Well, kinda
like this, but not really." I guessed incorrectly that he meant Dr. Green,
his mother, and me all watching him, intruding into his life.

"Why 'not really'?" I asked.

"In my story, the people watching me are other kids, and they're like,
bewitched or something, you know, about my penis. So not like this. I

know I called you a 'pervert.' You probably do find this fascinating, but I don't think you're bewitched, and I really know my mom and Dr. Green aren't thinking about it like that."

"But you have some doubts about me?"

"Yeah. I think any shrink is a pervert. No offense."

"How are you feeling about the whole thing now, Daniel?"

"Better. I don't feel like I'm a pervert anymore. I mean, like, I'm interested in sex, but who isn't? And I was stupid to listen to those guys. Real stupid."

It seemed to me that Daniel had to see me as a pervert during this period when we were looking at this explicit, embarrassing, and even shameful part of his life. He was also closely checking my reactions to his calling me a pervert. Was I embarrassed by this stuff, too? Was I stimulated by our talks? Did I think he was weird? A pervert, or even worse? Daniel was also using my feelings and reactions to guide his own; after all, much territory was uncharted for this thirteen-year-old boy. I knew my responses were important to him. He needed to know—was it okay to be a little "perverted"? Was everyone?

Daniel began to share some of his fantasies with me, ones that he was learning to combine with touching his penis, an important developmental process for many teens in the evolution of their sexuality. He was curious, and that led him to experiment. He had tried masturbating in front of a mirror and again while speaking to another member of the "jack" club, when they were talking on the telephone. He understood that the "stories" he told himself were as important a part of this activity as touching his penis was.

A few weeks later he finally decided to tell me more about the fantasy he'd had the day of the vacuum cleaner, the one that had been pushed so far back in his mind that he thought he'd forget it forever, except strangely, he kept thinking about it.

He said that he had decided to tell me because he felt like he had already shared most of it anyway. He began in his usual way. "This was in my mind, you know? It wasn't real, but a bunch of the jack club were, like, sitting there, jacking off, telling their ten-inch penis stories. I was getting really sick of them, totally sick. They always have the big penises. Then I tell them that I have this dad who's gonna come and take them camping. They don't believe me. Why should they? Like, I don't really have a dad as far as they're concerned. Anyway, I think I'm going to show them, dad or not. Then I go get the vacuum and turn it on. When my mom opened the door, I was so far into the story I actually thought it was my dad, coming to show those guys. She thought I looked shocked. I was. But not because she walked in. It was because she wasn't my dad."

Although Daniel had shared "parts" of this story before, neither he nor the two of us working together had been able to understand it fully until he was able to share this. He had felt desperately lonely, a boy without friends or a father. The physical touching of his penis soothed him, as did many of the stories that he told himself.

This lonely boy, far from his father and friends, needed more than simple touching, or even reassuring sexual fantasies. For him, things had to be "larger than life." He had to be able to impress his buddies and, more important, himself. The vacuum cleaner was an experiment along this path.

My meeting with Daniel's mother wasn't unlike my earlier meetings with her son. She felt stupid because she had thought the move across the country had been painless for her son. She now recognized that she had so much wanted to believe that it was painless that she had missed the signs of trouble. In retrospect, she could see them.

She remembered when Daniel, a very active boy, had begun hanging out in his room. This alone probably wouldn't have been enough to cause her concern, but then he stopped taking phone calls from his old friends. "They're at a different school with other friends," he told her. "They don't really want to talk to me."

Not long after this happened, Daniel's father was unable to take a long-awaited trip to California, a business trip on which he was planning to spend three days camping with Daniel—as Madeline spoke I heard pieces of Daniel's fantasies in the facts. His father promised to reschedule the trip, and Daniel said that he understood, but Madeline noted that Daniel stopped talking to her not long after this happened. When she asked about it, he kept saying, "No problem, Mom," but intuitively she knew that there was a problem. After she discovered his list of ten ways to have a good time, all forms of masturbation, Madeline recognized that she should talk about this with her son, but she found she couldn't. She admitted to me that the whole arena of her son's sexuality frightened her. She so much wanted to help him with it—she could see that he was struggling—but she was extremely fearful that anything that she said would only make his struggles worse. Even before the vacuum cleaner incident, she had spoken with Daniel's father over the telephone, confiding some of her concerns about Daniel's isolation, but she had felt that it would be a betrayal to mention Daniel's list to his dad. She also felt very guilty about moving across the country, escaping their problems—a move that had taken Daniel away from his father and friends at a time when she now realized that he very much needed them.

My work with Madeline focused largely on reassuring her that most of Daniel's fantasies and masturbatory activities were "normal." She was relieved that the episode with the vacuum cleaner appeared to be his one high-risk experience with masturbation. I further explained that her son's masturbation activity, like that of almost all young people, served many functions for him at this time in his life. First, it was, as he described it to be, his "special friend" in this time of need, providing a form of companionship that was soothing to him. It was also a kind of rehearsal for future acts, a test run that determined whether his penis "worked."

As we discussed the matter, Madeline became more open and was able to share some of her own misconceptions about masturbation. She had previously believed that masturbation could cause Daniel to lose interest in sex—he would become preoccupied with satisfying his own desires by himself rather than in the context of a mutual, giving relationship. She also thought he would become hopelessly addicted to his solitary activity, unable to stop. As we kept talking, Madeline admitted that she could really identify with the fantasy part of it—she understood how telling oneself "stories" or using visual images during any kind of sexual activity could be pleasurable and healthy.

She told me that she had learned a great deal. Not only that regular masturbation was a normal and expected activity for thirteen-year-old boys, but that Daniel was lonely, missing his father and friends after the move. Neither she nor Daniel could change this overnight, but she could talk with him about it. She felt she understood that issue better than masturbation, but maybe even that was changing.

Masturbation and Medicine

Daniel's and Madeline's uneasiness with the topic of masturbation is not unusual. In working with them, I'd been more surprised by Dr. Green's initial inability to be direct with me. Thinking about this, I remembered a lecture that I had given a few years previously to the medical students at the university where I work. I had lectured the same group of students on many sexual topics, but when I began to talk about masturbation, the looks on their faces were different. Adapting my lecture to the students' discomfort, I remember ending with a comment that since this topic was difficult for many, I would be glad to answer any questions about it in private. At this there was an almost audible sigh of relief from the usually boisterous students.

After the lecture, a lone student, Michael, came down to the podium. First he thanked me for the discussion. "We really need it. Most of us have already walked in on our patients masturbating, and we don't know what to do. It helps when you talk about it calmly, makes it seem more normal. I guess that's part of it, though. I still don't really believe it's normal. No amount of talking can convince me. I guess it's just too late."

"Too late for what?" I asked, not sure what he meant.

"You talk about the effect it has on people, like it isn't supposed to affect people's sex lives one way or another. You know, doesn't improve it, doesn't make it worse, but then you make a big point about how important it is to many people's sexual identity. I agree, it's really important for doctors to know that stuff. Then you mention all the people who thought it caused bad things to happen—D. H. Lawrence, Sigmund Freud, the Boy Scouts, even your professor in medical school who taught you that it was a disease." Here he paused before continuing. "Well, I still think that way. It goes really deep. If I feel like I'm gonna make myself sterile, or, even more ridiculous, my penis will blow up if I do it, how am I supposed to help other people think it's normal? That's what I mean by too late. I guess it's good that I'm not choosing pediatrics."

"Or worse yet, psychiatry," I added, and smiled at him.

"Yeah," he agreed, this time smiling also.

I told Michael that it was not too late to change his attitude about masturbation. After all, he had come to the lecture knowing the topic, and he did have the choice not to attend. Furthermore, he had been the only student brave enough to ask a question.

"Yeah, like I should have gotten Cliff's notes for the lecture on masturbation?" he joked.

"They probably have them, but you made the choice to come to this lecture. Even that shows your openness. It's not like you have to engage in every sexual activity your patients do in order to be able to help them, but it is important to examine your own attitudes about them, making sure that they're not interfering with the care you provide."

After this conversation I gave Michael my phone number and invited him to spend some time with me in the adolescent clinic on Monday afternoons. We spent several afternoons working together before the topic came up again. The situation was less than ideal. It was a particularly busy afternoon, and I remember that I was in a hurry to leave because one of my daughters had a musical performance at her school that evening. Our last patient was Jim, a fifteen-year-old who had been placed in a group home less than a week earlier. I had seen Jim before, and could see today that he was upset and wanted to talk. Hoping I could confine our conversation to a few minutes, I told him that I understood that being placed out of his own home could be frightening—it was for many kids in his situation—and I asked him how things were going for him at the group home. Usually pretty tight-lipped, Jim responded to my question with a flood of words. It was scary for him, and one of the scariest things was that the guys he shared his room with were "all jerking off" at night. He added some sound effects, giving us an example of some of the moanings. At this, I froze. I just hadn't been expecting this to be his complaint about life in a group home. I couldn't think of anything to say; I realized that my face was turning red. Michael, sitting next to me, asked Jim what scared him most about the activity of the other boys in his room.

"I guess that we'd all start doing it together, and it would mean that we were gay or something. Moving away from home is pretty scary, but then this stuff starts and it really shakes you. You don't know who you are."

This was followed by a longer conversation in which Jim shared his fears, and Michael and I both reassured him.

After the interview, Michael confronted me directly. "Boy, if I hadn't known better, for a moment I thought you, Dr. Comfort, froze in there."

"I did."

Michael softened at this. "Well, as you said, it happens to everybody."

I complimented him on the way that he had kept the conversation with Jim going, and he told me that it made him feel good to see me get embarrassed about the same subject that he felt so unprepared to deal with. We talked about how counseling for masturbation is easier when you're prepared for it—like giving or going to lectures—but it can hit you hard when you don't expect it. We also agreed that acknowledging the embarrassment makes it easier to discuss.

I knew that at least some of my embarrassment that day stemmed from my education in Catholic schools. I remember a fourth-grade teacher discussing the risks of both physical and psychological damage from masturbation. Sin and shame color these memories, and became fixedly woven into the fabric of my own attitudes despite years of education, therapy, and life experience that have contributed to many other, more positive feelings about masturbation. When I am tired, in a hurry, or taken by surprise, they can still appear. The questions that I had at the age of eight—how you "did it" and why, if it caused such terrible things—went unasked and unanswered.

Like many aspects of adolescent sexuality, masturbation has suffered from long-standing taboos. Dating back to the Book of Genesis, in which the Lord took Onan's life because he spilled "his seed on the ground," *onanism,* a term frequently interchanged with masturbation, has always been sharply criticized. Misunderstandings about the physical acts themselves have been present from the beginning, however. The sin of Onan was actually withdrawal before orgasm and the subsequent spilling of semen. Although it shares some similarities with masturbation, it is not necessarily synonymous.

As I'd mentioned in the lecture that Michael had attended, more recent opponents of masturbation have included the Boy Scouts of America, the Christian Coalition, and the Roman Catholic Church. Even well-known liberals in the sexual arena, authors D. H. Lawrence and Norman Mailer, have opposed masturbation, saying that it interferes with an individual's sexual development by precluding the emotional growth that comes with partnered sex. More recently, Dr. Joycelyn Elders, the United States Surgeon General, was pressured into leaving her position after she had voiced her ideas about teaching masturbation in high school.

The medical world has also been of two minds. On one side, Dr. Max Huhner, the author of a book entitled, *Sexual Disorders,* introduced the idea that masturbation was "the most widespread of all sexual diseases, not even excepting gonorrhea." This idea, promoted by Dr. Huhner and others, had tremendous impact on physicians trained in the decades that followed, and on their patients. Yet this viewpoint was balanced even by early psychoanalysts. Wilhelm Stekel wrote that all bad effects attributed to masturbation exist only in the mind of the doctor. And Sigmund Freud wrote extensively about masturbation, describing both healthy and unhealthy patterns. Dr. Peter Blos wrote that masturbation in adolescence was essential for promotion of growth in the area of attachment to others, and believes that a lack of masturbation in adolescence may indicate an inability to handle developing sexual desires.

The important role of fantasy in masturbation also has been acknowledged recently. In understanding how fantasy operates in our lives, however, we need to understand that fantasies are not just sexual. Dr. Ethel Person underscores the role of fantasy in everyday life, and notes that important fantasies contribute to both external and internal roles and identities, and even act as powerful catalysts, guiding many of the choices we make. Understanding fantasy as a process whereby we form mental pictures of many things helps us to understand how much a part of our lives it is. We often "dream" or "daydream" about experiences before we live them. And even if we never live out our fantasies, they perform an important function. Many patients, both teens and adults, use their fantasies to fire their imagination and feed their creativity; it can be an essential part of one's identity. For others, fantasies are a refuge to which they can retreat when life becomes difficult. They return to the everyday world both stronger and calmer.

With respect to sexual fantasies in particular, Dr. Person points out that masturbation fantasies are much more than simple aids to assist in arousal. Yes, some of these fantasies can enhance sexual development, but they, like nonsexual fantasies, can also become central factors around which identity is organized, and determine the main events around which an entire life is organized, such as choice of partner, career, or geographical location. They may also account for the major portion of someone's sexual life. After all, more than 10 percent of people are celibate, and everyone experiences periods of celibacy.

The teen years are crucial for the development of a healthy, satisfying capacity for fantasy of all kinds. For many, masturbation and fantasy combine in adolescence, drawing on aspects of childhood fantasy and genital activity. This process of integrating these two activities, which were in childhood quite separate, does much to lay the groundwork for adult sexuality. It is therefore not only beneficial, but really necessary for healthy sexual development. In addition, a well-developed capacity for sexual fantasy promotes many other aspects of a healthy self, including imagination, self-esteem, and body image.

So fantasy and masturbation, both separately and in combination, amount to much more than "jacking off." They serve many functions for children, adolescents, and adults. Daniel intuitively understood this. He knew how important the "stories" that he used to stimulate himself were. "The jack club," ten-inch penises, and his father were all important parts of this world, a secret world dramatically exposed by the vacuum cleaner incident.

Masturbation is commonly reported by teens, though more by males than by females. A study of more than four hundred high school students in Australia indicated that 59 percent of the boys reported at least one episode of masturbation compared with 43 percent of the girls reporting that they tried it. Even sharper contrasts between genders are found in the area of frequency. Thirty-eight percent of the boys reported that they masturbated three or more times per week compared with 9 percent of the girls. These differences continue through late adolescence into early adulthood. A study of university students reveals that twice as many boys as girls report having tried masturbation, and boys who masturbate show a frequency three times higher than girls. These differences reflect how boys and girls report their masturbatory fantasies, too.

Since no gender differences were noted with respect to nonsexual fantasies, this gap is curious, although not surprising. It may indicate physical and emotional differences, or the fact that girls are more reluctant or even unable to identify their fantasies as masturbatory or sexual. Identifying fantasies as solely for their own sexual pleasure may be too threatening for many reasons (see Heather's story later in this chapter).

Although Daniel was excited and proud about much of his sexual life, both fantasy and feelings, he recognized the danger of his adventure with the vacuum cleaner. Robert Benson, a urologist who has studied men and boys who injure their penises, believes that erotic stimulation by vacuum cleaner or electric brooms is common, especially in the very young or the very curious. Daniel fit both of these descriptions. Dr. Benson notes that unfortunately, and contrary to popular awareness, injury, including loss of the tip of the penis, may not be unusual. This is not the only type of masturbation associated with physical risk. Teens, both girls and boys, may insert objects into their urethras, vaginas, and anuses. These objects can cause pain, discomfort, tearing, and infection. Helping adolescents to understand the physical risks, but not be frightened by the activity itself, requires that adults listen to teens and be able to communicate about sexual matters, including the healthy role of both fantasy and masturbation.

After all, it is difficult to learn about something that is never discussed. Daniel didn't need my help with this part; his fantasies were active and stimulating. The use of the vacuum cleaner was not a good idea, but his fantasies gave him confidence and courage, helping him discover who he was, separate from the rest of the guys in the "jack club." His fantasies were also a work in progress, reflecting his search for his sexual identity and his masculine identity. For example, Daniel was sexually big and successful in his fantasy. His father's appearance in the fantasy was multifaceted, representing both the promise of his father's recognition and affirmation of Daniel as a man, and Daniel's fears about being exposed and vulnerable in front of his father.

Finally, it isn't necessary to disclose the details of one's own fantasy life in order to help an adolescent develop one of his or her own. It is important, however, to acknowledge that fantasy exists for people of all ages, and is a significant component of a healthy sexual life.

Heather's Story

Fifteen-year-old Heather's story is different from Daniel's in many ways. First, unlike Daniel, who was using both external props (the vacuum cleaner) and internal ideas (fantasy) to heighten his sexual desire and pleasure during masturbation, Heather wasn't in my office because of anything she or anyone else thought she was doing to or for herself. Second, she actually wanted to come and talk to a psychiatrist. Heather believed that someone, although she wasn't sure who, was putting thoughts in her head. As these thoughts entered her awareness, she would actually lose consciousness. She had fainted in this way at least a half-dozen times in the past four months, always at school, either in math class or, twice, at school dances. She didn't understand what was happening and wanted some answers—now. Who was doing this to her? Even more important, could I stop them from doing it?

Chewing on fingernails covered with icy-blue polish, Heather let me know that this was a serious problem. It was interfering with school— she had missed days, maybe weeks. Even worse, these thoughts, and especially the fainting, were interfering with her social life. No one wanted to go out with a girl who fainted. She had already been to "medical-type" doctors who had done all kinds of tests. She wasn't sure that they believed her. I was her last hope.

Listening to Heather's story at first made me want to smile. It was certainly a break in my afternoon. Our first hour together occurred right after I saw an eighteen-year-old girl who was slowly starving herself; following Heather, I would see a nineteen-year-old who had found a faster way to die, having taken an overdose of pills. Still, Heather's situation was serious enough to have brought her to see me, not something that most teens do as willingly as she seemed to.

She began by saying, "The past few months have been like a bad dream." I was struck by her metaphor. As I felt myself being pulled into her story, I wondered if the almost physical sensation I was experiencing—a kind of pull toward dreaming—paralleled the feelings that she experienced when these "thoughts" would enter her head.

"How has it been like a bad dream, Heather?"

"It usually starts when not much else is going on. Like when I'm standing around at a dance, or mostly when I'm staring out the window in math class, and, like, it's really boring. There isn't much to do. Then this feeling comes, and this thing starts taking over. It's slow at first, then it's, like, moving faster. I start getting hot, really hot. I feel like I'm drowning. Then I can't breathe. Then I—I wake up after I've fainted." She paused and looked me right in the eye. "Someone has got to be doing this to me."

"So who do you think it could be?" I asked.

"My priest says it's wicked angels."

"Is that what you think?"

"Is it important?"

"*Here* it is, Heather."

Reluctantly she said, "I don't think it's angels. The priest might be right about some things, but not this." Then she added quickly, "But I do think it's someone. Could a guy be doing it to me, like even my math teacher?"

"I still don't understand exactly what you think the guy is doing to you." I realized that she might think I was expressing disbelief, so I added, "It will help us both solve this mystery if we know exactly what *you* think is happening."

"I don't know what is going on, but it *feels* like a guy or something is taking over my body." Heather stopped chewing on her nails and looked at me, as if waiting for me to provide the solution. I had some ideas about what might be going on with her, but I didn't want to voice them too quickly, losing an opportunity for her to think more about what was happening to her, something that was obviously hard for her to do. Thinking about this, I asked her if it was difficult for her to stay focused on the fainting episodes.

She smiled, almost as if she was relieved I'd asked. "I wanna know, but it *is* weird, the whole thing is strange." She added, "At least I don't feel like I'm gonna faint here."

"But it's weird to talk with me about it."

"Yeah, kinda, the opposite of fainting, though. It, like, works me up."

"Curious," I said.

"Yeah."

I thought about Heather long after she left my office. I talked with the physicians who had evaluated her, and they were pretty certain that there wasn't a medical cause; they believed it was psychiatric. On that score, I had already found out some important diagnostic information. I had asked Heather certain questions in order to rule out the possibility that she was experiencing any kind of psychotic thinking—a break with reality that often causes people to hear voices or feel that others can read their minds, penetrate their minds, control their thoughts, and so forth. Although Heather felt incredibly alienated by what was happening, she was not the first adolescent to have trouble understanding that certain fantasies were actually coming from within him- or herself. These thoughts or fantasies are even harder to accept, especially in girls, when they are sexual.

I thought about Heather's comment in reference to our conversation, how it was "the opposite of fainting." I had an idea what she meant. Talking with me would be quite different from actually experiencing the fainting, which Heather still seemed largely disconnected from, at least consciously. I knew that one of my tasks would be trying to help her recall one of these powerful episodes, maybe going through it out loud with me step-by-step, and stay fully conscious without succumbing to fainting. We had made a start. My sense was that the power of her fantasies didn't stem from their content. Rather, these fantasies were so difficult for Heather to "own" that she would lose consciousness rather than recognize how she had brought them into being all by herself.

I had spoken with Heather's mother, Melana, only once, over the phone, to set up the appointment. She was a polite, soft-spoken woman who desperately wanted her daughter to get well. "Whatever this is, Dr. Ponton," she had said, "please help her." I usually like to get background information from the parents, and meet one or both of them at least once when I begin working with a new patient, but Melana asked if we could postpone that meeting. "My husband and I own a small restaurant, and we've both already been gone so much for these appointments, or to pick her up from school after one of these fainting spells. We just really both need to put in some very long days, you know, as much as possible. Could we wait a few weeks?"

After my first session with Heather, I called and left a message on her parents' voice mail, telling them I didn't think there was anything seriously wrong with their daughter, but I would keep them posted.

When Heather arrived for her next session, I found that I wasn't the only one who had spent a lot of time thinking during the intervening days. Heather had had another fainting episode, at a dance, this time in the arms of the boy with whom she was slow-dancing. He had been surprised, but was proud he hadn't dropped her onto the floor. Heather was also surprised, but she told me that this time she had remembered what we had talked about and so, after she was taken home by her friends, had tried to write an account of what had happened. Somewhere, buried inside her recollections, was a fleeting description of having felt "kinda attracted" to the boy with whom she had been dancing.

I asked her what she remembered about that part.

"Well, I know I was attracted to him at least a little bit." Then she looked shocked. "You think I'm fainting because I'm attracted to these guys? You gotta be crazy. Most of the time it's in math class, and no one in their right mind would be attracted to that math teacher. You should see him!"

I told Heather that I wasn't exactly sure why she was fainting. It did seem to be happening at two specific times, though—math class and school dances.

"Well, I don't think they have anything in common. In math, I'm usually bored out of my mind. At the dances, I'm usually having a good time. At least I was until I started fainting." She eyed me angrily. "What's happening to me? Why haven't you solved this yet?"

"It makes you angry that I haven't solved it for you?"

Fighting back tears, she said, "The other doctors, like, give you this idea that there is this one answer, like a bad gene or a seizure."

"You really wish there was an easy answer."

"Yeah."

We sat in silence for a while before she spoke. "There is one thing."

"What?"

"In math class, you know, I'm spacing out all the time, even before the thing, like, takes over—getting hotter, finally fainting, I, like, remember spacing out a little at this dance."

"What do you think is going on when you're 'spacing out'?"

"I'm thinking about my life, trying to make it better, I guess. It's so weird that I can't remember it when you ask."

"What seems weird about that?"

She laughed. "Like, why *would* I remember—good question."

"Heather, there's nothing wrong with your memory, but it is interesting that you forget what's going on right before you faint. It may have a lot to do with *why* you faint."

"Maybe it's about sex."

Even though I had been waiting for this moment, it came much more quickly than I'd thought. Still, we had to move slowly over this delicate ground.

"Why do you say that?" I asked.

"I've thought it before, like why I faint when I'm at dances, if I'm nervous about boys or something. But math classes, though—it doesn't fit. They are boring. Maybe I've got to do something to make them more exciting. Fainting sure does that."

"Anything else you're doing to make them more exciting? Maybe before the fainting?"

"Like the stories I tell myself to keep from getting totally bored?"

"Maybe."

"My little stories could make me faint, huh? So no guy is doing this to me?"

"What do you think?"

"It feels like something outside of me."

"Is it hard to think it could come from inside, from you?"

She nodded and again seemed close to tears. "It makes me want to believe in those wicked angels the priest was talking about."

"Sometimes they're a lot easier to believe in."

When Heather had said, "Maybe it's about sex," she was testing me and, I believe, herself. She had remarkable difficulty even letting herself think that her fantasies—or any of her thoughts, for that matter—could be sexual in nature. Testing this idea out with me, she may have wanted to know what it felt like just to say it. She also wanted to test my reaction. Would I jump on it immediately, saying, "That's it!" and, at the same time, frighten her? She hadn't taken long to invoke the "wicked angels" again.

Generally, when teens talk with me about sexual matters, it is something that they want kept private from their parents. Although Heather never told me this directly, I believed that this was the case with her. She was having enough trouble talking with me about this.

She and I continued to meet for several weeks. The fainting episodes stopped, but we continued to struggle with their meaning.

Most of Heather's fantasies had not been explicitly sexual. They covered a full range of feelings and activities, not unexpected for a fifteen-year-old girl—or any person for that matter. She usually placed herself at the center of the fantasy. In these "stories" she traveled widely, leaving her Catholic high school, her parents, even her friends, far behind.

She remembered imagining these stories when she was very young. She acknowledged to me how much they expanded her world. Her family—mother, father, and three brothers—had never left Northern California. Heather spent a lot of time in Australia in her fantasies. In math class she often had Australian odysseys. They would start with traveling to Australia with boys, sharing hotel rooms or campgrounds. She wasn't sure how and when the sexual stuff started, but the stories had started to change, probably a year or two before she came to see me. Some of the boys in the stories started to have names and faces, and she wanted to kiss them. She told me that she held back for a long time because for her, kissing was taboo, even in her fantasies. Then she remembered the first time that she had a fantasy with an explicitly sexual tone. She had just finished reading *The Thorn Birds,* a novel set in Australia that includes the story of a young girl's sexual awakening. Heather felt that this could be her story, too, and unlike fantasies, which came "by accident," this time the fantasy was by her own choice. Australia had always been the setting for these stories—interior desert, a rugged coastline, and far away from her San Francisco life. The novel helped her add other things to it. The girl in the book feels desire—a desire to be sexual with a man, to touch him and have him touch her. Heather felt those desires, too, at least within the framework of her fantasies. As she wove her story, first having a boy start to touch, then finally kiss her, followed by her touching him, the fantasy would stop short. It wasn't that she couldn't remember, or that she couldn't tell me, but this was the point at which she would lose consciousness.

She wasn't sure why. Earlier she had even tried to stop the stories altogether, thinking that dreaming about desire was wrong, even in such a limited way. The fantasy certainly didn't fit with what she was learning in her religious classes—postpone and procreate, "the Catholic guideposts to sexuality," as she termed them.

When she said this, I realized that maybe the reason Heather's parents weren't seeking involvement was more complicated than Heather's wish for privacy. I filed away the thought as she went on.

"It's funny that I thought a guy had to be doing it, putting those ideas there. It's like I couldn't be coming up with this stuff myself."

"When you were thinking that, you didn't have anyone to talk to yet. It also didn't fit with what you're learning at school or in church," I said.

"Still doesn't," said Heather, and I wondered if now wasn't a good time to contact her parents and see if we could meet.

The Parents Enter the Picture

Heather's parents, Melana and Dmitri, were several minutes early for the session that I had called to arrange. Through my half-cracked door I could hear them talking in the waiting room, inspecting my office and planning strategy. "We have to tell her Heather's doing better. She's not fainting anymore, Dmitri."

"Look at these books—they're all about sex."

"They're not all about sex. Here's a whole bunch on adolescence."

"Probably the same thing. I don't want her talking with Heather about sex."

"Someone has to talk with her about it, Dmitri. We don't."

At this point I opened the door, introduced myself, shook their hands, and invited them in. Melana and Dmitri were true to their plan. They did tell me that Heather no longer fainted. "We really appreciate how much you've helped her," said Melana right away, as if to counterbalance, or delay, the protest she knew was forthcoming from her husband.

Then Dmitri spoke, his face reddening almost immediately. "If you're talking with our daughter about sex, we'll need to stop these sessions."

I thought about what was at stake for Melana and Dmitri. They were worried about their daughter. The fainting had been a serious problem for her, but also for them. They had taken Heather for many medical appointments and scary tests, worried that she was struggling with a dangerous physical problem. Then they had been told by the doctors that no medical cause could be found and, furthermore, that their daughter needed to see a psychiatrist. When the fainting stopped relatively quickly after their daughter first came to my office, they realized then not only did Heather not mind coming to see me, she wanted to come—she took two buses to get to my office and started to keep a journal that she brought with her. I could understand how they might feel left out. This was only part of the problem, though. They had beliefs—some religious, some cultural, some simply personal—that prevented them from talking with or having anyone else talk with Heather about sex. All of this helped me to understand their position, but I was still puzzled about how to respond to Dmitri's explicit proscription. I decided to ask them why they thought their daughter was better.

"Talking," said Melana. "She says the talking has made her better." I couldn't know for sure, but I suspected she was doing her best to find some kind of middle ground between directly encouraging me in my work with Heather and directly contradicting her husband.

Sensing his wife's reluctance, Dmitri moved the discussion back to his major concern. "Dr. Ponton, are you talking with her about sex?"

"I'm talking with her about her fainting. It's clear that you seem worried that talking about sex might be part of that."

"I just don't want you talking to her about sex, that's all."

"What if I can't help her with the fainting unless we do talk some about it?"

"Is that the way it is?" asked Dmitri.

"Dmitri, what worries you about me talking with Heather about sexual matters?"

"It's simple. I believe that you don't talk to kids about sex. She's an innocent girl. I want her kept that way."

"You believe that my talking with her about sex would take away that innocence?"

"I do, and I won't have it. That's all I have to say." He stood up, apparently ready to leave.

"Is there a reason no one mentioned this concern to me when I first began seeing Heather? It seems to be very important."

"We didn't think it would happen." He looked at Melana for the first time.

She said, "We wanted her to get better, and they told us you could help her."

At that point I realized that they had had this concern all along but had held back, their fears about their daughter's health overriding their beliefs. Once they knew she wasn't gravely ill, though, they were ready to start asserting themselves. Or at least Dmitri was. He had gone straight to my bookshelf as if he was looking for the incriminating evidence he knew must be lurking around my office.

I spoke again. "Melana and Dmitri, Heather is better, but she still needs more help."

"Not if she's talking about sex," said Dmitri, leaving the office.

By now I knew we couldn't have an open discussion about the matter. I started to ask Melana to think about how much treatment would continue to help Heather, but I could see that she was struggling to hold back tears. She would have made that choice if it were up to her alone.

"Dr. Ponton, thank you for helping her. She is so much more open, not so spacey. I wish you could continue to work with her, but he's not going to let it happen. When the doctors told us she could faint in front of a car, then it was a matter of life and death. I guess you can't lie to him and say that you're not talking about anything sexual, right? I guess not?"

"No, Melana, I couldn't lie, but I'm willing to try to speak with Dmitri again. It's also very important that I see Heather one more time to talk with her about it."

"I'll make sure that she comes, and I'll try to talk with him."

Melana wasn't very hopeful. She left my office, leaving me to question whether I could have handled this situation in a better way. I had to acknowledge to myself that I prided myself on my ability to work with parents, but I knew that it was not always easy, and in this case I was not even being given the choice. More important, neither was Heather. It was also unfortunate we weren't going to be able to keep working together in light of the fact that so much was finally falling into place for Heather.

In the weeks we had been working together, she had said very little to me about her father. Now I wondered if she was afraid of his disapproval, even anger, if he ever suspected she was not "innocent." It certainly added a thread to the tapestry of reasons she had to repress her sexual fantasies. Like many girls, she struggled with her own prohibitions and internal conflicts about having sexual feelings, but combining these with explicit prohibitions from her father and her church could make the struggle impossible. Was Heather consciously aware of her father's prohibition? That I didn't know yet. And I might not have a chance to find out.

I also sat in my office after Dmitri and Melana had left, thinking about my own reactions. Like Heather, I had attended parochial schools. My parents were not Greek Orthodox, but Heather's situation was similar. I had sat through many religious classes that outlined the virtues of celibacy. In elementary school all the girls were asked on a yearly basis whether we felt a calling to become a nun—to remain celibate permanently, to become a bride of Christ. In first grade all hands were raised. By eighth grade many no longer raised their hands, including me. Then the questions changed—a sneak attack, from my perspective. The girls were asked whether we were still chaste, having no impure thoughts, and then, directly, if we were virgins. Although I personally knew the truth to be otherwise, not one girl ever failed to raise her hand, all the way until graduation. I remember watching my friends raise their hands, always watching the hands, never their faces, which told the truth. I also remember what they were concealing. Valerie, for instance, hadn't slept with any guy, and she wouldn't, ever, because she was in love with Maria, the most beautiful girl in our class. Debbie had gone "away" for long weekends twice. She believed that her two abortions had made her sterile and that she would never again be able to get pregnant. In desperate attempts to answer that question, though, she kept trying. The saddest case was Yvonne's. After her "friends" told on her, Yvonne's stepfather was ordered out of her home for having sex with Yvonne and her fourteen-year-old sister. The rest of the hand raisers were just the usual young girls filled with "impure thoughts" and hopes for equally impure actions. What girl was going to fail to raise her hand and be judged by the nun, or even the other girls, even herself?

Had things changed so much in thirty years? I bet Heather, a girl who fainted when she had sexual thoughts, would have raised her hand, too.

I also thought about how my own past was related to my failure to talk with Dmitri and Melana earlier. I could have pressed for a meeting sooner. I certainly had done so plenty of times with other patients. Somehow, though, with this case I was still afraid to raise my own hand, to admit to sexuality in some form. Not my own sexuality, but as a topic, a real part of real life, of their daughter's life. Someone like Dmitri, whose ideas were so rigid and fixed, didn't care whether his daughter acted on her fantasies or not. The fact that the fantasies existed at all would have met with his resistance and anger. The last thing I wanted was for that anger to result in any more restrictive consequences for Heather.

I was still thinking about this when I met with Heather for the last time. She was furious—how could her father order her to stop therapy because she was talking about sex?

"Where is his mind? I wonder what *he* is thinking about. He sees me like some virginal creature. It's gross."

"Heather, I'm very sorry about his decision. You are working hard in therapy to understand yourself, and it has not been easy. The fainting was upsetting, but also mysterious. You've hidden your sexuality from yourself. I will talk with your parents again, but I'm not sure anyone can help your father understand this and change his mind. I tried to."

"Oh, he understands, all right. It's like my sex life belongs to him. I should show him. I should just get pregnant. Then he would know."

"Heather, you are right—your sexuality belongs to you. Getting pregnant to show him that, though, isn't a very well-thought-out approach."

"I know," she said, sighing, and I knew she did. I wasn't going to have to worry about this with her. "But he makes me feel so weak."

"It doesn't help that your mother and I, two grown women, aren't able to change his mind, either."

"Oh, I see how he is. It's not your fault. It's just—"

"Just what, Heather?"

"Well, it's like, I can't go back to how it was before. I don't want to."

I smiled. "I'm glad you don't want to. And I don't think you have to."

"Maybe you're right. I mean, I'm sure not gonna tell them anything, but I'm also not gonna keep secrets from myself anymore. At least not if I can help it!" She smiled.

Dmitri did not change his mind, and I did not see Heather again, although I continued to talk with Melana occasionally by telephone. She said Heather was doing fine, still free of fainting spells. I wondered how fine things really were, though.

Heather was deeply frightened of her sexual fantasies, so much so that she was unable to identify herself as their "author." This was not a girl out of touch with reality, but a girl unable to get in touch with herself. Would this pattern continue to haunt Heather in different ways? I couldn't know. I have seen many times the damage it caused when young people are not permitted, let alone encouraged, to explore sexual fantasy. Many of those people became adult patients of mine, decades older, with failing marriages, difficult relationships, problems with intimacy, sexual dysfunction. Sometimes those problems cause other problems, like turning to alcohol or drugs to ease the pain.

I could still hope for Heather. I still do.

Fantasies and Masturbation

Fantasy is a healthy component of a person's life. It can even be considered a useful skill. Sexual fantasy in particular is typically a very private arena for both young people and adults. Respecting a teen's privacy is vital. It is neither necessary nor healthy for parents to be "in on" the content of a young person's fantasy life any more than it would be appropriate for a child to be aware of a parent's. If a parent is concerned a child's fantasy life is somehow dangerous or unhealthy, she may want to consult a professional before speaking directly to the child, but in any case, she should remember that this is often a new experience for young people, regardless of the frequency with which it may seem to be taking place, and he or she is apt to feel—quite rightfully—vulnerable. It is important to be extremely gentle and accepting, bearing in mind that he or she may not even be fully aware of the fantasies and the role they may be playing.

Masturbation is still a largely taboo subject in our society. Yet, like fantasy, it is a perfectly healthy component of both adult and adolescent life. While parents may be comfortable offering their young children instructions about "touching themselves" in public, addressing this still naturally occurring behavior with adolescents can be much more difficult. After all, at older ages, it is much more likely to be intertwined with the beginnings of adult sexuality. The problem of addressing this subject may be compounded if the adult has minimal experience speaking of it. Here, again, you want to consult a professional before talking to children about masturbation, if only to gain some practice at addressing the topic directly and without embarrassment.

Many of our problems with masturbation relate to the shame and guilt that have come to be associated with such activity, rather than the activity itself. Because masturbation is still largely a hidden topic, children and adolescents are not exposed to a lot of information about it. For many teens, this area of sexuality offers them an opportunity to develop a private perspective, including preferences, rules, and ideas. It is also still an area in which misinformation abounds, and because it goes undiscussed, these same teens are still vulnerable to those concepts, too.

4

Safety in Numbers
The Guiltless Mosh Pit

It's like the music is in your body. —Ricky

"**D**r. Ponton, what do you think of Smashing Pumpkins? Would you let your fourteen-year-old child go to one of their concerts unsupervised? I'm sure you wouldn't. I mean, I wouldn't, I haven't, not yet anyway. What would you do? We're not letting Ricky go," exclaimed Mercedes, an expressive and worried mother who was meeting with me for the first time. Ricky, the object of her concern, was sitting on the floor playing with the stud that pierced his lower lip and examining my stack of CDs.

"*Salsa Moderna, Cesaria Evora,* Chopin . . . you and my mom should get together. She likes this kind of music."

"What kind of music is that, Ricky?"

"You know—old people's music."

"What kind of music do you like?"

"You heard it from her—Smashing Pumpkins. Bet you don't have any of that."

"Not here, you're right. But I have listened to them, and I would be interested in listening to your music if you want to bring it in."

This surprised him. He stopped playing with his lip ring and started looking at his mother and me.

"You want to choose something?" I asked him, pointing at my stack of CDs.

"Not me." He backed away from my CDs like they were suddenly poisoned, and said, "Let my mom choose."

"I couldn't." Then, I think feeling put on the spot, she said, "Is this really why we're here?" She was eyeing me suspiciously. Her son smiled slyly.

"You brought me here, Mom. That was your choice, too. Go on, pick one. You like salsa. You're a great dancer, too."

"I'm not going to get up and dance, Ricky. Not here."

"No one will ask you to dance, Mercedes. And I wasn't trying to make you uncomfortable. Like you and your son, I love music. It helps me relax. Besides, you brought him here to talk about whether he should be able to go to rock concerts. Music is part of it."

Mercedes smiled. "Having all these teenagers in here, you probably need to relax!" She had picked up a few of the CDs and was flipping through them when she paused. "Where did you get all the Cuban CDs?" Her face had changed suddenly, and she looked down at my carpet, but not before I saw her eyes fill up.

Ricky chimed in, "I knew you'd like 'em, Mom." And then to me Ricky said, "My mom was born in Cuba."

After several moments Mercedes looked up at me. "I would like to play Maraca or Silvio Rodriguez."

"Mercedes, you can borrow them if you'd like."

"I will, if it's okay. After all, we're here to talk about Ricky's music. We've already spent quite enough time on mine."

"Yours is important, too, Mercedes. Maybe Ricky loves music so much because you do, too."

"But the Smashing Pumpkins, Dr. Ponton."

"A far cry from Silvio Rodriguez, admittedly," I said.

"But you're right, he probably has a passion for it, so he should be able to go to the concert. I guess that's what you're saying."

"It's this weekend," chimed in Ricky, looking first at me, then back at his mother. "So you have to decide fast. Like right now."

So many of the decisions that have to be made with teenagers are urgent. Ricky was acting like many adolescents, trying to speed up the process. But one of the keys to a well-thought-out decision, especially about a potential risk, is to slow the process down. This might be something Ricky still needed to learn.

He egged Mercedes on. "Ma, they're only going to be here this Saturday night, and I have a free ticket."

"Ricky, I just don't know. Their concerts are so dangerous." And then to me, "They have this mosh pit. I even read that a kid got killed at one of their concerts."

"Mom, I'm not going to hurt myself. So what do you think?"

"Well, I think you could hurt yourself. I let you go to that concert two years ago, and you came home all bruised up, and now you wear that lip ring."

"Oh, man, what about it?" Ricky scowled. "Do you think I'll get in more trouble because I wear a lip ring?"

Ricky and Mercedes were headed into old patterns. Trying to steer them back to the main issue that they had presented to me, I suggested we keep our focus on the upcoming concert in particular.

"Dr. Ponton, Ricky had bruises all over him after the last concert."

"That was years ago!"

"It was six months ago. You're not going to be down there on the floor, promise me that, Ricky."

After several seconds her son said, "I can't promise that, Mom. I mean, that's where it's at, the floor, that's the concert." Then to explain to me what his mother had referred to, he added, "I was just a kid back then, and this guy ran into me. I was stupid."

"So what you're saying is that you're not going to be slamming or surfing or grinding, and that you'll use good judgment and move away when you see others doing it?" I asked him.

"Well, yeah, do you think I want to get myself killed or something?"

The "or something" rang in my head when Ricky and I were sitting alone together several minutes later. I knew that I needed to ask him about it, but I decided to start slowly. If I rushed him the way he tried to rush his mother, I could lose the chance to gain his trust.

"Ricky, your mom seems to have some pretty reasonable concerns about your going to the concert, yet it really seems to set you off if she brings them up. What do you think is going on?"

He half smiled at me, and I could see a full set of bright green braces on his teeth; together with the gold lip ring, they were quite an arresting reminder that teenagers are stuck somewhere between the child and adult worlds. Sheepishly he said, "I like my mom a lot, but I feel like she's forgotten what it is like to be young. I really want to go to those concerts, especially the Smashing Pumpkins."

"Why do you like concerts so much?"

"I dunno. I feel different when I'm at them."

"How so?"

"Well, for one, like I'm not just some skinny guy who has to stand on his skateboard to be as tall as the other kids. And the Pumpkins play . . . just so righteous."

I smiled at this, thinking of how vague teenagers can be when they're trying to be specific.

"When they sing, 'You make me feel real'—*I* feel real, like they're singing to me."

"It sounds pretty amazing."

"It is. She wants me to sit up there in the stands; it's not the same up there. It doesn't feel the same."

"What's it like on the floor?"

"Everyone is into the music, moving like one big wave. This warm feeling spreads over everyone. It's spiritual or something. I feel so high"—here he looked at me—"and it's not drugs. I don't do drugs, you know. That's not what I'm talking about. But then my mom starts talking about everyone slamming into each other, how I'm going to get hurt. She just doesn't get it."

"How it feels to be transformed . . ."

"Yeah. Your body feels so different. You feel like you're joined with everyone there, but like you really feel your own body. That's what's so fantastic about surfing the pit. Yeah, there are bruises, but you're not feelin' any pain. At least not in the moment! You just feel like you and the music and everyone else there are all one . . . body, I guess. And the music is the heartbeat or something. I don't think my mom gets that at all."

"Have you tried to tell her?"

"Nah. But I sorta think she should get it, you know? Something about how into music she is, and when she was young, but maybe not. I just get this feeling about it, you know? She loves Cuban music, that's why she was almost crying when she saw your CDs. Sometimes I come home at night and she's sitting in the living room with all the lights off, listening to her music. I know something deep is going on."

"So you think she might be able to understand."

"No, I don't. When I talk with her about it, all she says is always about the risk, about what could go wrong. She's always thinking about the danger. She's the one thinking about how I'm going to die in the mosh pit, not me."

Risk and Revelation

Ricky's description of how he felt up close at the Smashing Pumpkins concert was familiar to me. Many teens talk about the intense pleasure that they experience at rock concerts, different from the pleasure that they have listening to their music in their bedrooms at home. For young teens, music is one of the first things that they come into contact with that helps them define themselves differently from adults. For more than a hundred years, adolescents have had "their music." Often, that music speaks to issues adolescents are struggling with: the power of sexual feelings, anger at adults whom they feel "control" teens' lives without listening to them, the first awareness that one is a unique and separate person with special feelings, strange and powerful attractions to other people, the thrills associated with having a strong adult body, among others. Adolescent music is powerful. It speaks to universal feelings that teenagers have, and it also speaks to specific issues that affect a group or even a generation of teens—protest songs addressing the United States' involvement in Vietnam, the role that swing music played with teens in prewar Germany, the way that sexual risk and HIV is woven into teen music today. Adolescent music also helps teens understand sexual feelings with which they are struggling.

Ricky was also experiencing the music sexually, even if he hadn't put it in so many words. He described it "moving as a wave" and "the warm feeling" spreading over his body. The presence of special phenomena associated with adolescents and music and dancing have been known for centuries. Reports of adolescent groups dancing themselves into trance-like states date back to the thirteenth century. "Tarantism," or outbreaks of dancing mania, reportedly centered on the teens' shared beliefs that the bite of a spider during the night caused them to forget who they were and to dance tirelessly. Adolescent girls were believed to be especially vulnerable to this type of behavior, but boys were not excluded.

There are many aspects to this group phenomenon. First, music and dancing are in themselves hypnotic. They allow teens to experiment with their bodies, to feel things that they have never felt before. Ricky describes this. A range of spiritual, sexual, and other feelings can be experienced at the same time. The presence of other teens feeling the same things and acting the same way allows teens to experience forbidden sensations such as wavelike pleasure. Billy Corrigan, the lead singer in Smashing Pumpkins, gives that permission directly as he sings, "You make me feel real." Teens like Ricky allow themselves to experience the changes that they are undergoing—beginning separation from families, taller, more powerful bodies, as well as the emergence of sexual feelings. Ricky told me that it was easier for him to have those feelings when he is at a rock concert with other kids. He had some of the same feelings when he listened to CDs in his bedroom, but he "couldn't feel them all the way," something fell short.

As a society, we focus a great deal of attention on the dangerous aspects of rock concerts—the mosh pit, easy availability of drugs and alcohol, dangerous folk who might prey on naive young people—but we also need to talk about the benefits. Large concerts are very attractive to teens. Providing more than the obvious unity, they serve as a bonding force with teens in other parts of the world—the band they're seeing was just in San Francisco, New York, Seattle, or London. Yet the concerts also mean that other teens are right there, their sweaty bodies pressed close to yours. When the music is playing and the dancers are moving and the lights are going, it is magical. Ricky and other teens discuss how powerfully liberating this experience is. It is also frightening to parents who may not want their son or daughter or the other kids to feel that "free"—what are the kids going to do then? Dangerous things for sure.

In addition to entertainment, connection with teens around the world, and liberation, rock concerts are social events where friends gather, where kids meet other kids. The floor allows for much more socializing than the seats in the stands. Finally, rock concerts encourage teens to develop their identity, separately and as a member of a group. Sexual identity is part of that.

Mercedes's Music

Two weeks after our first meeting, Mercedes returned my two Cuban CDs. After gently laying them down on my desk, she stood there for a few seconds, looking at several other CDs spread out there.

"Did you like them?" I asked.

"Yes—umm, thank you so much."

She seemed relaxed without Ricky. This time she chose to sit on my faded gray couch rather than the ergometric but stiff chairs, and she started the conversation. "So how are the Smashing Pumpkins like Silvio Rodriguez?"

Even before she asked me the question, I had the feeling she and I were going to enjoy this session together. My first signal had been her calm face, then the way she took her time looking at my CDs, then her choice of the comfortable velvet couch, all of it tranquil. Teenagers, with their gold nose rings and high energy, can put parents and other adults on edge, and after years of working with and parenting teens, I'm sure that teens don't mind knocking parents a little off balance. It probably reassures them some. They often tell me that they feel off balance, and "sharing" this feeling, if only by causing it in others, evens things out.

Still, being alone with Mercedes was not the only reason I felt more at ease. After all, it isn't always relaxing for me to meet alone with parents. Many times it's more stressful. Some parents are overwhelmed and are "eager" to tell their parental saga to anyone who will listen. I listen, but often at the peril of "catching" their stress—which, like teens provoking feelings of discomfort in others, may be the result of parents hoping to relieve themselves of the burden of those stressful, anxious feelings—and having it weigh heavily on me at the end of a session. Already, I knew that this wasn't going to be the case with Mercedes. She hummed as I made tea for us. We began by talking about the music of Silvio Rodriguez, and it became apparent to me that the music had played a part in helping her to relax with me. Ricky was right about his mother. She not only played Cuban CDs when she was sitting alone in her living room with the lights turned low, she really listened to the music. I asked Mercedes how it made her feel.

"Sometimes I'm numb. Teaching all day in San Francisco high schools is a nightmare. Sometimes I need to listen for an hour before I even have the energy to take my shoes off, but after a while I forget where I am . . . then it's off to a beach in Cuba where my father took me as a child. I am sitting in the sand, watching the waves move toward the shore. My family is there, too." Mercedes was staring off and she looked up, surprised to see that I was there, too, in the room with her.

She smiled at me. "Listening, I almost forget that I spent my entire day teaching sophomores Spanish verbs."

"That time sounds very relaxing for you."

"It is. It's more than relaxing. The problems float out of the room, all the struggles with Ricky, the gold lip ring, all gone."

"Left on the beach?"

"Yeah, one CD and I'm back in Cuba."

Mercedes's music helped her in two important ways. First, it obviously helped her to calm down. Equally important, it provided a connection to her birthplace. I understood that, too. I often spend hours listening to French-Canadian music, feeling a similar connection to my family. As we talked more about it, I recognized the ways that she and fifteen-year-old Ricky were alike. Ricky felt "transformed" at rock concerts. The music made him feel real, more connected. I wondered whether Mercedes would feel differently about the concerts if she understood what Ricky was experiencing. Would it shift at least part of her focus away from risk?

She and I discussed this, and she readily agreed—she could see the connection. Her music was relaxing, Ricky's transforming—each had a powerful draw.

"Mercedes, what's your picture of Ricky at the concerts? What do you imagine he's doing or feeling there?"

"The worst or the best, Dr. Ponton? When I think about Ricky there, I keep imagining him trampled at the pit, impaled by another kid wearing a spiked dog collar and heavy black boots. Weird, huh?"

"You think so?"

"I know it happens to kids, but I also know it isn't typical. Why am I so stuck on it? I guess my other thought, about the feeling part, is that he loves music the way I do. Music is special for me. Of course I relax with it, but it's a lot more than that. I feel freer with it, although I'm not sure I would tell Ricky that."

"Why not?"

"Too dangerous."

"For you or for him?"

"Both, maybe. I'll think about it."

Just what was going on? Mercedes thought it was strange that she couldn't put these images out of her mind. Why did she keep thinking about these things? Ricky's lip ring was upsetting to Mercedes, but it was not a spiked collar—not even close. Why the image? In fact, Mercedes did not even know kids who wore spiked collars, not even her students. I found it a curious image, but I have come to accept that parents sometimes have jarring visual pictures of their children that they can't get out of their minds. Sipping our tea on this relaxed evening, I thought Mercedes might be that way.

We began talking about Mercedes's teenage years in Havana during the early 1960s, formative years for Mercedes and Cuba. Mercedes, at thirteen, felt sophisticated, her newly feminine body learning secrets, changing, as she put it, beginning to feel like a Havana woman, and most important, she was going to her first dance. She and her female cousins were planning a nighttime party with music. She never got to her dance. One morning her mother and father awakened Mercedes and her brother and told them they were moving far away. They left that day, and several weeks later, Mercedes found herself relocated, living in a part of the United States where few Cubans lived—no Cuban music, certainly no dances. The American dances were not the same. She never felt that she fit in with the other kids. She was an outsider. Mercedes was in her twenties when she moved to San Francisco, with its Latina community, and rediscovered her love for Cuban music, but by then her adolescent years had passed, and she hadn't danced very much in the interim.

Why worry so much about Ricky now, so many years later? As we talked, she realized maybe she was worried that someone or something was going to disrupt Ricky's teen years as hers had been disrupted. Was she trying to stop that from happening by stopping Ricky first? Or was she envious of her son, somehow using her worry about the dangers of the mosh pit to try to keep him from enjoying what she had missed during her own adolescence?

Her memory of the past and the idea that this affected how she was treating her son made Mercedes stop. She didn't move for several minutes. Her tea grew cold in its cup. She didn't say anything. It grew dark in my office, the sun having moved past the large redwoods that stand in the backyard. I didn't say anything, either. I didn't turn on the lights. I thought about what Ricky had said about his mother—*sits in the dark, a lot . . . don't know what's going on, but it's strange. . . .* On that night I felt that she needed someone to sit with her. Eventually she left, thanking me for not saying anything. I sat there in the dark for several minutes after she was gone thinking about those lost dances before I locked the door and went home.

Real Risk

Like his mother, Ricky brought a CD to his solo session with me—no "Latina" music for him. It was the Smashing Pumpkins *Adore*. In contrast to his mother, he popped in the CD as soon as he entered my office, no question about whether or not now was the time. He wanted to listen to it, and wanted me to listen to it with him. "Remember you said you'd be interested in hearing my music," he said, as if to remind me. "Do you like it? You can see why I do, right?"

I could. Sensitive to my older tastes, he chose songs that he and I would both appreciate. He wanted me to be comfortable. In this way he was like his mother—music meant a great deal to him. It allowed him to experience feelings he often otherwise kept hidden, not just from others, but sometimes even from himself. We had been listening for several minutes when I decided to ask about the concert, the one his mother had let him attend after all. "How was it?" I asked.

"Did my mother call you?" He grimaced and began to twist the lip ring in little circles.

"No, Ricky, she didn't."

He looked surprised but then hid a quick smile. "I thought she would, that's all."

"Is there a reason why she might have?"

"Yeah." The tough edge was back in his voice. "There is."

He paused, and I waited.

"If I tell you, does it mean she's always right?"

"I'm not sure anyone is always right."

"Not even my mother?"

"Not even your mother."

By now Ricky was no longer hiding his smile, and I saw a full grin with its arresting picture of plastic braces.

"Well, she's not always right, but she was kinda right this time. See, I take this friend, Chloe, to the concert, and she is so . . . stupid. She gets herself hurt! We're down in the front, not the pit, the front. I'm watching Billy, the lead, and I look over and Chloe gets herself lifted up by these guys. Right as I'm watching this. Then they drop her. I push my way over. It's impossible to get to her. When I get there, she has this dumb smile on her face, but she can't move. Her leg—it's all warped, pointed at this weird angle. I needed to do something." Here he paused, checking my reaction. I am not surprised by his story of Chloe—he and I both know things like this happen at rock concerts. I am mostly interested in finding out what happened next, and in what Ricky's reactions were.

"So what did you do?"

"At first I didn't do anything. I'm just looking at her. I'm worried someone is going to step on her, the thing that my mom is always telling me is going to happen. Then I try to get people to move back."

"Do they?"

"No." Remembering, he was frustrated and angry. "I don't know what to do, but I take off the shirt I'm wearing around my waist and start to wave it and point. I'm hoping someone sees me, the band, the people working there, anyone. I think they do, because they stop playing after that song and three guys come over. It is a big deal. They carry her off, first-aid station, lots of questions. She's out of it, so I answer. Then I had to call my mother."

"That bothered you."

"Well, she was cool, but the whole thing was really embarrassing."

"Sounds like you handled it really well."

"That's what my mom said."

"I agree with your mom." But even after I had said it twice, I didn't get the sense that Ricky believed me or his mother. "Do you think you handled this well, Ricky?"

He paused, chewing his lip right around the ring for several seconds. "I feel real bad about taking Chloe to that concert and getting her hurt. She acted stupid, but I took her there."

"And you acted responsibly."

"But, Dr. Ponton, if I hadn't taken her there in the first place, it wouldn't have happened to her." By now Ricky had stopped chewing his lip. I could see that he was trying not to cry. I barely heard his next words.

"It's all ruined."

"What's all ruined?"

"The good feelings I had at concerts. They're all gone." At this point I could see that he was trying to unobtrusively search my office for Kleenex. I handed him the box that was sitting right next to him on the table between us.

"Ricky, can you tell me more about what is all gone?"

"The way it felt . . . so good . . . I can't feel that way anymore, ever."

"Ever" is a word teens use all too frequently. Many things seem like they are going to be "forever" the first time that they happen. Telling teens that most things are not forever is not usually helpful.

"Have you had those feelings anywhere else?"

"You mean besides concerts? Uh, I guess." Here he paused, having stopped crying. "I feel so stupid complaining about this." His Kleenex was now a mound of little pieces at his feet. "All the bad stuff going on in the world, and I'm upset about this."

"Surprises you that the feelings mean so much?"

"Yeah, I guess I can see that it is more than the way I feel at concerts."

"How's it more?"

Ricky was sitting straight up in his chair at this point, but he was still unable to look me in the eye. He was staring instead at a picture on the wall behind my head.

"I've had feelings like these a lot. You're gonna laugh when I tell you about the first time." He started smiling himself.

"I'll try not to." I knew that it was going to be hard to keep a straight face when a grinning Ricky was going to tell me a silly story. "Okay, so I might laugh a little," I admitted, smiling, "but tell me anyway."

"Well, it happened last year, when I was spying on this slumber party my sister had. It's late at night, all the girls are up, and my mom tells them they can't use the telephone anymore to call guys like they had been doing." Ricky looked at me, his expression serious now. "Okay, so its two a.m., and they have nothing to do, so they decide they're gonna have this séance game and conjure up sex genies. What's so funny is that everybody's sex genie is so different. . . . My sister's best friend, Kim, her family came here from Vietnam, and she comes up with this giant Buddha. She is so tiny, she gets straight A's, and she tells this amazing story about sex with this Buddha, some cross between a god, a person, and a giant dildo. I'm laughing so loud I hope they don't hear me. It isn't what I would even think about with Kim"—Ricky starts laughing again in the room with me—"but it kind of makes sense, too. Apparently giant Buddhas are great sex partners—the best, the way she was telling it!"

He looked at me. "Do you believe all that medieval stuff that you were talking with my mother about—teenagers who become possessed with a strange spirit after they're bitten by a spider, kids who can't stop dancing?"

"Or feeling?" I asked.

"Yeah."

"Well, it doesn't matter whether I believe it. It seems like you do."

"That's the thing—I'm not sure. I just think it's the same sorta feeling. It was so strange when you and I started talking about rock concerts. I kept thinking, How can you know that I feel those kinds of things?"

"Let's go back a minute—what's 'the same sorta feeling'?"

"It's like the music is in your body."

"So the feelings you get are the same as other feelings in your body? Like sexual feelings?"

"Well"—he turned crimson—"not exactly. Not like I would know, exactly. But kind of the way it feels to be—you know—turned on, I guess."

"I think I understand."

"Look, Dr. P., it's not like every time I put a CD in I pop a boner or anything." He was grinning again, pleased with himself, I imagined, for finally being so direct.

I understood more than Ricky thought, though. He was not the first adolescent to describe "feelings" in their bodies when they listened to music or danced, feelings that were "warm" and "good."

"What would happen if you told your friends about your feelings?"

"They'd go with it, and we'd all get up and dance, possessed by the dance genie."

"Pretty amazing."

"Yeah."

"So you're going to give up those powerful feelings because of a friend's accident at the mosh pit?"

"You don't think there's a chance, huh?"

"Not much of one."

"But why do I feel bad about the feelings now?"

"Ricky, I'm not sure. I think it's more than feeling guilty about Chloe's leg. I guess the feelings you have around music are very strong and make you feel very good. It can be scary to feel that way for all kinds of reasons—you can feel like the genie is gonna take over."

Here he laughed. "That's what I thought about the girls at their little séance. The sex genies were going to take over."

"They do," I joked with him.

"Yeah, sure. I'll bet." But both Ricky and I could see that he was relaxed, and both of us knew he wasn't finished flirting with the music genie.

The Edge of the Pit

Dancing frenzies tend to be heightened in groups. Unlike the thirteenth-century view of such dancing as mysterious, I tend to view group dancing—and moshing—as potentially healthy outlets for all kinds of feelings, including sexual. Certainly not all teens are ready for sexual relationships, but they still have bodies and psyches that are developing sexually. Dance and music provide young people with alternative outlets for exploring, experiencing, and practicing new feelings and sensations. The group atmosphere can be exciting, but it also—usually—provides a safe atmosphere for such exploration and practice. Parents have reason to be concerned when moshing goes awry, of course, testosterone can easily switch from playful to aggressive. Girls and boys should both be forewarned about this risk, as young people of both genders can find themselves suddenly in an unsafe situation.

The risks are more than the potential for suffering injury. Testing sexuality is one of the riskiest parts of life. Like Ricky, many teens are beginning to "feel" sexual feelings for the first time. This is a precarious process. Many things can shut down or turn off these feelings completely. Ricky was ready to stop going to concerts because he felt that his strong desire and self-centeredness had caused a friend to get hurt. He forgot that his friend and a mob of other kids played a crucial role in the injury. He couldn't control the whole group, but maybe, he was thinking, he could control his own feelings. Coming to see me, he started to realize that even if he could stop his feelings—and he and I both had questions about that—was it even desirable to do so? Probably not.

So are mosh pits without danger? What can parents do, if anything?

Parents are not the only ones worried about the physical safety of teenagers at concerts. Ricky's story shows that teens themselves are. In addition, the singers and those who put on concerts are. These are major productions that millions of teens attend each year. Almost twenty-five years ago, when I was a pediatric intern in New York City, I met Shelley Lazar, who was then working at the Palladium, the premier rock emporium of the seventies. She was the backstage manager for the rock concert that my future husband and I chose for our first date. When we met, Shelley and I shared our mutual interest in teens and dangerous risk-taking. I was interested in understanding why they did it, and she was interested in containing it, at least at rock concerts. Over the years we have had continued opportunities to talk, mostly when I have brought my two teenage daughters and their friends to concerts.

In researching this book, I put in a call to Shelley. She had just returned from Woodstock III, where violence had erupted. While my two daughters and I had watched parts of the four-day concert on television, Shelley and others were live on the scene working hard to make it an exciting and safe experience for thousands of teens. For several days it was just that—young people enjoying music, sun, and each other—a giant summer picnic that went on for hours. What changed, and what could have stopped the rioting, if anything? Most important, what do teens and parents need to know about concerts before they go?

Both teens and parents need to be informed, says Shelley. A key factor that altered the course at Woodstock III was the violence encouraged by bands that played. When they got onstage, their cry went up: "Let's tear down the towers!" A short time later, thousands of teens at the concert rioted—fires started, clothes were torn off, the kids were hurt and, yes, the towers were torn down. The days-long picnic had become a nightmare.

What could have been done differently? Shelley has observed that bands have considerable influence. Those bands that promote heavy moshing and violent activities seem to come in waves. Then the wave seems to ebb. What stops it? Lawsuits that affect the band monetarily; bad publicity; kids and parents becoming wiser; and, yes, even bands becoming more responsible and changing their music and/or its delivery.

Shelley said that concerts in Europe are safer. "The crowds in front of the stage and in the mosh pits are generally filled with more men and boys. European men are more comfortable with this closeness—men dance together, they kiss openly—it isn't scorned by their cultures." What's different in the United States? Violence, for one. Although crowds are more closely packed in Europe, a violent episode is more likely in the United States. Violence at rock concerts should be no surprise to American parents or teens. Adolescents are learning how to take risks in a culture filled with violence. This increases the potential danger of all activities in which they participate. Violence can also occur in school when a teen is planning a party with friends, at home when they are excited, or on the streets. Violence in this culture is epidemic, and alters many teens' experiences with sexuality.

Parents can help their teens make better decisions about concertgoing and other activities. They can find out what band(s) will be playing, and whether they condone or even promote moshing or other dangerous activities, and whether there is a known history of violent activities at a band's concerts. Ideally parents and teens should talk about it together. In any case, the information is readily available over the Internet.

Although moshing is predominantly an activity for boys, there are dangers for girls, and it is very important that they, too, be encouraged to develop good judgment. Girls, like Ricky's friend Chloe, can be pulled into the pit and encouraged to "surf," unaware of the dangers that might befall them should they slide off the wave. Shelley also said that she saw several girls at Woodstock removing their clothes before a crowd of boys. The girls' faces registered shock when they were then roughly grabbed and mauled by these same boys.

Parents can help their teens learn to assess the risks at concerts and other group activities by talking it through with them before they go. They can also review what happened at any given concert afterward. Mercedes and Ricky spent a lot of time talking about that Smashing Pumpkins concert, and Mercedes also called Chloe's mother and encouraged her to talk about it with Chloe.

Shelley's and my conversation ended on an upbeat note. We acknowledged how important it is for kids to have the opportunity to go to concerts—in addition to great musical exposure, concerts provide a place to experience all kinds of "feelings" that can be extremely positive. It is also important to remember the tale dating back to the thirteenth century—the tarantula might bite, and they might forget who they are, dancing tirelessly into the night. It is up to parents to help them remember.

Return of the Genie

My work with Ricky was winding down when the sex genies reappeared. Changes were apparent even before then. Ricky and Mercedes began playing their CDs when they did the dishes together, transforming a formerly gruesome task into one that was tolerable, sometimes even fun. Mercedes was trying to teach Ricky to salsa. "He has potential," she told me. Also, Ricky's life was developing in other areas.

"Dr. Ponton, things are kinda changing with Chloe."

"How?"

"Well, I was going over to her house, bringing her flowers after her accident. Okay, I was being real nice, but then she starts acting weird."

"What do you mean?"

"She's wearing this pink sparkly lip gloss, her hair's brushed, and she's smiling whenever I go over there. It's not just Chloe, though. I'm different with her."

"What do you think is going on?"

"Well, I was thinking about those genies we talked about. I think the sex genie has got her and she likes me."

"A surprise, huh?"

"Yeah, the weirdest part is what's happening to me. I think I might like her, too. I'm having some of those same feelings I get at the concerts, you know? The sex genie must have me, too."

"Maybe. You act like you didn't think it was going to happen."

"Well, I kinda did, but not with Chloe. Man, she was so stupid at that concert."

"The sex genie is sometimes unpredictable."

"You can say that again. The concert stuff was easy compared to this stuff. It can strike any time, huh?"

"Sounds like you might want to control the genie."

"Well, maybe a little. You're gonna tell me it doesn't work like that, right?"

"I'm not going to tell you anything here, Ricky. You're doing a pretty good job figuring it out for yourself."

"At the pit, I really didn't even have any idea what was going on. I just had those 'feelings.' Now that I know what they were—are—it's even more confusing. Crazy, huh?"

"Well, you're working on it."

Kids need to keep on working. Being "possessed" by feelings in one's own body can be hard to understand sometimes, and are especially difficult when young people experience them for the first time. These powerful genies can make their first appearances on many stages, rock concerts just being one. These situations offer teens a place to experience feelings that they may not have known they have, but it is important to break through old-fashioned ideas that the genie will possess them and they will forget who they are.

Any self-exploration seems to hold the inherent risk of losing oneself in the process. In fact, healthy self-exploration leads to discovering and defining oneself. Adults can help by allowing an open atmosphere in which adolescents can explore normal feelings—this is not the same thing as encouraging overly risky behavior of any kind, sexual or otherwise. When their feelings are acknowledged as normal, there is less risk that children will get off track in the process of exploring their feelings.

5

Coming and Going Online
The Interface of Sex and Technology

There's lotsa stuff I wanna know about. —Stacy

I can't talk to girls. I'm not so sure I can really talk to anyone. —Tom

Grandmothers occasionally bring their grandsons and granddaughters to therapy. Some have sat quietly in my office after having driven or ridden the bus a long distance in order to make sure that their grandchild comes. Most frequently, though, they are quiet voices in the background encouraging mothers and fathers to bring their children for help. Often they are the ones who say, "Something's wrong. They shouldn't be acting that way." Seldom do they take center stage.

I knew Vera Pomeroff was different from the first message that she left. "This is Mrs. Pomeroff. I am calling about my granddaughter, Anastasia. I am the child's sole guardian, and I have discovered some disturbing information. I would like to arrange a meeting to speak with you directly. I will call back at another time when I can speak with a real person. I do not believe that it is safe to leave my number on this answering machine."

I played the tape over and over, listening to her voice, trying to understand her careful but heavily accented speech. She sounded annoyed, her polite comments failing to hide my lack of consideration in not providing "a real person" to receive her call. Later that morning, I had the pleasure of speaking with Vera Pomeroff directly, and discovered that some of my hunches about her were correct. She was not a quiet grandmother, content to offer her support gently. She was not only comfortable taking the reins in her granddaughter's life, she seemed to like doing so.

First she wanted me to know that her problems with her granddaughter were serious. She herself had minimized them when she first discovered them, she said, and now the consequences were dangerous for both her granddaughter and herself.

More than a little curious, I asked this articulate, long-winded woman to get to the point. "Exactly what is the problem?"

Vera then asked me a surprising question. "Do you read—erotica, Dr. Ponton?" I was so startled that I wasn't sure that I had heard her correctly and asked her to repeat the question. Irritated that I had failed to understand her the first time, she shouted into the phone. "Erotica . . . materials devoted to or intending to arouse sexual desire."

Momentarily I stumbled, feeling barraged by her loud voice as well as the question itself, but I recovered and answered that yes, I was familiar with erotica. Then I had to ask myself what she had really asked, and whether I had really answered. "What kind of erotica do you mean?"

"That, Doctor, would best be discussed in person. If you need to see samples to familiarize yourself, I will bring some with me." Opening up slightly, she then said that several months earlier she had discovered her copy of Anaïs Nin's *Delta of Venus* in her granddaughter Stacy's room. Of course, she forbade her to read it, and then hid the rest of her own limited collection of such books. Since Stacy was apologetic, she thought that the matter was settled. Yesterday, however, she had discovered a letter in the mail addressed to her granddaughter. She had opened it, of course, because she "had no choice." Reading the letter both embarrassed and confused her. A hand-tooled bookmark with an inscribed poem fell out of the envelope as Vera opened it. It reminded Vera of a gift she herself had once received, but her granddaughter was only fourteen years old, and though the letter was no more than a postcard, it looked like "that technological chat business" Vera had noticed Stacy engaging in on the computer. Obviously a boy had sent her granddaughter this letter, a boy Stacy had "met" on the Internet and given their address to. Vera was worried. Who was this boy, anyway? Was he even a boy? She had read stories in the news, girls who met their Internet "friends" in person and disappeared forever. She thought she should probably call the police, but read the poem first. It was a love poem. She decided to confer with her granddaughter's school counselor, who had referred her to me.

As I listened to Vera unburden herself, I recognized the fear in her voice. And, I guessed, as with many parents of adolescents, she wasn't just afraid for the teen in her life, she was afraid for herself. She wasn't prepared for the romantic communication her granddaughter had received. As the mother of two teenage daughters, I sympathized. When, if ever, are parents prepared to discover that first romantic advance made toward their child?

I suggested that she come and see me, and bring her granddaughter with her. She asked if she should tell Stacy about the letter. I said that I believed that she had to tell her; Vera had felt betrayed upon realizing that their home address had been shared with a stranger, but Stacy would feel betrayed by her grandmother's opening of her mail.

Two days later, in a canceled hour, I met Vera and Stacy for the first time.

In my waiting room, I could feel a powerful energy between this grandmother and her teenage granddaughter. Stacy was seated in the chair by my assistant's computer, drawn to the movement of the screen saver. Her hand was poised—waiting for my okay to push the button on the mouse and inject herself into cyberspace? Vera was holding what appeared to be a stack of books wrapped in brown paper, no doubt the erotic literature. Even with their different objects of focus, I was aware of the strong connection between these two.

Stacy jumped up first, rushing past me to enter my office, brushing my shoulder with a thick mane of purplish hair shot through with silver. "You wired in here, too? Hey, you've got an Ethernet! But you're not hooked up! You want me to hook it up? You shrinks need to be hooked up to each other, chat rooms for shrinks, that's a place for me to be, of course I wouldn't say anything."

"You wouldn't?" I asked, charmed by this avatar of the chat rooms and doubting that she could ever be quiet, either online or off.

"Sometimes I'm quiet, even when I'm wired."

As Stacy and I chatted, I noticed a remarkable change in Vera's facial expression. It had started with her granddaughter's mention of "Ethernet," at which Vera blinked and then fell back into her chair, now clutching rather than holding her books. The computer terminology seemed to silence her. I saw that her granddaughter didn't just speak their language, she was fluent. It appeared to be her passion. Recognizing this communication gap might help me work with both of them. I asked Vera what she had brought with her, although I already had a pretty good idea already. Without a word, she handed the stack over, but not before I saw a slight smile. I slowly removed the books from their brown paper bag. There were six or seven, all hardcover editions, all worn with age. Vera was partial to Anaïs Nin—*Delta of Venus, Little Birds*—but there were others. I sensed this was her treasured collection.

Silver bracelets flashed as Stacy reached across me for one of the books. Reflexively, I hung onto them, but Stacy was not put off. "Grams loves these books. I'll show you the good parts. I underlined a bunch of 'em. They're great!"

I had to give her credit. This girl was unabashedly enthusiastic, whether it was computers or literature, but I also noticed that she was blissfully unaware of her grandmother's glare. Perhaps Vera hadn't realized yet that Stacy had marked the pages.

"Vera, Stacy is right. You have a wonderful collection here. Thank you for bringing it. You mentioned that you and your granddaughter share a fondness for Anaïs Nin."

"She is a well-respected author, although her writing is not meant for children. I intended to share them with you alone, Doctor."

She emphasized the word "doctor," giving me a certain authority, but all the time she was speaking, I felt myself directed—directed to follow her command. I wondered if she wanted me to espouse a censorship code. Hearing the steady humming of metal, those silver bracelets tapping on my desk, I again focused on Stacy. She looked as if she wanted to leave the room after her grandmother's comment about Nin's writing not being meant for children. My own thoughts were speeding along. Vera's rigidity and her need to control brought up many feelings for me, and they weren't comfortable.

I decided to bring up the Internet situation right away, mentioning what Vera had told me on the telephone and leaving it open.

Stacy spoke first. "Grams and I already talked about it. I shouldn't have given Nick my address. It was stupid."

"How did it happen that you did, though, Stacy?" I asked.

"I liked him a lot. Still do." She blushed and turned to look at the computer screen.

"So why do you now think it was stupid?"

"Well, uh, the risk, I guess. Nothing bad has happened with him, and it won't. He's not a weirdo. But I know that there are weirdos out there." She tapped the computer screen with her hand.

At this straightforward admission of Stacy's, Vera's face relaxed, and the small muscle on the side of her mouth stopped twitching. She spoke slowly, and I sensed she was choosing her words carefully. "Things—people—are not always what they seem to be. The feelings are so strong. . . ." Then she paused for several seconds as if even saying that much had taxed her, adding, "I just don't want Stacy to get hurt." The muscles around her mouth started quivering again, but I could now see that it was because she was trying to hold back tears.

Still unsure how to support her, I mentioned that I noticed how much she cared for Stacy, and said that it wasn't easy to talk about these matters at any age. Vera set her books on the floor and started to cry before she could get her handkerchief out of her purse. Stacy rose from her chair, went over to Vera, and put her arm around her, saying tenderly that she hadn't wanted to do anything to hurt her. Vera cried for several minutes, Stacy's arm resting on her shoulder the whole time.

The session ended quietly with Stacy, Vera, and me agreeing to meet again to talk about Stacy's relationship with Nick, the Internet poet. As they were gathering Vera's books, together this time, Vera's brow furrowed. "Doctor, I would like to meet with you alone." Stacy looked crestfallen. Vera saw this and patted her granddaughter's hand. "This is not about you, Stacy. There are some things that I have to talk to Dr. Ponton about."

At this point Stacy was holding her grandmother's handkerchief and Nin's *Delta of Venus*. She lifted the book in the air a bit and handed it to Vera. "More things not for me, Grams?"

The Telling

Two days later, Vera appeared in my waiting room carrying another book—a worn, silver leather photo album. The lines around her mouth were set, and she walked through my office door as if she was arriving at an inquisition.

This Vera was not the tearful woman I had seen with her granddaughter. She was polite, but let me know her agenda immediately.

"Dr. Ponton, I have come here to share a family situation with you and ask your advice about what to do."

After Vera said this, I realized that she had wanted to tell me something from the time of the first phone call—the small clues, "can't talk with you over the phone . . . must do it in person"—but then she had experienced overwhelming difficulty in following through with it.

"My granddaughter is illegitimate." Then, perhaps thinking that I had not understood what she meant, she added, "Baseborn, out of wedlock, a bastard."

I was stunned by this woman calling her granddaughter a bastard.

"Her mother, Anna, was my only child." Here the tears started again. "Anna met a man. She was only nineteen, a student. She became pregnant. It was humiliating to her, and to me. She did not tell me until it was too late to obtain an abortion. They were available in Russia, if she had only asked in time. We had been waiting for visas for America. The visas came through when she was six months along. I thought they were a godsend. I pleaded with her to come with me, telling her that we would avoid the shame and tell people that her husband had died. I convinced her to come. I never asked her about the baby's father. She never told me, but understand that I did not ask, did not want to know. So we came to America, and Anastasia—Stacy—was born a month later."

Vera and I sat quietly for some time after she told me this. She was not crying now, but still looked stunned. I did not ask her questions or comment on what she had said. Knowing when to be silent is an important part of therapy, one that I am, by nature, not adept at. Here, it felt intuitively right.

Vera slowly calmed down, and then opened the photo album to show me faded pictures of Anna—a slender teenager standing in front of her Moscow high school, holding a bookbag . . . a much younger Vera with her arms locked around her daughter's waist . . . the two of them leaning over a stove with several steaming pots, cooking dinner together. . . . The photos on the last page of the album were so worn that I could barely make out the figures, but I finally saw a mother and an infant, Anna and Stacy. As we looked at the album together, Vera told me pieces of her story, and I knew that she had waited a long time to share this with anyone. Anna's father had died when Anna was four, leaving Vera to struggle, raising a daughter alone, yet, Vera told me, those years had been the happiest in her life.

I looked her in the eye and spoke softly. "Where is Anna now, Vera?"

"It was pneumonia, but she was heartsick, depressed. Stacy wasn't even a year old. I couldn't afford an apartment with heat when we first arrived. Anna didn't tell me she was sick for weeks. I would have made her go to the doctor no matter what it cost. We are not a backward people, Dr. Ponton. She shouldn't have died."

"No," I said. "It's never right when a child dies." I asked her what it had been like to raise Stacy alone. Vera's eyes barely registered this question, and I realized how much she was still back living with her memories of Anna. I wondered how much of her time with Stacy was spent there. I now understood that I was going to have to help Vera with Anna first if I was going to be able to assist her with Stacy. All of this was playing a role, however unspoken, in Stacy's involvement with Nick, her Internet boyfriend and poet.

Behind the Photos

After this meeting with Vera alone, I again met with Stacy and Vera. In a quiet voice Vera told her granddaughter why she had wanted to meet with me alone. She said that she still missed Anna, that she had not gotten over her death, and that she needed to, especially because Stacy was growing up. After Vera said this, Stacy again patted her shoulder.

"I'm not going to leave you, Grams. I won't get pneumonia like that.

Look at me—I'm healthy as a horse!" Stacy smiled and widened her kohl-lined eyes, her magenta hair shifting back and forth. We all laughed at the welcome comic relief.

"Maybe once your grandmother and I have had a chance to talk more, things will be clearer, Stacy. Do you think about your mother a lot?"

"When I look at the photos with Grams I do." After a long pause in which she played with her bracelets, Stacy added, "I think about my dad a lot, too. I look for him everywhere. That's how I got into the Internet, searching for him. That's how I met Nick."

"You met Nick searching for your father?" Vera asked. I could feel tension again filling my office.

"Grams, what did you think?"

"I didn't think anything. Kids your age like the Internet."

"Yeah, they do."

"Did you find him?" I asked.

"No, not so far." A silver bracelet flew off her wrist and hit the doll-house under my desk. Stacy slid off the couch onto the floor, picked up the bracelet, and began to play with the little plastic children in the house. Yet another adolescent riding the line between childhood and adulthood. "Do you play in this dollhouse with kids who lose their parents?" she asked very slowly.

"Sometimes, Stacy."

"Does it help?"

"Sometimes."

Although I hadn't taken my eyes off Stacy, I could hear Vera fumbling in her purse for a Kleenex. She was crying again. "I wish I knew where my father was, Grams, but I miss my mother, too. Is it weird to miss people you've never met, or can't remember?" she asked, looking up at me.

"No, Stacy, it isn't weird at all. Can you say a little more about what you miss about your mom?"

"I don't know, just having her with me, I guess. It's gotten to be a bigger deal lately. I'm not sure why."

"Well, you're getting older."

"Yeah, I guess that's part of it. There are things I just wish I could ask her."

"Like what?"

"Well, like what it was like when she was in love. What it felt like. What it was like to be pregnant with me. That kind of stuff."

"Stuff about being a woman."

"Exactly," said Stacy.

After several minutes of silence, Stacy finally turned around, leaving one of her silver bracelets in the dollhouse, and looked directly at her grandmother. "Mom didn't get pneumonia on purpose, Grams. And it wasn't your fault, either."

The muscles in Vera's face relaxed. Forgiveness from Stacy was a wonderful gift to her, but it might not have enough strength to beat back Vera's own powerful tendency to blame herself.

"I know I'm not a very good substitute, Stacy."

"Oh, Grams, of course you're good. It's just . . . ."

"It's just that there are certain things you don't want to talk about with me. And I understand. Things are a lot different now than they were when you were my age."

"What things are you talking about, Stacy?" I asked.

"Well, computers, for one," she said, smiling up at Vera, who smiled back, just a little. "But you know, Dr. Ponton's right. I'm fourteen. I have a lot of questions about . . . sex, I guess. And boys. And love."

At this Vera coughed out over a kind of half sob, half laugh. "Things aren't so different as you'd think, Anastasia."

"Well, *you* never want to talk about it."

"What makes you think that?"

"You don't even want me to read about it!"

"You're so young, Stacy—"

At this point I interrupted. "Vera, Stacy really isn't that young to be interested in learning about sex and boys and love. Most girls start becoming interested in these topics a lot earlier than fourteen. Is there something specific you're worried about?"

"Anna was only nineteen when she got pregnant with Stacy—"

"Grams, I'm not gonna get pregnant. God. At least not for a really long time. But I might want to go out on a date sometime, you know?"

Then Stacy asked her grandmother exactly what I wanted to know. "Do you blame yourself for my mom getting pregnant?"

Vera didn't even looked surprised by the question. "I guess so, Stacy. I know I worry about that with you and that Internet—Nick. When I saw that letter—"

"God, Grams, he's just a friend. I mean, I can see I shouldn't have given him our address. I've done it before with guys." Then, seeing the expression on her grandmother's face, she added, "Give them my address, I mean."

"Any ideas about that, Stacy?" I asked.

"I don't know why. I guess I want people to know about me."

"To know where you are?"

"Well, yeah, but first to know who I am."

"So, first to know who you are, and then to know where to find you."

"Yeah."

"Do you sometimes think about whether your father might be using the Internet to look for you, too? First to know who you are, and then where to find you?"

"I guess so," said Stacy, looking back into the dollhouse, back at the tiny plastic family with a mother and a father. "Is it crazy? Am I crazy to wonder if he's out there?"

"No, you're not crazy. But there might be a way to look for him that is safer for you and your grandmother."

"Safer than what?" asked Stacy, bewildered.

"Safer than offering your address to people you don't really know so well, even if it sometimes feels like you do. Maybe you and your grandmother could team up and look together."

"I would like that," said Vera.

"You hate computers," said Stacy.

"No, Stacy, I just don't understand them."

"It's easy, Grams. It's like when you were teaching me Russian—you said not to be afraid of another language, remember?"

When grandmother and granddaughter walked out of my office that day, Stacy was explaining how the screen saver worked. Not only had Vera's face loosened; her whole body seemed lighter. I was glad to see it. She was going to need energy for what lay ahead with Stacy.

Internet Adventures

A week later, Stacy and Vera were back, and the picture had reverted back to quivering facial muscles and flashing silver bracelets.

"Have you seen that stuff on the Internet, Dr. Ponton? I mean, really sat down and looked at it? It is absolutely disgusting. There are people advertising that they want to have sex with you online, people actually having sex online, and now even interactive sex. You can call in and choose whatever you want, and they do it! It is totally unregulated. It's completely—" Here, Vera was speechless. Stacy rolled her eyes.

Thinking about the five X-rated e-mail messages that I had just deleted from my account that morning, I had to concede that some of what was upsetting to Vera upset me, too. Sex on the Internet can be both graphic and unregulated, and kids can have too-easy access to things they aren't necessarily ready for. I told Vera and Stacy that I agreed, but then asked them what it had been like to be online together.

Neither responded. Deprived of her role as censor, Vera did not know what to say. Finally, Stacy spoke.

"I liked it, Grams. You were different . . . fun. Did you really go back and do that interactive thing?"

"Of course I didn't, Stacy," Vera said. "Really."

"Did you enjoy it, too, Vera?" I asked.

After another long pause, Vera said, "Well, yes, anyway, parts of it."

Here Stacy started laughing. "It seemed like you were having a good time, Grams. You were so funny when we found that interactive tape, suggesting they have a Russian version. I mean really funny." She looked at her grandmother and smiled, then added, as if she had to justify what they had done, "Look, we weren't hitting on those sites. We were just surfing them, just looking, that's all."

"So it was special for both of you."

"We were doing something exciting together. . . . You asked me if I was looking for something on the Net. I was. I still am. I've gotten tons of great information from the Net—stuff I really wanted to know but didn't want to ask anyone."

"What kind of stuff?" asked Vera.

"You know," said Stacy, looking at me rather than her grandmother, "information. When I'd get my period, whether it was normal not to get it sometimes, finding out what guys think about girls' periods. More than people . . . my father, or guys, that is. I do sometimes look at the sex stuff. I mean, I need to know. I guess it would be different if I had a mom. She would know that kind of stuff, and I could ask her."

"And she would talk with you about it?" I asked.

"Yeah. There's lotsa stuff I wanna know about." Then she added, "Like how my mother felt when she got pregnant."

Here I paused to think. I knew that I was going to have to speak next. Vera looked as if she had just been slapped, and Stacy was waiting for an answer from her. Remembering back to the first moment that I had met Stacy, her hand poised over my mouse preparing to send herself into cyberspace, I had the same sense here that she was really looking for something. What she had just revealed seemed to be an important part of it.

"What are your ideas about how your mother might have felt?"

"I'm not sure, but I think about it a lot, you know, a real lot. She wanted to have the baby, uh, me, yes. I was the baby for sure. What I don't get is what about my father. I mean, whoever he is. Was. Is. I guess I wonder what their relationship was like, and whether—"

She fell silent.

"Whether what, Stacy?" I asked.

"Whether they loved each other. Whether it was just sex."

Vera interjected strongly. "Stacy, you need to know she loved you very much. With your father—I don't know. They were young. I don't think your mother thought about the consequences, but once you were born, she was absolutely devoted to you. Looking back on it, I believe that she and I shouldn't have left Russia then. I shouldn't have let my feelings about how she got pregnant push us to leave, but I can see all of that only now, looking back. I don't want to make the same mistake with you."

"What mistake?"

"A teenage daughter gets pregnant, and you think a lot. I didn't talk with Anna about sex until it was too late, and then I worried too much about what other people would think. I guess I felt like it was my shame, like I had caused the pregnancy. I've felt like that for a long time."

"How did you cause it, Vera?"

"Well, the books that I brought to show you the first time. Anaïs Nin, the others. They, or others like them, were around the house when Anna was growing up, after my husband had died. I was still young. I never stopped being interested in sex."

"Whoa, Grams, are you sure you want me to hear this?" Stacy smiled, clearly teasing Vera.

"No, Anastasia, I'm not. These books—they're a private part of my life. I never thought your mother should see them, either. I had no idea she would—I kept them in my room. I thought she would respect my privacy."

"Vera," I said, "you're entitled to privacy, just like Stacy is." I flashed on the letter addressed to her granddaughter that Vera had opened. "But it seems that you're facing the same stumbling block with Stacy as you did with your daughter—that Anna was, and Stacy is, also interested in sex. Curious about it. Like you. Is that so hard to understand?"

Vera didn't reply.

"I just always thought these things are private. And for adults."

"Well," I said, "any sexual act should be private. But wondering about the topic, wanting to learn about it, that isn't wrong. It's natural."

"What's on the computer is *not* natural."

"Grams," said Stacy, "how did you learn about sex?"

Vera laughed. "From your grandfather."

"What about your books?"

"My books are not just about sex. That's what makes them literature, and not just crude pornography. But it's also why they're complex, the relationships, the language—"

"So I'm too young for all of that, huh?"

Here Vera was silent.

"Well, I know I'm not ready to have sex. And if I were, which I'm not, mind you," said Stacy, emphasizing her words, "I'd use birth control. I definitely want to be married when I have kids. But I'm still curious about it. Where *should* I get information?"

I spoke. "The Internet is out there, Vera. You can't change that any more than you can change Stacy's curiosity. If what scares you is the idea of Stacy getting pregnant, she's already told you she isn't ready for sex, and that if she were, she'd use protection."

"But the Internet could give her ideas."

"Yes, it could give her ideas, and thoughts, but not feelings. Her feelings come from the inside. And the ideas—well, it's helpful for young people to have someone they can talk to about new ideas and information, someone they trust."

"Anna never came to me until it was too late."

"But Stacy is here now, Vera. And you said yourself, the books didn't get Anna pregnant. She had sex because she believed she was ready. Certainly she isn't the first young woman to feel ready for sex and forget about whether she's ready to be a mother."

"The books didn't make her pregnant, I know . . ."

"Do you know that, Vera?"

Here Vera laughed. "You're right to ask, maybe I still don't know."

"So you blamed yourself for at least part of it, and you don't want to make the same mistakes with Stacy."

"I do, and I won't. So, then, how do I deal with this Internet stuff, just let Stacy go for it?"

"Vera, there are some guidelines, some of the things that you're already doing—learning about the Internet yourself, letting Stacy know that it isn't safe to give out her address, using it together with her, and most important, talking with her about what she is looking for and about what she finds. She's told you a lot already. You've also been a whole lot more honest with her."

"Can I stop it from happening again?"

"God, Grams, again with me getting pregnant? Why are you so obsessed with that?" Stacy started drumming the silver bracelet on her right hand.

I interjected again. "It's not yours to stop, Vera. Stacy makes the choices."

"There must be something I can do."

"Vera, I think you're doing it."

"What if I just stopped her from using the Internet? You've seen the stuff—it's crazy."

"Is that what you tried to do with my mom, just stop her?"

"No, I didn't do it with your mother. That's why I'm trying to do something different."

"You think *that* will work?"

"No, but I feel like I have to do something."

"Look," I said, repeating myself for what felt like the hundredth time, "you're already doing a lot, and you can't control everything. It just won't work. But you can be there for Stacy as a guide and resource."

"I wish that I could get a 'filtering system' for adolescence for Stacy, like those filtering systems they sell for the Internet."

Here Stacy nearly fell over laughing. "Like you're really going to get me to wear it, put a chip in my head, maybe? Sounds like the KGB."

"Vera, you and Stacy together *are* the filtering system. The Internet is technological—you're a real person in Stacy's life. There's no substitute for that."

"I think you're right, if I could just believe it."

"It is scary, but you are doing what you can. Remember that you and Stacy have a good relationship, that she's lucky to have you as a resource, if you'll agree to be available to her that way."

I kept in touch with Stacy and Vera for several years after they stopped coming to see me. When Stacy left to go to college, she and Vera stayed in touch by e-mail. During the summer of Stacy's sophomore year, she and Vera traveled to Moscow and, after much effort, finally located Stacy's father. He had known about Stacy's birth and had written a letter to Anna in San Francisco. He told Stacy that he had never heard back from Anna, and had moved on with his own life. He had a wife and three other children. He did not have a computer. So he began to correspond with his eldest daughter by regular mail, with Vera translating when his English failed him, and Stacy using as much of the Russian as she had been taught by Vera and was continuing to learn in college.

Christmas Call

Three days before Christmas I received a call from Dave, a single father of an eighteen-year-old son with whom I'd worked briefly a couple of years earlier. Now Tom was a sophomore at U.C. San Diego, and Dave was calling upset because Tom's grades in college weren't the A's and B's that he had received in high school. Dave wanted me to meet with Tom during his son's winter break. When I asked him what was wrong, thinking it had to be more than grades, Dave said it was "more of the sex stuff." Then he stopped, falling into an embarrassed silence. Finally he added, "It's got to be my fault again. I let him rent those stupid sex videos—well, 'let' isn't even the right word. God, Dr. Ponton, I encouraged him."

Even before Dave had mentioned the sex videos, I remembered them. In fact, I remembered quite a bit about this father and son pair. I had first seen Tom when he was sixteen years old. He'd had sandy-blond hair and the permanent tan of the teens who surf the California coast. I had met him in the adolescent medicine clinic at the university, where I work on Monday afternoons. Tom was worried that he might have VD, maybe even AIDS, but he wouldn't tell me why. When I pushed, he revealed that he had been having sex but he wasn't using condoms. I asked him about the risks of not using condoms, and the following conversation took place, a crucial one for me. It helped me understand some of the ideas that teens have about sex and how easily they acquire misconceptions and behaviors that lead them into danger.

"Doc, are you going to bug me about not using condoms like that other guy did?" The other guy was a pediatrician who had decided Tom should see me.

"'Bug' isn't exactly the way I'd put it, but I am curious about why you don't want to use them. I bet you've got a reason."

Suddenly Tom's angry expression changed, and he asked me whether the clinic had any sex videos. "You know what I mean. Not educational stuff, I know you got those, but real sex, so you can see how to do it."

Intrigued but still not quite understanding, I asked him exactly what kind of videos he was talking about. "The university probably hasn't purchased them, but I would like to know what you're interested in."

"Well, my dad lets me rent these videos. That's how a guy really finds out about sex."

"Is that how you found out about not using condoms?"

"Sort of, yeah . . . All these guys on the videos have sex with women, sometimes with a condom, and then pull out and take the condom off, for the pleasure, you see. I guess that's where I got the idea." He stopped, surprised, I think, that he had told me so much.

"So let's see if I follow you. You remove the condom for pleasure—your pleasure, the girl's—and then you ejaculate?"

"Yeah, that's what the videos show."

"You've tried this out?"

"Yeah, but that's where I've gotten into trouble. The first two girls, no problem, but this last girl screamed about getting her pregnant, giving her AIDS, didn't I know this was San Francisco. . . . She kept mentioning infections."

"Is that why you went to the clinic?"

"Yeah, I started to believe I'd gotten an infection, maybe even AIDS."

"Your dad knows that you watch these videos?"

"Yeah, he gave me his card, told me they'd help me, be educational. When it comes to sex, guys have to know it all, be able to do it all. It's not easy to figure out."

"No," I agreed, "it's not."

Following this conversation with Tom, I saw him alone and also met with father and son together. In our sessions, Dave admitted that he was just beginning to find out about relationships himself. He had slept with many women, but felt that he had never let himself be a part of the relationships. He told me that he was only just beginning to establish a relationship with Tom's mother, from whom he was divorced. Dave felt hamstrung by what he saw as gender roles, both his own and what he hoped would be his son's "as a man." He wanted his son to have a rich sexual life. He also hoped that his son would not repeat the mistakes he had made—a lifetime, or so it seemed to Dave, of passionate, brief relationships lacking friendship. He wondered how he could help his son learn about sex. Having intimate conversations with his son about the nature of relationships simply was not something that he could do, at least not at that point.

Now, two years later, Dave told me that things with women, with sex, were changing for him, but he was worried about the legacy he had left his son. Not only were Tom's grades falling, but Dave had recently received a credit card bill that showed that Tom was visiting online sex sites while he was at college. "Visiting" is not quite accurate. Judging from the bill that Dave had received, Tom was all but living at online sex sites. Why was Tom spending so much time at these sites? Dave hadn't asked Tom yet, but he was asking me now. Could a kid get addicted to these sites? Was it Dave's fault? After all, he had started his son out on the sex videos by loaning him his credit card. Even back then, this wasn't what Dave had expected when he said that he wanted his son to "be a man."

I agreed to see Tom again, and Dave scheduled an appointment during his son's holiday break. Tom arrived at my office several days after Christmas, bearing the signs that I have come to know so well with teens home from college. His California tan was gone, and he wore the pallor that I associate with college dormitory rooms, a haggard appearance that comes from many hours of studying or participating in other indoor activities. He looked like he had just rolled out of bed, wearing the clothes he had slept in; a shadow of a beard darkened his chin. He scanned my office for food—where were the Granola Bars that he used to eat by the pair?

"They're still here, Tom," I said, opening a cupboard. "Of course, it is only nine in the morning."

"You mean, I should have had breakfast, Doc? Like what am I doing eating Granola Bars before eggs? The office looks the same. So do you."

"Thank you—I'll take that as a compliment."

"Yeah. You should. So what, my dad told you I'm a sex maniac now, I bet?"

"No, he didn't tell me that you were a sex maniac, but he is worried about you. Why don't you tell me what's going on?"

"It's kind of hard to get back into it. I know I used to talk about a lotta stuff here, but with this stuff, it's really . . . weird."

"If you're referring to all the sexual stuff, I don't expect you to just start talking about it; maybe you could begin by telling me what college has been like for you."

Tom looked relieved and spent the rest of the session telling me about his college dorm—the food was disgusting but he was eating too much and gaining weight; the laundry room—he had been there only once, and all his clothes came out of the washing machine dyed red; the college swimming pool—too much chlorine and it was not Ocean Beach, where he used to love to surf early in the morning before high school. While Tom talked, he ate four Granola Bars.

Something was missing from his stories. He didn't mention any people—no professors, no roommates, no girls. I thought back to why he had first come to see me, his failure to use condoms, a terrifically risky behavior in the 1990s. When we had first talked about his "problem," another story emerged. Tom was being raised by a single father who was often away on business trips. Tom knew that his dad had a string of girlfriends but did not have much of a friendship with any of them. Was Tom headed down a similar path?

Dave called me after Tom's first session. "I mentioned before that things have changed for me in the past couple of years. I met Rachael. I think that she and I are friends." Here he struggled. "This is the first time I can talk to someone. She encouraged me to get help for Tom. She said this porno thing of his is way out of line. Although, Doc, even without her I would have done it anyway. It was rocky for me, and to see him struggling with this—I don't even mind paying for the enormous bills—but what's it doing to him? Do you know?"

I told Dave that quite honestly, I didn't know what hours of watching Internet porno was doing to his son, but I would try to find out.

Although Tom hadn't talked about sex in our first hour together, he didn't waste much time bringing up the subject the next time he came in. I heard about an education of a very different type.

"You hear all those stories about freshmen guys, so into sex; it's like people think we're animals or something."

"What's it like for you?"

"I'm not dating. Well, I *had* two dates in college, then it was like I froze or something. I don't know. I just didn't want to do it anymore."

"What happened?"

"The first girl was real smart. She was 'just visiting' U.C. San Diego from some East Coast school—Smith or something. We're hanging out together in my room, and then she starts telling me about these rules for sex—she knows this school back East that came up with 'em. Rules for sex. Like he-says, she-says kind of stuff. If the other person says this, then you gotta say that kind of thing. Scary."

"Why scary?"

"All I could think about was the stuff in high school. Then I start thinking, does she know about me, about my stuff with girls in high school, how I wasn't using condoms. Then I think she can actually see I'm the kind of guy you gotta have rules for." Tom started shaking his head. "I just didn't know what to say to her. She left after about an hour, probably thinks I'm some stupid California guy who doesn't know anything." He paused for several seconds, staring at his feet. "There was another date. I froze with her, too."

"Maybe you're not ready to have sex, Tom."

"Doc, I had a lot of sex in high school."

"Yes, but things seem different for you now."

"Yeah, it's funny. I don't even miss the sex I had in high school."

Remembering some of Tom's nightmarish high school dates, I could understand why he didn't want to go back there. "So, how did this computer thing start?"

"Well, I wasn't into it in high school, if that's what you mean." Here he looked wary, staring at me, and I had a feeling that I often have working with teens, that the teen is wondering, *If I really tell this doctor what's going on, what is she going to think of me?*

"I don't know what you think, Tom, about coming back to see me, but I'm not here as a censor. I'm only trying to help you figure out what's going on in this area."

"Okay, I don't need a censor. It's like I've got one in my own head, going all the time."

"What's that like for you?"

"Bad. It's worse since I started visiting the sites. First it was Danni A., she's red-light district. I thought I'd just see a few digital photos. After that it was videotapes online, and then, finally, online sex . . . a lot of it. I felt like I was going crazy. I got this voice in my head telling me to stop it, and I just can't get it to stop. I'm hitting on the sites all the time. I'm driving myself crazy with it."

"It changed for you?"

"Well, at first I liked it. It was so easy. I was in control. I knew what was going to happen next. I even felt like I was getting experience. I'm not sure when it started to change, but it was like it started running my life. Like I *had* to do it. I sure wasn't in control. Then the voice started— *Stop it, Tom.* I guess I was glad when my dad got the bills and finally talked to me about it."

"You say that you felt like you were getting experience."

"Yeah, I think I started needing it more after that thing with the Smith girl. I felt stupid."

"So you were gonna learn more about sex, or at least the rules that she had been talking about, on the Internet."

"Well, both, I guess."

"With Danni A.?"

"I know it sounds weird."

"What kind of things were you hoping to learn?"

"How to not feel so messed up about sex, I guess. At first it worked. It was a lot less work than the East Coast girls. I didn't have to impress Danni. I just feel like I'm gonna screw it up with girls—high school, college, it's all the same. My relationships with them are a mess."

I wasn't going to disagree with Tom—his relationships were a mess—but I also recognized that he was here, with me, talking about it, not having Internet sex or looking for another girl. I told him that, and he looked relieved. "At least I'm doing something right. You know, I guess I thought it would work last time talking with you; I learned to use condoms. I stopped watching videos, at least so many of 'em, but still I'm messed up with sex."

"What part is messed up?"

"I don't know. I can't talk to girls. I'm not so sure that I can really talk to anyone."

"You talk here, and you're starting to talk to your dad."

"So you're saying I should keep talking and get myself unaddicted to sex on the Internet."

"Is that what you think?"

"It's what I think, but sometimes it seems impossible."

Tom stayed in therapy for several months this time. When we ended, he was going out with a girl. They had not had sex yet, although he was thinking about it. His "addiction" to the videos, and then sex on the Internet, did not disappear, although it had decreased. Tom and I have concluded together that he might always have to struggle with it. Being given open access to sex videos at the age of fifteen blazed a trail for Tom from which it is hard to veer. As he says, "It's so easy—all you have to do is lie down and plug in—no thinking. It's only afterward that you know you got screwed."

The X-Rated Files

Vera had been right. There is a lot of sexual material online. It is vital to screen it.

In cyberspace, adolescents and adults chat, flirt, talk dirty, and have what has come to be known as "cybersex" with people they will never see or meet. The unbelievably rapid expansion of the Internet has raised complex ethical issues and parenting questions both. Should the Internet be regulated? What do I do when my son or daughter gives out our address to an Internet friend? What if I don't want my child viewing sexually explicit material?

As an individual, one might strongly be opposed to censorship, therefore believing that the Internet should not be regulated. On the other hand, as a parent, you might feel quite differently, wishing that your child could not readily access sexual material, invitations, pornography, and potential partners for real or cyberspace liaisons.

Yet even if the Internet remains unregulated, parents and teens do have options. The questions raised by those choices speak to the broader issue of parental control over adolescent sexuality. First, what kind of control can parents really have over adolescent sexual behavior? Ultimately, most sexual behavior, on and off the Internet, is a personal choice. Vera had a great deal of trouble accepting this. She believed that she should have been able to "prevent" her daughter Anna from becoming pregnant somehow, and felt that she had failed in not doing so. Fifteen years later, she believed that she should prevent Stacy's Internet contact with Nicholas. She came to understand that although she could influence her grandchild's sexual decisions, she did not really have control over them. They had been, and would continue to be, Stacy's. Dave also felt badly as a parent. He wasn't as interested in Vera in controlling the behavior of the teen in his life, but he, too, felt extremely guilty about what had become a kind of perversion for his son.

Parents cannot control the behavior and choices of their adolescent children, despite the cultural belief that adolescents are "out of control." The principles of influence and guidance get lost, and any discussion can rapidly degenerate into a painful power struggle.

Sexuality is not the only area where this type of conflict occurs between parents and teens, but it is often the most difficult, resulting in screaming arguments or, more frequently, strong feelings that can never be fully expressed. Yet the most effective tool parents have in assisting their adolescent with developing a capacity to assess and negotiate *any* risk, sexual or otherwise, is their relationship with their child. In order to communicate with their child about sex and sexuality, parents must confront their own biases and overcome the societal taboos that prevent a more open exchange on this topic.

The intersection of sexuality and the Internet raises interesting questions for teens and their parents. Yes, the Internet offers adolescents the opportunity to participate in online sexual activity, but it also offers the opportunity for teens to learn important educational material about sexuality and health. So while there are threats, there is also promise. Stacy's and Tom's stories show this. The computer assisted Stacy with her growth. Lacking a mother and father, she had used it to explore many questions about herself and her world. The computer was never critical or judgmental, never shocked by her interest, curiosity, or ignorance. The Internet provided her with accurate information about her first period, the pace of her physical development, and the mechanics of kissing, all areas about which she had questions. She never once felt embarrassed while using it. It helped her build her self-confidence.

Things changed when she began to use the chat rooms. Stacy herself felt the risks increase. As she said, who were these people she was talking to? She knew that some adults were poseurs and talked their way into child and teen chat rooms. She was cautious but at the same time curious, trying to discover information about her parents and herself. It was also easy. She didn't have to report to her grandmother.

Nick and Stacy had been online with each other for several months before she gave him her address. They shared a love of poetry and had shared other poems before they finally settled on sonnets. One could argue that Stacy was missing out on "real-life" relationships because of her involvement with Nick. My experience with teens and Internet romances has been different. The Internet provides many young people with a place to practice relationships. Many of these friendships parallel those that used to develop with the now nearly lost art of letter writing, a form of communication that allowed a slower expression of feelings with important lapses of time, time that allows teenagers to figure out what they are feeling.

For Tom, the issue of anonymity and lack of judgment also played a huge role. Whereas the explicitly sexual aspect of Stacy's online activity was limited to discovering more or less factual information—about menstruation, about kissing—Tom was actually engaging in sexual activity. And clearly he *was* opting out of relationships with real women. Tom was struggling with more pathological behavior than Stacy, but it's highly likely that he would have been troubled by conflict in the arena of sexuality and intimacy whether the Internet existed or not.

The National Center for Missing and Exploited Children has written some excellent brochures on child and teen safety on the information highways. They caution adolescents about keeping their identity private, emphasizing that they should never get together with someone that they meet online. Stacy had given her address to Nick, and she would have chosen to get together with him if her grandmother and I had not intervened. Stacy eventually chose not to, even after her grandmother had offered to supervise a meeting if she had wanted to have one, deciding that she wasn't ready for it.

One of the main concerns that parents have about the Internet is that it will expose their child to unregulated violence and sexuality. Two psychiatrists concerned about this and the potential for abuse in chat rooms observed and documented aggressive and sexual comments in a kids-and-teens-only chat room. They found that in the kids' chat room, there was only one aggressive comment per hour, and in the teen rooms, two per hour. This compares favorably with television, where there are an average of twenty aggressive comments per hour. I am still concerned that the impact may be different. Online media is more interactive than television. Online aggressive comments can be aimed directly at a child, and the impact may be more severe even though the frequency is considerably less. Sexual comments (one every twenty-one minutes in the child rooms, and one every four minutes in the teen rooms) occur more frequently. Monitored rooms have very few, and are more appropriate for younger children.

The Internet is changing the frame for adolescent sexuality. It gives teens a chance to ask questions and experiment with different roles; it is also fast, less supervised, and anonymous. It offers benefits and dangers. Parents have to understand it and show interest and curiosity. There is no substitute for learning about it at the same time that your teen does. Like everything else about the Internet, its interface with sex and sexuality is an area of rapid evolution. We do not know how it is going to affect adolescents over the long term. Ongoing education, teaching risk assessment, and good communication are still the best tools we have to offer our teens.

It is important to educate your own child. An "obnoxious" child or teen in a chat room can be placed on "ignore" and have his or her communications blocked from the other kids' computer screens. Children and teens who are persistently offensive can lose online services permanently. I have worked with families who have lost online services because of the computer activities of their child. So you can see that parental knowledge and involvement with the Internet is crucial.

Unnatural Partners?
Intimacy and Intercourse

I feel a whole lot more peaceful. —Miriam

I guess I never expected this was gonna happen. —Joel

I'm very sexual. I'm just not going to have sex with him. —Mai

No guy lasted under a minute in any of the movies I saw. —Rory

Brown-eyed, brown-haired Miriam first came to see me when she was fourteen. An early developer, she had had her first period at age nine, and carried large, rounded breasts by age ten. Self-conscious about her body's appearance, she hid her womanly shape behind a large bulky brown sweatshirt and oversize pants, and wore tinted oval glasses, also brown, showing a monochromatic picture to the world. In our first session, she told me that "brown" was her personal statement, revealing what she thought about the world: "depressing, dull, and scary." Wearing brown offered her protection—others couldn't see her body or her face. She was safe. Trying to initiate an alliance with her, I mentioned that I had seen many teen girls who hid themselves behind a black facade, but never one shrouded in brown—she was unique. I could tell that my comment pleased her, and I saw the beginnings of a smile spread across her face, a streak of brown lipstick before her hand reached up to hide it. Then she slowly lowered her hand and began to talk.

"The girls in black are not the real ones, you know. They just wear black to get attention, but they don't know anything."

"Know anything about what?" I asked.

Silence. I tried again. "Girls in brown know more than girls in black about what?"

Silence again. Most of our first session went that way. I asked, she was silent. I waited and tried again.

Miriam's mother, Sonia, was not silent. I could tell even in our first five minutes together that this woman could not only talk, she could tell long, interesting stories about the lives of her family, stories of her sister's struggle with her mother, how her family moved to California, stories that drew me in and made me lose track of the hour. Many of them were about her daughter.

Sonia was worried about Miriam's self-esteem. She had gone through puberty earlier than her friends, and she was overweight, hard to see underneath that baggy sweatshirt. Sonia was worried that Miriam was getting teased about her body and was hiding it. Also, what was the story with the brown? Sonia wasn't worried, she just wondered about it. I discovered in later meetings with Sonia that she wondered about a lot of things. She confided in me that she wanted her daughter to feel good about her body and added that she knew those "good feelings" were an important part of a healthy sexual life.

"Healthy sexual life." Few parents are able to say the words, let alone acknowledge that this is one of their aspirations for their child. I was impressed.

If Sonia impressed me, Miriam bowled me over. Even at fourteen, she had a strong presence and powerful energy. Our second session together introduced me to this. I was a minute or two late coming from the clinic to my private office. I guessed that something was up by the grins on my assistant's and Sonia's faces when I walked into my waiting room, and their laughter when I opened my office door. The lights were dimmed, a dozen candles were sparkling, a woodsy incense burning, and my fireplace was flaming. Miriam was sitting in front of it in a long brown robe, chanting. She invited me to join her in a Wicca spell for friendship.

"This will help our work together," she said confidently, her brown eyes glowing in the light, the tinted glasses gone. "I do this with all my friends."

"Miriam, I am honored. You have transformed my office."

"You've got a lot of cool books, but this room definitely looks better with candles."

She led the ceremony that followed, where her prayers and spells wove together, asking for a long friendship with me. Miriam was not the first girl in my office who believed in Wicca—white witchcraft or good magic, enchanting spells designed to make life more peaceful.

Miriam and I worked together for a year. I saw her conduct other spells, one to make herself thinner—it didn't work—another to get back at a popular girl in school who had been cruel to her. It worked. The girls changed her behavior toward Miriam.

We did more than indulge in ritualized magic. We had my magic, too, in therapy. We talked and talked. We worked on her body image and made collages of bodies—the body that she would like to have, the body that society wanted her to have, and the body that she had. We pored over magazines for teen girls—*Jump, Seventeen, YM (Young Miss)*. Miriam wrote a scathing review of *Cosmo Girl* when it first appeared, highlighting how it trained young girls to become successful objects and manipulators of a patriarchal system. When she read it, she got a standing ovation from her English class. I encouraged her to keep a journal and write poetry. She brought some of her poems and read them to me; others, she said, were too private to share. I recognized that several of her poems were about sexual desire, both its pleasures and curses.

I also continued to meet with Sonia. She continued to talk, too, but she listened and did a lot for her daughter. They joined a gym and went together a couple of times a week. They took a self-defense course. They went on a mother-daughter trip to Mexico, looking for sacred places. I could hear them walking down the path to my office long before they arrived, laughing at each other's stories.

Slowly my sessions with Miriam began to change. The brown was gone, most of the time. She wore form-fitting tops, some of the time, and was clearly proud of her figure and her strength, acquired from the weights that she and her mother were lifting. I heard more about friends, then more about boys, so I wasn't completely surprised when she came in and told me that she was planning to have sex with her current boyfriend, Julian. I walked her through the questions that I encourage boys and girls to ask themselves before they have sex. Was she doing this for herself? Did she trust this partner? Could she talk to Julian? Would she be comfortable saying no, even at the last minute? Had she and Julian practiced with other sexual experiences before deciding to do this? What was her plan for protection from pregnancy and sexually transmitted disease?

I already knew the answers to many questions I might have asked. I knew that she was comfortable with her body, and even though she was young, she had experienced and had knowledge of her own desires. I also knew that she had probably talked about this with Sonia. Their communication was very good at this point. I encouraged her to think about whether this was the right time for her, whether she was feeling pressured by anyone—friends, boyfriend, anyone at all.

Miriam gave me thoughtful answers. This was her choice. Listening to her, I caught some of her energy and enthusiasm for what was coming. I remembered the friendship ritual that she had created for our second meeting together. Meeting with Sonia, I learned that she knew about Miriam's plan. Sonia was anxious, but she had an intuitive sense that Miriam was prepared for this. She also recognized that this was, ultimately, her daughter's choice.

First-Time Tales

Karen Bouris has written a sensitive book, *The First Time,* about the first intercourse experiences of 150 women. She divides their experiences into several categories—traditional wedding nights, pressured choices, getting it over with, women loving women, violation, and what she terms a romantic minority. Less than a fifth of the women in her study thought their first sexual experience involved conscious choice, good communication with her partner, and physical and emotional readiness. The experiences were described in different words, but all felt that they had made the choice to have sex without pressure, and all felt love for their partners. They had chosen partners who were physically and emotionally caring. Even in this category, few women experienced orgasm their first time, but all said they and their partners had cared mutually for each other's pleasure. Reading *The First Time* is illuminating not only for the stories of the 20 percent who experienced rewarding sex their first time, but for the stories of the 80 percent who didn't. Those stories offer some important clues about what not to do: (a) prematurely rush into intercourse; (b) use it as a commodity to trade for something else (e.g., status, money, popularity, or even affection); or (c) accommodate to pressures in a relationship.

I also was familiar with the results of many early studies in this area involving thousands of adolescents. Large numbers of adolescent girls (63 percent in one study) reported that they felt afraid of their first sexual experience, compared with only 17 percent of the boys. In that same study, 43 percent of the boys reported that they felt thrilled after their first experience, compared with 13 percent of the girls. Sixteen percent of the girls reported that they felt used after their first experience. No boys reported this. In 1994, the Alan Guttmacher Institute found that 74 percent of the girls who had intercourse before the age of fourteen and 60 percent of those who have had sex before the age of fifteen reported having had sex involuntarily.

Statistics like these do not inspire confidence, but I also knew Miriam, and the months of effort she had put into preparing herself for this experience.

If I expected an answer about how it went the first time, I was going to be disappointed. Like many teens in similar situations, Miriam was shy, and I decided not to ask her directly. Midway through our session she asked in a joking voice, "Dr. Ponton, aren't you going to ask?"

"Miriam, aren't you going to tell me?" I joked back.

"Okay. But I wouldn't want to shock you."

"You've got to worry about that?"

"Sure. Well, it was great. Well, I think it was great. My body was amazing. Julian said it, but I felt it, and his body—it wasn't like science class. Well, I had touched his, uh, penis before, but this time I touched it and he jumped, but I felt something, too." There was a long pause.

"And?"

"That's all I remember—just kidding. But kind of not. I was in this trance state after that, like Wicca. Better than Wicca."

Slowly other details skipped out. Most of their time had been spent kissing. Although Miriam had told me that she and Julian experienced oral sex before, it had been a limited version compared with what they enjoyed that evening. She was surprised that penetration was not more painful, and concluded that it must have been the trance state that allowed her to enjoy it so much. The lubricated condom helped, too.

I noticed that the quality of Miriam's voice changed as she told me her story, starting out like she was giving a book report, but gradually taking on a sensuous tone.

"Julian likes to play with my hair, see. He starts by touching the little hairs at the back of my neck, the curly ones. He kisses my hair and then sucks on it. I can feel him, his mouth pulling on it, moving in and out. He wanted to suck those little hairs around my vagina. I wasn't going to let him, but I changed my mind. I was glad I did."

"What was it like?"

"That's when I went into the trance. . . . Next time I'm going to let him try it again. I told him he has a hidden talent. What I don't understand, Dr. Ponton, is this whole virginity thing. It's like you're supposed to lose something."

"You don't feel that way."

"No. I feel like I've gained a lot. Crazy, huh?"

"Not so crazy, Miriam."

"I feel a whole lot more peaceful. Me, with all those Wicca ceremonies—strange that something could be more peaceful."

"It was peaceful for you?"

"Yeah, strange, with a lot of my girlfriends it's like some weird attack."

"You prepared for this, Miriam."

"Yeah, I did."

Miriam was not the only one transformed by the experience. It had had an effect on Sonia, too.

"Dr. Ponton, I've worked so hard to help her get to the point that she'll be prepared for sex and not feel bad or guilty about it. Now I wonder if I've done the right thing."

"What makes you wonder about it?"

"She's young. She turns sixteen next month! I hear this voice in my head saying, *How could you allow your daughter to do this?* It's driving me crazy."

"Did she talk with you about it?"

"Yeah, she did. Amazing. She has this transformative sexual experience, is at total peace with herself, and I'm the one who ends up feeling guilty!"

"What do you think about it, Sonia?"

"As a parent, all we hear is that it's going to be bad for them—pregnancy, physical force, broken hearts, AIDS. I know that's only part of the story, but I worry. So much can happen."

"A lot can happen, Sonia, but you're helping her a lot, and you're getting her ready to take care of herself."

In a culture that offers few rituals to its adolescents to mark their passage into adulthood, teens seek out and create their own. Engaging in risky behavior is one way that many teens define their own identity and create their own rituals. In a country where half of teens have sex at age sixteen or younger, and three quarters by age nineteen, the initiation of sexual intercourse has become a rite of passage.

Often, peers are the witnesses for the sexual initiatives, helping with preparations and hearing the stories afterward, but mothers play an increasingly important role with daughters. Two separate studies have shown they are vital in the formation of gender-role identity for girls, as well as body image, two crucial aspects of sexual identity.

It had been a challenge for Sonia, faced with midlife changes in her own body, to go to the gym and participate in kick-boxing with Miriam. The body collage that Miriam and I had worked on in my office inspired Sonia to complete her own. She also brought in magazines and critiqued those that I had in my waiting room. She helped her daughter to understand that the current female images in the media represent the body types of less than 5 percent of all women. She made changes that contributed to her daughter's positive experience. She, too, grew physically stronger, visible evidence of the time they had spent lifting weights together. She revamped her wardrobe, choosing to wear clothes that were more comfortable and trendy. She also read almost everything that was available on sexual education, becoming one of the most well-informed mothers I have ever met. Equally important, she shared both her long-held and newfound sexual knowledge with her daughter.

Do You Wanna Dance?

Seventeen-year-old Joel was late for his session, giving me some time to think. I had seen him only three or four times, and things were changing rapidly in his life. Just listening to what happened in the past week took up most of our time together.

Joel, an honors study at a local private high school, was seeing me because he had just moved to San Francisco with his parents and he wanted to get "adjusted." He had "done some therapy" in Chicago, where he had lived before, and after a few sessions he was already pretty comfortable talking with me. Joel and his therapist in Chicago had talked about Joel's strong feelings of attraction to guys, and Joel had decided that it was pretty likely, though not definite, that he was gay. He had experienced many fantasies about guys and very few about girls. Still, he had been unsure about these feelings until recently.

Starting high school here, he had begun writing for the school newspaper. One of his first articles, "Free Fall," was on skydiving, a passion of his, although he had tried it only once. He had received several compliments on it, including a phone call from the editor of another high school paper. The editor, Richard, had liked Joel's article and told him that he, too, had a passion for skydiving. They made plans to drive to nearby Napa Valley and interview some divers.

I finally heard Joel loudly stomping down the path to my office. His face was a deep red, sweat pouring off his forehead. He had been running. He threw two Polaroids down on my desk.

"Look at these," he gasped, still catching his breath.

The first photo was a slender young man with dark hair standing tall in a field, a white parachute flowing around him. The sunlight hid all but his silhouette, and I couldn't really see his face until the next photo—he and Joel were smiling at each other, their arms linked. I looked up at Joel, who returned my look expectantly.

"So what do you think?" he asked.

"Nice photos, Joel. What do *you* think?"

"God, I can't believe this."

"Can't believe what?"

"That this is my life."

"It's pretty good?" I asked.

"This was the most amazing weekend of my life."

"What happened?"

"What didn't happen? Richard and I went up to Napa. He already knew a bunch of the divers, so we hung out with them. They took us up. We got to dive. It was his first time. That's when I took the photo."

Then he looked down, and his voice became lower. "Two of the other guys were gay. Richard and I talked to them a lot. It was amazing watching them together. I just kept looking at them, these two guys—all of us went dancing Saturday night, just this country dive, but it didn't matter." Joel picked up the photo of Richard and said, "He's a great dancer, you know."

"I didn't know, but you do."

"Yeah." Joel laughed. "It's like I think everybody knows how wonderful Richard is. I want to tell the world about him, but—" His voice dropped off.

"But you can't?"

"I can't. I'm, like, really afraid to tell my friends at school. There's this big dance this weekend, four high schools, mine, his. I want to go to this thing. I even helped to plan it. But if he's there—"

"If he's there?"

"I'll wanna dance with him. God, I won't be able to stop myself."

"What do you think would happen if you did dance with him?"

His face looked tortured. "They would all see that I'm a fag."

"They might also see that you were in love with a great guy."

"Maybe. Some of my friends would see it that way. But the others, no way. A fag, Dr. Ponton."

"So you're not going to go to the dance?"

"I don't know."

Joel did go to the dance. And he met Richard there. They danced together in front of everyone, at least everyone in their world, a good portion of the high school population of San Francisco.

Joel said, "Just one dance, but I felt like everyone was watching."

"Scary stuff?"

"Yeah, real scary. I was talking with this great friend of mine, Emily, after the dance, trying to pretend like nothing was happening, but I was dying to know if she saw us."

"What did she say?"

"She said, 'Get real, Joel, we know—we think it's wonderful. What were you waiting for?'"

"How did that make you feel?"

"Better. When I was dancing with him, it was like the whole world was staring. Wish I didn't feel so different."

"It makes it harder. Just one dance, but it takes a lot of courage."

"There's more." Joel was talking very quickly. "It wasn't just one dance. We went to his parents' house afterward. They were gone. We were in his bedroom, fooling around with each other. We . . . we were sucking each other off, and there was this stuff shooting all over the place. So scary. Well, it was safe sex, but it was—"

"Scary?"

"Well, okay, more than scary. I guess I never expected this was gonna happen."

"What surprises you?"

"Don't get me wrong. This guy is so amazing. When I'm with him, I feel insane. It's going to sound stupid, I just never saw myself getting off with any guy." Here Joel looked straight at me. "I never saw myself getting off with any girl, either."

I could see that one of his hands was trembling. He tried to hold it. As gently as I could, I asked Joel what he thought would happen.

Shaking his head, he said, "I guess I just never took it that far."

Joel's reaction to his first sexual experience with Richard is not uncommon. Many adolescent boys, gay or straight, are surprised at their first ejaculation with another person. Prior to this shared experience, many boys see their own erections and ejaculations as something over which they have a large degree of control. In ejaculating in the presence of another boy or girl, they describe experiencing a loss of control, although most report that it also makes them feel powerful.

In addition, Joel's fears about being "outed" at the high school dance for being gay were troubling and very real. Stigma and verbal and physical harassment of gay teens by their peers are unfortunately quite common. Many gay youth run away, fleeing schools and families that are openly hostile, or that the teens fear will become that way if they know their identity. I have had the opportunity to work with many of these young people as they work to build a more supportive environment for themselves. Their struggles are often overwhelming, and point to the importance of families and schools building a network for these young people. Teens need the support of friends, teachers, and parents to handle the pressures. All too often, harassment of gay and bisexual youth is ignored in schools. Teachers and students commonly deny or do not even recognize that they have witnessed it. Joel's friend Emily was very positive, but most experiences are not so encouraging.

In a study conducted by Gilbert Herdt and Andrew Boxer, they reported that friendships like the one between Joel and Richard were the most common settings for the first same-sex relationship in adolescence. In their study, more than two-thirds of the youths' first homoerotic experiences occurred with friends of the same age. For girls, it occurred at almost fourteen, for boys it was closer to sixteen years of age. Over half of the gay youth in this study reported having had heteroerotic experiences, too.

Joel and Richard developed a friendship that lasted over several years, and it was still strong when they each left for college. They both were members of the Gay/Straight Alliance at their schools and got a lot of support from the groups and their friends. Joel's story also gives us important clues about how teens fall in love. Often they can't say the words, but the feelings are there—feelings that might bloom into deep intimacy or disappear as quickly as they came.

A Long Interview

Eighteen-year-old Mai flopped into one of the large leather chairs and threw her backpack on the floor. Like a growing number of high school students, she had chosen to focus her high school project on adolescent risk-taking, and, as part of that, had decided to interview me.

"You've got a lot of books on sex," were her first words. She avoided my eyes as she opened the backpack and set up a high-tech tape recorder. Pulling out a camera, she asked if I minded having my picture taken, commenting that this was standard procedure for all senior project advisers.

"No problem. Nice equipment you've got."

"Yeah. I wish I hadn't waited so long to get this done. I could have interviewed you twice."

She then flipped me a copy of her questions before she started firing them at me. I looked at the list. It might be a long afternoon, I thought. Mai was a careful student. She attended an academic high school with a lot of focus on grades, but she seemed to have a genuine curiosity about the motivations of teens and the interview actually went by very quickly. We were about three-quarters of the way through when we finally got to her questions on sexual risk-taking. Her strict interview format wavered, and she began to talk about her own experience.

"At my school a lot of the girls feel pressured . . . by the guys, but also by girls, to have sex," she said cautiously.

"How does it happen?" I asked, glad to let her answer a question for a change.

Mai's long dark hair fell down her back in a single braid. She took off her glasses and leaned back against the cushions on the floor. "My sixteen-year-old sister has a boyfriend, and they've already had sex. My mother knows, but she pretends like it's not happening. My father is traditional Vietnamese. I am the oldest daughter. I don't want to shame him."

"You would shame him if you had sex?"

"Yes. This is very important for him."

"How do you feel about this?"

"I'm not sure. If I wasn't the oldest daughter, would I be having sex right now? I don't know. The tie to my father is very important to me." She fell silent. Then she spoke even more softly. "My boyfriend wants to make love. He and I are very close. If it were not for him . . ." Her voice trailed off.

"If it weren't for him? Who's the him?"

She laughed. "Hey, this was supposed to be your interview!" Her eyes sparkled as if I had trapped her into talking in spite of herself.

"Just because it's my interview doesn't mean you don't get to talk, Mai."

"Okay, I get you, but I have to get this interview done. Anything else you think I need to know about sexual intercourse?"

"That choice matters."

Her eyes sparkled again. "You've been very helpful."

She packed up her oversize backpack, popping the tape recorder and several books I had given her inside. It was even heavier now than when she had arrived, and I was headed out myself, so I offered her a ride down the hill.

I know from years of driving teens that cars sometimes offer an easier place for kids to talk, but Mai said little until I dropped her at the street-car line. Getting out of the car, she came around to my window. "I don't know if you see kids that you mentor, but would it be okay if I called some time?"

"Sure."

A month later, Mai was sitting in my office, free of her backpack. She flipped a neat copy of her report, "Teens and Risk," onto my desk, but it was clear that she wasn't here to talk about that. "When you said that thing about choice, it clicked. With most things—friends, college, career—I feel like I have choices. Not with sex."

"Say more."

"Okay. Last Saturday night I'm at this winter formal thing with Ben. We are having this great time. I'm wearing a red silk slip dress." Looking down at her jeans and fleece jacket, she said, "I know, it's hard to imagine, but I looked really hot in it."

"Not too hard to imagine," I said.

"Then Ben and I are driving home and he said, 'Mai, I just don't get it. You are the sexiest-looking girl in school. You and I have been going out for two years, and we really like each other. What's going on? Why no sex?' Then he looked at me and said, 'You must be hopelessly asexual.' Dr. Ponton, I was fine, ready to tell him the same old stuff, until he said that. Then I froze. I couldn't think of anything to say, so finally I just got out of the car. I guess I was really upset. Well, pissed. I slammed the door to the house, and my father came running down the stairs. He starts yelling at me, 'If you're going to wear clothes like that, of course you're going to have trouble with guys!' Then I'm so angry I want to scream at both of them, but of course I don't."

"You don't?"

"No, I don't. Now I wish I had."

"Pretty upsetting, Mai, with both of them."

"When Ben said that, about me being asexual, I couldn't think of anything to say. Nothing."

"How were you feeling?"

"That's the thing. In that dress, I felt really sexual—like, I know I was turning the guys on, but I was turned on, too. Then, when he said that—"

"You froze."

"Yeah."

"All that heat was gone."

She laughed. "Well, yeah, until I got angry."

"Have you talked to Ben about this?"

"Nope, and I'm not going to."

"Why not?"

"I'm still really angry at him. I'm 'asexual' because I don't sleep with him! Pretty arrogant." She laughed, and then her smiled disappeared. "It's like they own it—my sexuality—my dad, too. I know he wants to protect me, but I'm going to be eighteen. It's not his to protect. It's mine."

"Are you going to tell him that?"

"I can't . . . I should, but I can't."

"Mai, you're pissed at your father and your boyfriend, but you're not going to talk to either of them."

"Yeah, my boyfriend calling me 'asexual' really pisses me off."

"Well, what would you say to him if you were going to say something."

"I don't know."

"Do you think he's right?"

"Definitely not. I'm very sexual. I'm just not going to have sex with him. If he thinks I'm going to change my mind because he throws insults at me . . ."

"Then he doesn't understand you. You feel very sexual even though you're not having sex."

"Yes. Ben and I hook up all the time. We kiss, we touch. It's probably because I won't give him a blow job. That's what he keeps talking about. Listen to him, and it's like I owe it to him because I'm his girlfriend." She paused. "It's hard with my girlfriends, too. We're all seniors; most have had sex or say they have. They act like I should be having it, too, like it's some kind of religion."

"With sex, many people think that everyone should be doing what they're doing."

"I don't think that way."

"What about your dad?"

"Maybe I can start by telling him it is not his business. I'm celibate, but it's my way, not his. He'd probably keep me locked in my bedroom."

When the Pressure Is On

In the halls of middle schools and high schools, girls and boys are being pressured to become sexually active. Among the inducements used are "Everyone's doing it," "You're frigid," "Be a man . . ." Written down, they don't seem particularly threatening. It is different when you hear them directed at you by a boyfriend or girlfriend, or by peers, as Mai did. Under those circumstances, they can leave you tongue-tied and doubting yourself.

A teen's peer group plays a strong role in determining his or her attitudes about sex and sexual behavior through the information and misinformation they provide, as well as the values they transmit. Parents also play a role in relaying their values, and a somewhat more limited role in transmitting information on the specifics of sexual behavior. Much sexual information is communicated nonverbally as teens watch and imitate their parents' sexual behavior. Parents often do not know what to tell their children about sex because they either lack information or are unsure of their own values. Fathers have been found to be particularly uninvolved in the sexual education of their children. Parents frequently deal with sexual matters with a single retort or threat, as Mai's dad did the evening after the dance, instead of taking part in an ongoing dialogue. There are many reasons parents have difficulty talking to their kids, including embarrassment, fears that a sexually explicit conversation will provoke teen sexual activity, or the absence or lack of a parental or peer support format. Taboo undoubtedly plays a strong role. Talking about sex is itself a sexual interaction, and as such, its avoidance may be part of the incest taboo.

Ongoing conversations are one of the best ways to address sex with children and teens, and can, over time, help to minimize the taboo and discomfort for both generations alike. In my own home, we have used select family dinners to discuss sexual terms and develop a family discourse, beginning when my teens were children.

Angry or humiliating retorts or commands can backfire. Angry teens can use sexual risk-taking to express defiance and autonomy. It can be used as a weapon to reciprocally humiliate parents. Mai was angered by her dad's comment, "If you're going to wear clothes like that, of course you're going to have trouble with guys," and spoke about having sex "to get him," but decided not to because it would conflict with her own values. She was choosing a sexual celibacy in which she experienced some sexual activity with pleasure and desire, but knew she did not want to have intercourse. This celibacy best suited her own needs and desires. She did not feel ready to have intercourse. Specifically, she felt pressured by girlfriends' comments, and she felt rushed by Ben, whom she wasn't sure she could trust. She didn't think that he appreciated or understood her sexuality, or her feelings that it was okay to look sexually "hot" without having intercourse.

In some important ways, Mai was ready if she had wanted to go further. She had a good knowledge about sexual matters. She had access to condoms and knew how to use them. She and her boyfriend had kissed and rubbed their bodies together, something she was quite comfortable with, but Ben's comment that she was asexual had quite the opposite effect from the one he wanted. It turned her off.

Mai's story brings up the issue of the sexual rights of girls and women. Not surprisingly, this is a relatively new concept, articulated for one of the first times by the Fourth World Women's Conference in Beijing in 1995. The document developed by this historic group states that "the human rights of women include their right to have control over and decide freely and responsibly on matters related to their sexuality." It is remarkable that even in this document there is still a taboo against using the words "sexual rights," and the words "human rights" are substituted. If an international group of women cannot agree to say "sexual rights," it should come as no surprise that a young woman struggling with her father and boyfriend is unable to express her own views about her sexuality.

Mai's choice to remain sexually celibate did not mean that she was "asexual"—quite the contrary, as she herself knew. Others in her life thought that they knew what her choice should be. Her story illustrates how important it is to not impose choices on teens, but to support and empower them to make the best choices for themselves.

Star Performer

Sixteen-year-old Rory, a wide receiver on his high school football team, did not come into the teen clinic expecting to see a psychiatrist. Far from it, he was there with a direct question, and he wanted a quick answer, no doubt to minimize his almost overwhelming embarrassment. He had spit his words out so fast that the young pediatric resident meeting with him asked Rory to repeat it. Turning crimson, Rory stuttered through his question a second time. "Can you slow down how fast a guy comes?"

When the resident—himself now crimson in sympathy—gave him a blank stare, Rory mustered his courage and asked, "You got this Viagra stuff for old guys, hey, what about me?"

The abashed young doctor, struggling to regain his composure, told Rory that this was normal. "What do you mean, normal? I come in less than a minute. That ain't normal, is it?"

Again, the resident attempted reassurance, which did not appease Rory. A half hour later, Rory was talking to me, the in-resident counselor for the clinic. At this point he wanted his question answered as soon as possible. After all, he had stuck his neck out this far. "Look, that guy isn't right, is he?"

"About what?"

Put on the spot again, he raised his voice. "Look, all I want is an answer to a simple question—is it normal to come in a minute?"

"Seems like he answered your question, Rory. He said that it was normal. Is there something else?"

"Like that guy doesn't know anything. You should see how he looked when I asked him. He probably has the same thing going on."

"This is a serious problem, and you want it taken seriously," I said.

When he saw that I was giving his concern fair weight, he lowered his voice. "Yeah, if there's anything you can do . . . I feel like there's something wrong."

"What do you think is wrong?"

"I see these guys in movies—they're at it for hours! Okay, it seems like hours."

"You want your penis to stay erect longer before you ejaculate inside your partner."

"Yeah, exactly. See, it's not just me. There's my girlfriend. Sometimes I don't even get inside her."

"You're concerned that in this situation she might not be receiving pleasure when you make love?"

Rory drew in his breath. "A long sentence . . ." and started laughing. "Yeah, I am. It sounds funny when you say it."

I smiled, too. "Well, try to put it in your own words."

"Your words sound great. I just wish I could say that kind of stuff."

"You think it just rolls off my tongue."

"No, you probably had to go to school a long time to learn how to say that stuff."

"Sure, a long time." We both smiled.

"What does your girlfriend say about all this?"

Sheepishly he started pulling on the corner of his jacket and finally decided to take it off. "She doesn't know I'm here. She tells me it doesn't matter. She just wants me to touch her more."

"What do you think about that?"

"I'm trying . . . She's like, real practical about it. 'Rory, it doesn't matter, I just like being with you.'"

"Many girls, and guys, for that matter, are very aroused by touch and can be excited to the point of orgasm by that alone. The amount of touch is different for everyone. Some like very gentle touching, hardly touching at all. Others enjoy very strong touching. It can vary day to day."

"I need light touch. It's me, I guess. I see this shit in the movies. I should be able to stay hard and not come."

"There are things that you and your girlfriend can do to delay your ejaculation. There are certain ways that she or you can hold your penis that will delay it. You have to work to understand when your penis has reached the point of no return and you're ready to come, then you stop the stimulation and wait for ten or fifteen seconds. You and your girl-friend can practice this together, but it's also a good idea to practice alone, Rory."

"Well, I want to keep practicing. I just don't want to keep making the same mistakes."

"You feel like you're making mistakes?"

"Yeah, yeah. I know Jen says it's cool, but it feels like I'm a big loser. I guess I want it to be really great."

"Why are you so worried about it?"

"Well, with Jen it's not any big problem, but if it got around school . . . well, you hear things about guys like that."

"What kinds of things?"

"Like it could ruin a guy's reputation." Rory laughed. "They could say there was something wrong, but then I guess I'm saying that about my-self." Then he took another breath. "You're saying I just need more prac-tice, and there are some special things Jen and I could do to slow me down. So yeah, what's the rush?"

He seemed relieved. "I gotta go practice. . . ." He laughed. "I'll call you. Thanks."

A couple of days later, Rory made a trip to my private office and bor-rowed a couple of books. Surprising himself, he also chose several books that focused on teen relationships rather than the mechanics of sex. Later, they were deposited in my office with a note. "They helped a lot. Thanks again. After all, what's the rush?"

Which Way In? Finding a Path

Rory's parents called me several months later to thank me for seeing their son. They had discovered that Rory was sexually active and wanted to know how to handle his request to have Jen "sleep over" when they were planning to be out of town. They decided to talk it over with someone because they had different opinions. When Rory, who was now seventeen, had posed the question, he had told his parents that he had seen me and suggested that they call me.

Waiting between sessions, I could hear Susan's and Mike's raised voices on the path to my office as I sat working at my desk.

"This is the door to her office."

"No, this way, over there!"

After a few minutes of this I decided to stand at my entryway to guide them.

Mike was a tall man with the same broad shoulders as his son, the football player. He looked like he knew where he was going, but he had already passed my office and was opening the door to the toolshed. Susan was still at the very top of the path. She was on her hands and knees, admiring an English ivy pushing its way out between two rocks. I thought she might be trying to take a cutting. I waved them both in.

Hurrying around my largest tree, Mike arrived first and shook my hand vigorously. "You need to post a map out there just to get around your backyard!"

"Good idea, it can be pretty confusing," I said.

As we sat down inside, I could see what Rory meant when he said that his parents were in different places. Mike coughed and complained loudly for several minutes while Susan cleaned off her ivy cutting in the bathroom. She seemed oblivious to her husband's frustration with the delay.

"That's an unknown ivy, Dr. Ponton, very unusual. Thanks for letting me take some."

Although Mike appeared eager to begin, I sensed that it would take some work with this set of parents to move into the topic of their son's sexual behavior. And I was right. Nearly half the session went by before we were even close to the subject.

Then Mike let me know exactly what he was thinking. "It's against my values to ever have this kid sleeping with some girl at our house. He says he's not going to have sex, but you can't trust him, Susan."

"Mike, it's his choice, his body. You can't control everyone," said Susan in a frosty voice that hid more than anger.

"I know I can't control everyone, but it's my house."

"It's our house, Mike." I heard the tenor of her voice rise to meet his.

"Let's see if I've got this straight. Mike, it is against your values for Rory to have a girlfriend sleep at your house. Susan, you have a different opinion. You think it might be okay under some circumstances. Mike, help me get the full picture here. What values does this violate?"

Taken aback by my question, Mike paused and stroked his beard. Susan smiled sweetly, seeing her husband on the spot. "Yes, dear, what values?"

"He's a kid. He's irresponsible, well, some of the time. And, simply put, I own the house. I can decide what goes on there."

"That's a value, all right," snorted Susan.

"Susan, we probably wouldn't even be here if you hadn't encouraged him to sleep over at Jen's house. Then he gets caught, and the Ludtmanns are not speaking to us."

"Mike, you've got that wrong. I knew about it, but I did *not* encourage it."

"Well, you didn't tell me it was going on. I thought he was at some football camp until Jen's dad calls me at the office, threatening to sue. I was left looking pretty stupid—sports camp, huh?"

Here Susan blushed and started fumbling in her oversize carryall.

"Susan, Mike, what was your communication like before this happened?"

Drying her eyes with a bunched-up Kleenex, Susan said, "Usually a lot better than this. After this situation with the Ludtmanns, everything has fallen apart."

"Exactly what was the situation with the Ludtmanns?"

"Well, in all fairness, we're still not sure. Jen had Rory and two other kids sleep over at her house when her parents were out of town. Then Mr. Ludtmann got sick, and he and his wife returned early to find four teens asleep on their living room floor. Apparently he went over the top and started shouting that he was going to have Rory arrested for statutory rape." Here Mike's tenseness relaxed, and he smiled. "The way Rory tells it, he had said, 'Mr. Ludtmann, there's nothing going on here, but I would like to remind you that if we had been having sex, your daughter is older than me. She's eighteen, sir.' The kid's got your sense of humor for sure, Susan. He's a winner."

Both of Rory's parents chuckled at the imagined picture of their son and Mr. Ludtmann. Hearing her husband's laugh, Susan relaxed too. "Mike, I feel like you're blaming me for this whole thing, and that's unfair."

"Not blaming you, Susan. I just feel like I was caught not knowing what was going on."

"I should have told you, I know. I just feel like it's impossible to talk to you about this kind of thing."

"Why, Susan?" I asked.

"Well, it's never a discussion. Mike acts like he knows what should happen. Rory tried to talk with his dad about it."

"How did that go, Mike?"

"Not very far, I guess, 'cause I didn't know much about what was going on. I figured he might be having sex with Jen when he brought those books home from your office. Uh, I read them, too. I was looking for answers, I guess, trying to find a way to talk to him. I knew it shouldn't all fall on Susan."

I thought about Rory's thirst for information, how helpful this dad might have been. "Did you ask him how things were going with Jen?"

"Maybe I think I've got to have all the answers. A simple question, 'How are things going?'—I tried. I did say I'd be willing to talk about any questions he had, but I didn't ask."

"Where's it stand now, after he was caught at Jen's house?"

"Well, I yelled at him after I got that phone call. I don't want him having Jen sleep over, but I don't want to sound like Mr. Ludtmann, either."

"Is there a way you could spend some time with him?" I asked.

"I could. Maybe I'll volunteer to be the parent chaperon for that away football game he's got coming up. I suppose we could talk about the whole thing."

"You both read those books. You could talk about them."

"Yeah, even getting started with the sex stuff is hard with Rory."

"You don't have to be an expert. Just try to start a conversation with him."

"For me, that's the hard part."

"Mike, that's the most difficult thing for a lot of parents."

Mike is like most dads, and even some moms, parents that have trouble even beginning a conversation with their teens about sex. For Mike, it was easier to tell Rory what to do—"Don't have Jen sleep over"— rather than find out how things were going.

I did hear back from Rory after he and his dad drove to the weekend football game. They had managed a conversation about sex. Mike stayed off the topic of Mr. Ludtmann, and Rory didn't ask if he could have Jen sleep over. Apparently, they touched on the subject of timing, and Mike shared information and, even more important, some of his own stories. The conversations had begun.

Intercourse: Starting Off

One of the most important things that I have learned from working with teens is that their sexual patterns are extremely diverse. Yet teens feel acute pressure to be sexually "normal," whatever that is, and struggle to make their own behavior fit into what they imagine fits that pattern. They keep much of their sexual lives hidden. There is often a story to share, though, and they are looking for someone to listen. Their reluctance to talk about sexual matters is combined with social taboos, and the end result is that they learn very little about what teenage sexual experiences are really like. Into this gap, television, movies, and music videos slide with dramatic stories that make it appear as if all teens are not only participating, but adept at sexual intercourse. This often infuriates parents, who view the media as aggressively seducing their children long before they are ready. The media's aggressive use of teenage sexuality to sell everything may infuriate parents, but it is more demanding to teens themselves who are struggling to find out exactly what is "normal" and if they are included. Rory is one of many young boys I have worked with who are critical of their own sexual behavior because it doesn't fit the media images. As Rory said, "No guy lasted under a minute in any of the movies I saw."

Rory did tell me that he had recently seen a television program that had shown the "trials" of another "minute man," but this character's entire life was portrayed in terms of trials related to expectations of sexual performance. Although Rory had watched the program with interest, he was afraid to discuss it with his friends, not wanting them to guess that this was his own situation also. After several conversations Rory was able to share with his father, Mike, his concerns about "timing." Mike shared some of his early experiences and told Rory that not only were his worries normal, they were to be expected. This conversation provided some of the reassurance that Rory was searching for, and the bond between father and son was greatly enhanced.

In this chapter I chose to include the sexual stories of four teens—Miriam, Joel, Mai, and Rory—instead of the usual one or two. My intention has been to emphasize the range of sexual choices for teens. Miriam started early with physical development and activity, and her first experience with intercourse occurred at the age of fifteen rather than the average age of sixteen. Both she and her mother put a lot of effort into preparation, and her story serves as a good example of a teen who understood the questions that needed to be asked of herself before taking this important step. I believe that asking and answering the questions is a very important part of sexual readiness for teens and adults both. Leaving out or rushing through any of the questions increases one's vulnerability. Parents and many sexual education programs focus on the issue in Question #7 from my suggested list of sexual readiness questions (in the Appendix to this book)—about whether any planning for protection from pregnancy and sexually transmitted disease has taken place—at the expense of some of the others. For example, if you can't tell your partner no, even at the last minute, then your choices are limited by those of your partner. This is an important issue, most typically for girls who don't know their own desires fully, and accommodate to the wishes of their partners, but a surprising number of boys also describe feeling forced in sexual situations.

Also important is the question that asks whether one has thought about the impact of the first time on one's life, and whether the decision being made is consistent with one's values. This was a vital question for Mai, who knew her boyfriend's desire and her father's wishes, but had to define and then defend her own path. Asking herself the question about her values helped her identify her choice as her own, and helped her gain understanding about why she was having such intense negative feelings about her boyfriend and her dad. Once she recognized her own choice, she was no longer as angry with these other people.

Rory and I indirectly addressed the question from the list concerning sexual technique. Many teens today go right to intercourse, neglecting the time-honored steps of fondling, rubbing, and stimulated intercourse without penetration that have delayed and enlivened the sexual lives of former generations. Rory was delighted to learn how to calibrate and adjust his excitability. Understanding that different individuals are excited by different degrees of touch gave Rory some control. Although he was a little fast, he found that he "fit" in the normal range, which was a tremendous relief.

Like Rory, Joel was grappling with issues related to sexual readiness, although he was exploring very different questions. Joel had masturbated, but he had never really thought in much detail about what it would be like to have sex with a boy or a girl. His inner desires were so hidden that he could not allow himself to have a sexual fantasy that included intercourse. He was stunned when he had intercourse with Richard, amazed at the strength of his erotic feelings. It forced him to pay attention to those feelings, clarifying an important part of his identity. Making his choices, he confronted many of the questions that are part of determining sexual readiness. Had he thought about the potential impact on his life? Did he trust his partner? But his surprise about what happened and the potential meaning of these events for his character indicate that even if one prepared carefully, there are always revelations in intercourse. The discovery of unknown aspects represents one of the largest risks. Perhaps the final question asked should be whether you are ready to experience something that may change you.

Sexual activity has many meanings for adults. It is important to recognize that this is also true for teenagers. No one template fits all teens, and most adolescents derive multiple meanings from a single sexual experience. Miriam's experience of intense physical pleasure revealed a greater intimacy with her boyfriend, Julian, but it also reflected personal growth and her developing spirituality. Like Miriam, Joel had experienced physical pleasure and intimacy, but he believed that the most important part of the experience was his surrender to desire. Mai learned from her exploration of the question that the freedom to make her own choice was vital. For her, it was important that it not be an expected part of her current relationship. Rory's story began with a focus on sexual intercourse to test biological equipment. In the end, it brought him closer to his girlfriend, Jen, who had already accepted what he was questioning, and led him to want a greater understanding of relationships. When both he and his father were able to share and communicate, Rory's sexual activity allowed for a greater intimacy not only with Jen, but with his father and with himself.

The sexual experiences described in this chapter help to identify how intimacy and intercourse are not always unnatural partners, but can be a positive formula that helps adolescents grow and understand themselves better. Sonia discovered that she believed in a healthy sex life for her young daughter in theory, but in practice found this a lot harder to deal with. Mike discovered that he had to learn to listen to his son. Once he tried this, Rory told him a lot more, and they grew closer. Teens' stories can teach adults a great deal.

Not My Child
Homosexuality, Bisexuality, and Sexual Orientation

I don't want a son who's a fag!
—Ian's father, Peter

Say a girl has sex with this guy . . . does it mean she's straight? —Noelle

My phone was ringing. It sounded very far away. It rang several times before my answering machine activated—a sharp click, followed by a barely audible sound. A woman's cry? She was struggling to say something, but all that came out were short gasping noises. Then she hung up, no name, no number, just leaving me with the haunting feeling that I should have reached for the phone.

I pulled myself up from the couch and looked at my clock. It was eleven-thirty at night. I had fallen asleep reviewing charts. Who had it been? A suicidal teen? A distraught parent? Several minutes later the phone rang again. This time I reached for the receiver.

"Hello?" No answer. "Hello, this is Dr. Ponton. I've been working late in my office. Is there something you want to say?"

An unintelligible cry followed. This person *was* struggling to talk to me. Finally, she spoke. "Dr. Ponton, please, don't hang up. Please."

"I don't plan to," I said, but I was really thinking, *It's so late—please tell me.*

Her story, once it started, fell out in bits and pieces.

"I'm so sorry, Dr. Ponton, it's so late, but I didn't know who to call. I was cleaning Ian's room." Her sobbing began again.

"Who is Ian?" I asked.

"My seventeen-year-old son. His diary was open, lying there on his bed. I read it." I heard a short gasp, but she kept going and forced the words out. "It said that he was in love with his science tutor, Josh, a boy at Cal. He's about two years older than Ian. They've kissed. I showed the diary to my husband. He confronted him tonight. Ian ran out of the house. My husband has been out looking for him for hours."

"And how is it that you called me?"

"My sister. I was going crazy. I kept thinking I caused it, that I shouldn't have read the diary. Shouldn't have showed it to my husband. She told me that you work with teens and parents in trouble."

"I do. What's your name?"

"Marlene."

"Marlene, how did your husband confront him?"

"It wasn't good. At first Peter—my husband—was trying to be calm, asking Ian to talk about it, but then he froze up. My husband, I mean. I could see Ian backing away. He just couldn't talk to us. My husband didn't see it, though. He kept pressing. Ian didn't say anything. He just walked out. Then Peter started screaming, banging things. Finally he said he had to go look for him, and then he left. That was three hours ago."

"Marlene, there are other options that might be helpful to you at this point, too. I know of two hot lines that help teens and parents in trouble. There's even a special line, LYRIC, for teens struggling with issues related to sexuality. The police are also sometimes very helpful around runaways, but it has only been a few hours. I would imagine that both Peter and Ian will return home soon."

Sounding relieved, Marlene added, "I think they will, too. That's what worries me. What will happen once they come home? Ian is so upset. The diary was so passionate. . . ."

Sensing that she wanted the priest's confessional as much as a psychiatrist's office, I listened for several minutes, trying to calm her, before I finally suggested that she call the next day and let me know how things had worked out and what she wanted to do.

Marlene's message was the first one on my answering machine the next morning.

"Dr. Ponton, this is Marlene. Peter is home. Ian came home, too, but only to tell us that he's leaving. He says he's moving in with a friend—I don't know who. I don't know if it's Josh or someone else. I think Peter and I should come see you. He is devastated."

I listened to it twice, noting how she underscored Peter's devastation. Judging from what I had heard the night before, he wasn't the only one who was devastated.

I met Peter the next day when I returned from rounds at the hospital with two medical students who had been working with me for several months. He had come early, by more than a half hour, and was seated in my waiting room when the three of us entered the office. He was crouched on the carpet before one of my bookcases, and had pulled at least half a dozen books from my shelves. He had already affixed post-it tabs to certain pages in some of them. My attention was divided between noticing this and taking in his white doctor's jacket, the stethoscope slung around his neck, and his university identification tag. Dangling from Peter's stethoscope was a tiny stuffed bear—the definitive sign of a pediatrician. I had worked with many fathers who were doctors, but none had ever worn their stethoscope into my office before. I wondered if he had forgotten it, maybe coming directly from the hospital. More likely, it helped him to feel more secure in a psychiatrist's office. I remembered that Marlene had said that he was extremely upset, although he did not appear so at this moment. When he rose to shake my hand, I read the ID tag—he was a pediatric surgeon—and I realized, now that I knew his last name, that I had heard his name before.

I also took in the titles he had chosen from my shelves—*Sexuality in Adolescence, Children of Horizons, Lesbian Lives, And Then I Became Gay.* I shook his hand, letting him know that I'd be with my students for the next half hour, but that he was welcome to look at my books, even mark them for Xeroxing if that was what he was doing.

"Your Xerox machine over there—it's also possible to use it while I'm waiting?" he asked.

Definitely a surgeon's personality—sure of himself, a little entitled, even.

"It is." Looking at the stack of books that Peter had already accumulated, I paused. "Perhaps you can wait, and we can look through them to-gether."

"Your office." He smiled.

"Yes, it is." I laughed. "You're welcome to borrow some of the books." This is a courtesy I extend to all the parents and teens I work with, but Peter seemed surprised by my offer. Was it that he had presumed as much already, or that he really appreciated it?

The little stuffed bear on his stethoscope wobbled, and he said, "Thanks. I guess I'll wait for Marlene before I make my choices. Better get to those students."

I walked in my office, thinking, *This doctor dad may say it's my office, but he still thinks it's his own.* I wondered what life at home was like for his son. I even began to think the polar bear was significant. Most pediatricians wear cuddly koalas and pandas. Peter was wearing a polar bear.

Thirty minutes later, the two students left my office, joking about the walk down the steep hill to the medical center—would they make it? They stopped their laughing as Marlene entered the waiting room with Ian. Peter looked surprised to see his son. Neither of them said anything, however.

Marlene finally spoke. "He was at home, Peter, packing. He wanted to come when I told him where I was going."

Still not a word.

Finally, I extended my hand to Marlene, then Ian, and thanked them both for coming. The books that Peter had collected lay piled on the floor as I suggested that they all come into my office.

The weathered room has a faded brown couch in one corner, and Ian commented on it right away.

"Dr. Ponton," he said, "that's a great couch. It looks like Freud's, or the photos I've seen. Who do you think should lie down on it, Dad, Mom, or me?"

I looked at Ian, whose eyes sparkled. He was nervous, but he had guts, too, or maybe just bravado. Somehow, I already admired him. He was not in an easy position, but he was meeting it head-on. He had come to this meeting, and he was acknowledging the complexity of the situation. I already saw that he and his father were more than a little alike—they would take charge of my office if I let them.

"Ian, I'm glad you came, but no one has to be on the couch. In fact, why don't I sit there? We can all sit up and talk, or at least that was my plan. Maybe you've got a different one?"

"Nope, we all need a shrink. We'd have to fight for the couch, anyway. Better to sit up."

"What made you decide to come here, Ian?"

"Doc, I thought you were supposed to welcome me with open arms." Again, the eyes sparkled at me.

"I'm trying to, Ian, but I'm curious about why you came."

"Well, my mom's a snoop, but she asked me to be here, and she's cool." He flashed her a look that said, *Your turn.*

Marlene responded. "I guess I thought it was really important that Ian come. I guess I feel as if I pushed something ahead of where it should be by reading Ian's diary. I am very sorry that I violated his privacy, and not just because of what was in there." Ian looked gratefully at his mom as she spoke. Still, Peter said nothing. He was sitting in the corner, looking out of my windows. He looked like he was fighting back tears. He adjusted his glasses so that I could no longer see his eyes.

"Peter, I'm glad you came here, too."

He shrugged. "What choice do I have? My wife's a snoop, my son runs off, and I'm a fool. Good enough reasons to see a shrink."

Sidestepping his other comments, I asked, "Why do you think you're a fool, Peter?"

"Uh, I've acted like one. I can't talk about this." He stood up, excused himself, and moved to my waiting room.

Marlene, Ian, and I talked quietly for several minutes. I then walked into the waiting room to sit with Peter, who was shaking his head. He spoke as soon as I sat down.

"I can't do this. I know what I have to do. I have to go back in there and make it real, say to my son, 'It's okay.' I can't do that. I want him home. He needs to be back home. He needs to be home, with us, but I can't pretend everything is normal."

"Peter, you just found out about this. It's really difficult to deal with it—for all of you."

He shook his head and his tears started to flow, but he kept his voice low, as though not wanting his son and wife in the next room to hear him.

"But I didn't just find out. Not really. I've known about this for years—I just didn't want to believe it. I could see the signs when he was three or four. He was so close to his mom. He would rather sit in the house with her than go outside and run around with the guys. I should have brought him in for that therapy that turns boys around, the kind they use on kids whose gender is screwed up. They're more likely to be gay, and that's what's happened here. He showed the signs, but I didn't do that."

"No, you didn't do that, and you're here with him now, Peter."

"I don't know what I'm gonna do."

"I'm not so sure you have to *do* anything right now."

"I keep thinking about what I should have done. I feel like I really let Ian down. I'm a doctor. I saw this coming. I was a fool."

"It sounds like you feel responsible for your son's sexual orientation. I don't know how much you've read already," I said, nodding toward the stacks of books, "but you are not responsible."

"Maybe not, but it was my responsibility to correct things, wasn't it?"

"I don't know about that," I said.

He was quiet for a minute before he spoke. "We have to go back in there, don't we?"

"Peter, you do have some choices in this."

"It doesn't seem that way."

"You have choices about yourself, not Ian. I think you need to talk with your son about all of this, but today may not be the right time for it."

"So what can I do?" Peter looked down at the books scattered at his feet.

"You could say that you need more time to process this, and read some of these books in the meantime."

"Sounds like a cop-out to me, but I don't have any better ideas." He smiled. "You're the psychiatrist."

"You also mentioned that you want your son back home. You can ask him."

"Ask him to come home while his old man learns something? Think he'll do it?"

Peter and I got up and entered my office together. He asked Ian immediately, and his son agreed to come home.

Ian's Story

Several days later, I met with Ian alone, which he requested and his parents readily supported. I was pretty sure Peter's support was still a function of believing I could fix things, fix his son.

Ian was quieter than he had been during the session with his parents, but he was still pretty forthcoming.

"I checked you out with a couple of kids. They said that you see a lot of street kids."

"So you think that means I'm okay?"

"Well, no, I think it means you can handle me."

"Have you ever seen anyone, a psychiatrist or therapist?"

The gray eyes narrowed. "Let's get one thing clear. I am not seeing you, a shrink. I am here"—and he looked around my office—"to help them adjust to this." Then, dramatically, he added, "You can ask me anything."

At this point I was quite sure that I couldn't ask him anything. I decided to follow his lead, though.

"So how do you think we can help your parents with this?"

"My dad would probably say get a new son. He's home reading all those books you gave him. It's crazy."

"What's crazy about it?"

At this question Ian looked out the window so that I couldn't watch his face.

"He thinks something's wrong with me. It's like he's looking for the answer, something to repair, like when he does surgery. I knew he would act like this. It's why I never told him."

"How long have you known?"

Ian looked right at me. I wasn't sure if he was surprised by my directness.

"Since I was eight or nine, maybe earlier. You know, I admire that guy so much. He saves kids' lives. I wanted to be just like him. Does he know this? Just like him." Ian started crying openly.

"Ian, it was brave of you to go back home. Have you or your dad been able to talk about all this?"

"No. He just keeps reading those damned books. It's so funny. A few years ago, I was reading those same books."

"What's so funny about it? You were trying to learn then, and he is now. What was it like for you, the reading?"

"Well, not like it is for him, I'm sure. He's trying to figure out a way to make me straight."

"That's what you think he's doing?"

"Yeah. It makes me feel like a pervert. You gave my mom the number for the youth hot lines, for LYRIC even. She called them, and they sent her a whole lot of stuff. She's reading it, too."

"Have you ever talked to the folks at LYRIC?"

He looked at me and said, "You don't tell them everything, right? You gotta keep some stuff confidential?"

"There are certain things I tell parents when it's about their child's safety, but it's my job to keep a lot of things confidential."

"I worked for them. It helped me handle my own stuff, talking with other kids. I felt like my dad when I did it, like I was helping kids."

"You probably were. And you probably are a lot like your father."

"Oh, God," he groaned, but he was smiling.

I laughed. "Would that be a bad thing?"

"Now isn't the best time to ask that, I guess. I mean, I've always admired a lot of things about him. But I've also always known he would freak if he found out about me, and that's not exactly a testimonial to his being open-minded, or openhearted. It's weird. He fixes children's hearts. Why is his own so closed off?"

Ian's metaphor was a powerful one. But I didn't want to lose track of something else he'd said.

"Ian, you said 'if' your father found out."

"If, when, whatever."

"Well, how would you want him to act?"

"Supportive, I guess. Like it wasn't all about him."

"Do you think he believes it is?"

"I know he does. He can't help it. But that doesn't make it right."

Several days later, I met with Marlene and Peter for the second time. I asked Ian if he wanted to be there, but he declined, wishing me good luck. He said things were okay at home—tense but okay. That's how they felt to me, sitting with Marlene and Peter—better, but the tension was still right there beneath the surface. It took Peter only a few minutes before he started grilling me.

"Dr. Ponton, I've read some of your stuff. You believe that identity changes in adolescence—is changed by risk-taking and other things. So you must believe that Ian is going through a phase."

"What phase are you talking about?"

Peter's face colored quickly. He was supposed to ask the questions, and I was supposed to answer. I wasn't being fair.

"Well, he's going through a homosexual phase, and with your help—"

"With my help?"

"I guess I want to know if he can come out of it. If he can't, I'll have to accept it."

Finally, he asked the question I had been anticipating. "What causes this?"

I struggled for words. "Peter and Marlene, I wish there was an answer to that question. You've read a lot about adolescent sexuality in the last week or two. There are many ideas about how sexual orientation develops and how it changes. There are several studies that point to biology's role. Many teens have experienced strong feelings of attraction for the same sex as children. Relationships, culture, society, and internal feelings are believed to play important roles, too. It appears to be different for everyone."

Marlene spoke for the first time. "So Ian has his own story here—"

Peter interrupted. "What I want to know is whether he's homosexual or whether it's going to change."

"Marlene," I said, "you're right. Ian's own story is very important, and he has only begun to share it with you, from an accidental start that he didn't choose. His story is very important." Then I turned to Peter, whose agitation I could sense. "I don't think I can answer your questions, Peter. I do believe that sexual orientation can change during a lifetime, but those changes are up to the person him- or herself, and have more to do with their interests, preferences, or life events than with someone else's. I think it would be a serious mistake to treat what you've discovered about Ian as a phase."

"So you think he's gay? Permanently?"

"I don't know, but I think you need to listen carefully to what he is saying right now, and support him as much as you can."

"So you can't help him change?"

"Peter, he doesn't want to change! And no, I can't make him straight, if that's what you're asking." Then I thought I should try again. "Peter, this is a very important time for Ian. He needs your support."

Peter sank back in his chair. I could see that he was trying to focus on what I had just said.

"What support could I give him?"

"Even though this situation has been forced, your son is acknowledging his sexual desires, and is starting to talk about them with others. This is a very important time."

Marlene spoke again. "He told his best friend at school—Martina."

"He did?" Peter sat up straight.

"Yes. And I think he wants to talk more about it with us."

"He does?" Peter looked shocked.

"Why does that surprise you?" I asked.

Peter smiled grimly. "Well, it's ironic, don't you think? I'm here asking you questions about wanting to make my kid straight, and he wants to talk with me about being gay, get my support . . . walking into the eye of the hurricane, in my humble opinion."

"Your son has a lot of courage. He's a lot like you—like both of you." I looked directly at Marlene.

"I don't think it was very courageous of me to read his journal," she said.

"Marlene, you called me, and you are insisting that your family deal with this. That takes some will. Yet you're pretty quiet when you're here. Any ideas?"

She shook her head. "I was so scared the night Ian ran away. I wouldn't be honest with you and Peter if I didn't say that I hadn't already guessed about Ian's sexuality before I read his journal." Then she looked at her husband and said, "Why I ever told you, Peter, I don't know. After what's happened."

"Marlene," I asked, "what did you hope would happen?"

She sat quietly for several moments. "I'm not an impulsive person, but I felt impulsive that evening. When I read that Ian had kissed Josh, something happened. I felt like Peter should know. What did I hope would happen?" Then she looked straight into her husband's gray eyes and said, "I think I hoped you would say it was okay, you know. 'It's okay, Marlene, it's hard but we'll get through this together. We'll help our son.'"

Peter didn't respond. I decided to give him time. When he finally spoke, he said very slowly, "I've let you down, too, Marlene. I wish I could have said that."

Less than a week later, I was attending a grand rounds in pediatrics because the topic was of interest to me—"Gender and Children." I was already seated when someone tapped me on the shoulder and asked if I would mind if he sat next to me. I was surprised. Surgeons hardly ever attend nonsurgical grand rounds.

"I'm glad to see you here, Peter."

"I must seem pretty unsophisticated to you, a cardiac surgeon who screws up his own family. It's hard for me. Ian's my only son."

"How are you and he getting along?"

"We've been talking more."

"That's good to hear."

An hour later, I turned to him again. "What'd'ya think?"

The talk had noted, among other things, the phenomenon of parents bringing boys who avoid rough and tumble play and show feminine behaviors to their pediatricians, wondering what's wrong with their child.

"Well, it's not my area." Then he paused. "Maybe it is after all, huh? Okay, let's get into it. Are they saying that some doctors think it's okay to change kids' behavior if they don't fit the standard gender roles?"

"I think that's one perspective, Peter, but it is very controversial. I think, though, that's not so far off from what you were asking me about when you first saw me with Ian."

He nodded. "Yeah, but I've thought a lot about it since then. They imply that parents who do it to protect their kids from social stigma are different from parents who believe that homosexuality is immoral."

"That's what they said, Peter. What do you think?"

"Hey—I'm a cut-and-stitch man. Some of the problems I face are tough, but I'm beginning to believe it's a lot easier than the stuff you do."

"Your work is crucial, Peter, life and death, every day. Many people don't recognize that this can be, too."

Several days later, Ian and Peter and I met together at their request. Marlene felt okay about not coming; she made the request by telephone and told me that she thought that they had a lot to discuss.

When I entered the waiting room, Peter was telling his son about a child whom he had just operated on. I listened several minutes as he finished his description of the surgery and was struck by the expression on Ian's face. He didn't take his eyes off Peter, and I realized from the questions he asked that he had been in the operating room many times with his father. How had Peter's new idea to modify the shunt worked? Did it give him the extra time he needed to help the child? What were the implications for the anesthesia?

I was impressed. It takes years to develop this type of knowledge. Peter had shared a lot with his son, and Ian had absorbed it. I wondered if Ian could share as much with Peter.

Once they were in my office, all conversation stopped and they both stared at the floor. "Whose idea was this meeting?" I asked. They both said, "His," and we all laughed.

"How are things going?"

"Okay," again from both of them, and then a long silence.

"Our last family meeting was pretty hot, and now things are okay? That's a big change—"

"We don't talk about it," said Ian.

"What do you think, Peter?"

"Ian's right. I haven't wanted to say anything after the way I acted before. I guess I don't want to rock the boat."

At this, Ian looked irritated with his cautious dad. Trying to protect whom?

"What *boat,* Dad?"

"Ian, I wasn't very supportive when your mother and I found out about you and Josh."

"No, you weren't." Ian looked down. "It's not like I expected it to be different, though."

Peter took a deep breath. "Why not?"

"I figured you, like most dads, would want your son to be straight."

"I did, Ian. Look, we're really close, you and I. At least I thought we were. I did think—*Hey, my son likes science, he even likes medicine, seems interested in surgery* . . . I thought about what it might be like to operate with you someday." Here Peter's voice cracked. Ian was looking away from his dad, but he was listening. "Ian, this whole thing has made me realize that you're not a carbon copy of me." Then he added, "I've started to realize that it's weird of me to want you to be. I have to tell you that I still don't get the sexual stuff, but I know that part of it is because I can't imagine myself there."

"Why do you think it's so hard, Peter?" I asked. I could tell he was surprised by my question.

"I don't know. For me, you spend your whole life knowing you're *not* something. It's part of who you are. Then this happens and it makes you question it—everything. I realize I don't like to ask myself those kinds of questions."

"I didn't like it, either, Dad. When I first had these feelings, it drove me crazy. I kept thinking, 'Why me?' I doubted everything about myself, not just the sexual stuff. I was even thinking that I shouldn't go to med school."

"It made you think you shouldn't go to med school?" Peter asked the question slowly.

"Yeah, Dad. *I* started questioning, even medical school."

Peter was shaking his head. "I can't believe that this . . . made you think you couldn't go to medical school."

"You can't even say it yet, Dad. Why's it so hard to think it would make me question myself, what I want?"

Peter's eyes had a faraway look, and he winced.

"It's okay now, though. I'm fine about being gay, and I'm going to apply to med school."

It was quiet for a long minute or two. Ian looked at Peter, who was looking at his own hands, the careful, clean hands of a surgeon, hands that touched the hearts of children every day. Finally he spoke.

"I think part of what's so hard about this is feeling estranged from you, excluded even. Though I know you knew I'd have a hard time with it. When I was a little older than you, Ian, this doctor I had been working under during internship told me that he didn't think I had the right stuff to be a surgeon, whatever that is. But what he said made me doubt myself. I put off applying to surgery, thinking something was wrong with me. I didn't go through the kind of thing you've been through, but it made me question myself."

"It's not the same thing, Dad."

"No, not exactly. But I still know what it's like to doubt yourself. And I hate that you couldn't come to me."

"Dad, what did you expect? Look at what's happening. When Mom told you about Josh and me, you screamed, 'I don't want a son who's a fag!' You screamed it. I heard."

Peter flinched. "Ian, I'm trying."

Learning that a son or daughter is gay is often a time of upset for teens and parents alike. Not everyone can communicate in the way that Peter and Ian did. Most of these "conversations," if they occur at all, are short and take place without the presence of a supportive third party, let alone a therapist. Although this was just a beginning for Peter and Ian, it was important. Peter understood his son's struggle better when he could identify and describe the pain of an experience during his own youth. Ian was right—it wasn't "the same thing"—but his father was trying to identify with him in some way. He may even have felt compelled to identify with Ian about something else because there was suddenly such a huge, deep place in which he couldn't identify with him. Many parents cannot remember the struggles that were an integral part of their adolescent sexuality. Also, Peter probably did not experience the intense sexual questioning that his gay son had gone through. This lack of shared experiences makes the issue even harder to understand. In addition, the culture does not help fathers at such a moment. A masculine heterosexual orientation is often achieved at least in part by stigmatizing and devaluing a homosexual orientation. I was saddened but not surprised when I learned that Peter had said he didn't want any fags in his family. Old patterns die hard. They change only through the type of painful conversations that Ian and Peter were beginning to have.

Sexual Orientation and Sexual Identity: Fitting the Pieces Together

Sexual orientation is an even more cloistered part of a larger taboo subject—sexuality—and is a mystery to many, teens and parents alike. Peter is one of many parents who ask very specific questions about their child's orientation. Parents ask these questions for many reasons—to further their own knowledge about sexual matters, out of fear that their child will be gay, and more rarely, to support their child with whatever sexual orientation he or she has. Defining terms is important. Often one is exchanged for another, and this can make a confusing topic even more difficult to understand. *Sexual orientation* is used to describe a person's underlying sexual preferences—homosexual, heterosexual, bisexual. It is usually defined as a consistent pattern of arousal toward persons of the same and/or opposite gender. *Core gender identity* usually develops in childhood and is the sense of oneself as male or female, a boy or girl. This is a task completed early in life, except in rare circumstances. *Sexual* or *gender roles* are characteristics, behaviors, and interests defined by society or culture as appropriate for members of each gender. As Peter did when Ian was young, others often mistakenly assume that a boy with a more feminine gender role will have a homosexual orientation. Many aspects of these roles are psychological. *Sexual identity* is an inclusive category, which refers to how a person describes, expresses, and feels about his or her sexual self. Sexual orientation, core gender identity, and sex/gender roles are all important parts of sexual identity, but no one of these make up the entire story. This vital topic is discussed at length in the summary of this book.

Sexual/gender roles are changing, and many of today's teenagers are more androgynous, adopting a combination of masculine or feminine traits, and redefining gender roles. Girls with a combination of masculine and feminine traits are reported to show greater self-acceptance and be better accepted by their peers. This is not the same for boys. Peer acceptance is greatest for boys with masculine traits, and not surprisingly, self-acceptance is also better for sharply defined masculine boys. Interestingly, this is not the case in either childhood or adulthood, when a combination of masculine and feminine traits is associated with good health.

Psychologist and author Lawrence Steinberg puts forward the theory that although girls experience greater pressure than boys to conform with gender roles and adopt feminine traits in adolescence, they are not as pressured to give up their masculine traits as boys are to give up feminine traits. So while girls may be pressured to wear makeup and act nice, they are also allowed to pursue sports and other more traditional masculine areas. Steinberg believes that boys are pressured from early childhood not to behave in feminine ways; their gender-role socialization does not intensify during adolescence because it is already so strong to begin with. In short, boys adopt strong gender roles in childhood, girls in adolescence.

The gradual identification of one's own sexuality is a process that frequently involves sharing information with others—most notably family and friends—about one's sexual orientation; this is commonly known as "coming out." During the past twenty years many have written about this important process. Troiden describes coming out as a lengthy process often beginning in childhood and extending into adulthood. He divides it into four sequential stages: an initial sensitization or gradual awareness of feelings of attraction to the same sex; identity confusion; assumption of identity; and, finally, commitment. Troiden's use of the term *identity* here implies that sexual orientation plays the largest, if not total, role in determining overall sexual identity. I have seen its importance from my experience with many teens. For gay, lesbian, and bisexual youth who struggle with a growing awareness of a world that is often unreceptive and prejudiced, their sexual orientation is often the defining factor.

Other researchers, most notably Gilbert Herdt and Andrew Boxer, question Troiden's staging of coming out, and believe that a model focusing on life-course transitions rather than specific stages best explains the coming-out process. Their study of gay and lesbian youth in Chicago showed that many of these young people struggled alone for a long time with a gay sexual orientation. They then chose to participate in a variety of supportive groups and services, working with a group of peers who were struggling with similar questions. Cultural factors do play an important role. For example, a teen growing up in an urban environment often has greater access to like-minded peers and gay services than a teen living in a rural environment. Ian, at seventeen, had already volunteered for a teen hot line that addressed sexual issues, and had attended a support group. However, it must be remembered that many teens struggle alone, without support.

For many teens, coming out is a lengthy process lasting on the average three and a half to four years. Ritch Savin-Williams, who has conducted several major studies, believes that the coming-out experience is quite different for boys and girls. Girls may have more heterosexual activity, and the process may take longer. He reports that among adolescent girls, being female has precedence over being gay in the context of their sexual identity, while among boys, being gay is more important then being male. For both boys and girls, the coming-out process is challenging, and parental support is vital.

In a position paper developed by the American Psychoanalytic Association, Bertram Cohler and Andrew Boxer emphasize that models which identify specific stages such as Troiden's are locked into a defined time and, to some degree, a specific culture or place. They encourage greater flexibility in thinking about the process of coming out, and underscore the vital importance of individual teens' narratives about their sexuality. For myself, knowing that each teen has his or her own unique story still unfolding helps me to be cautious with parents like Peter who ask direct but unanswerable questions, such as "Is my child gay?" I do tell parents that their attitudes toward and reception of information about their child's sexuality make an important difference. One study indicated that a lack of parental acceptance of sexual orientation is the most common reason homosexual youth attempt suicide.

Not Me: What's Going On Here?

"I'm not here for the reason my parents gave you," whispered fifteen-year-old Noelle.

"Why are you here?"

"Because I'm seriously turned on by my best friend." Now her voice was even lower.

This was my first private encounter with Noelle after we had left her concerned parents and her field hockey stick in my waiting room. Her parents had telephoned and said that Noelle was feeling depressed after a bout of mono and had asked to talk with someone. They were pleased at her request, a teen asking for help, and agreed to call me and to bring her to the first session, just in case they were needed. After everyone shook my hand in the waiting room, Noelle quickly suggested that her parents go get some coffee. They seemed surprised. Didn't Noelle want them to stay for her first time in a psychiatrist's office? No, she didn't want them there. I recognized that she didn't want them to hear anything that she was going to tell me. What if my soundproofing wasn't good enough? I suggested that they wait at a neighborhood coffee shop. I knew she was in a hurry to tell me something, but I hadn't expected her to drop it in the first minute of our session.

I paused and asked, "Okay, do you want to tell me more?"

"That's enough, isn't it?" She looked disgusted with me, and I had that feeling I get when I'm losing the struggle for a brand-new connection with a teen.

"What's she like?" I asked, trying again.

She was playing with her shoelace. "She's great. She's the other forward on the team. It is amazing to watch her run. Torie is passionate about field hockey. So am I." Noelle's cheeks had turned pink, and a trace of sweat appeared on her upper lip. "Do you play?" she asked.

"I don't, but I like to watch."

"You've seen it. Good. Not too many people watch girls' field hockey. Of course, the stadium's right here, that's cool."

"I am nearby Kezar Stadium, but I also really enjoy watching women's sports." I didn't tell Noelle that I had a daughter who played for one of the teams.

"Maybe you've seen Torie—number 18, she's really tall, almost six feet, and she has this amazing hair, reddish brown, hanging down to her waist? You wouldn't forget her. When we practice at Kezar, runners stop going around the track when she runs for a goal—they watch her instead. Everyone watches her. . . ."

"You do, Noelle. Is that what worries you?"

"Part of it." She took a deep breath and pulled her knees up to her chest, smoothing her blue and yellow plaid skirt. She was still wearing her field hockey uniform.

"Two weeks ago Torie slept over. She's done it before, but this time it was different, really different. We had just won the play-offs, city championship. After the game the seniors had sprayed us all with whipped cream. It was so much fun. Then Torie and I go back to my house. We're still getting sprayed by the others in the car on the way, even on the street outside my house. The whipped cream is all over us, in our hair, all over our uniforms. Inside, we're standing in my bedroom, and Torie just pulls off her shirt. This whipped cream is running down her breast, and I can't stop staring at it! Then she smiles and says, 'Hey, Noelle, wanna taste it?' I just about fall over before she says, 'Just kidding!' But I knew she wasn't. That night I'm lying there next to her, and I can't sleep. All I can think about is licking that cream off her breast." She stopped for a breath. "Nothing happened. After Torie goes home I feel sick. I want to jump my best friend. What's wrong with me?" She looked at me for the answer.

"Noelle, does it feel like something's wrong?"

"She's a girl. Don't you see that as wrong?!"

"I see that you're pretty unhappy about it."

She faltered. "I have a boyfriend, you know. He's a soccer player."

I wondered if Noelle got as excited about her boyfriend running down the soccer field as she did watching Torie, but I didn't ask that.

"Are you worried about something specific, Noelle?"

"I'm worried about *me*. What if I like girls, really like them?"

"That would bother you?"

"What world are you living in?!"

Again, that sense of losing her. "Noelle, I'm sorry if I don't understand what's going on. I do see that you're really worried about these feelings, that you didn't expect to have them for Torie."

"Yeah." She relaxed again. "All the other girls in the school are calling each other 'lesbo.' You don't even have to do anything to get called a lesbo!"

"And you feel like you've done something?"

"I haven't done anything, but I can't get rid of this idea. I'm licking this cream off her breast—oh, it's so crazy." Noelle had hidden her face from me, but I could still see part of one red cheek.

"Talking about this bothers you?"

"Are you telling me that I don't have anything to worry about?"

"Noelle, I'm not sure anyone can reassure you about the feelings you've had. They seem to be really upsetting to you, maybe because they're about your best friend, a girl, or maybe because they're pretty shocking, not things you ever expected to think about."

She took her hands down from her face but still stared at the floor. "They don't surprise you?"

"No. I've seen other kids with similar feelings."

"Do they mean I'm gonna be gay?" Her blue-green eyes met mine. "I don't want to be gay," she added.

"Noelle, I don't know whether or not you're going to be gay. You have had some strong feelings for another girl. It is a pretty common thing. It happens to many girls and boys. It can be pretty exciting, but also pretty scary."

"It definitely scared me. Still does." A long pause. "I think I was excited, too."

"What do you think about that?"

"I don't know. Since the thing with Torie happened, I've tried not to have the thoughts."

"You're able to talk about them with me, though."

"Yeah," she admitted, "I am. It's not so bad with you. I can kinda let myself think them. Plus, you ask me about 'em."

"But if I wasn't asking, there would be the thought police?"

"That's it—the thought police. I start thinking about Torie, seeing her breasts, and then I'm like, *Noelle, don't go there.*"

"You want to keep the thoughts secret from yourself?"

"Yeah, I do. I'm scared about anybody knowing."

"That includes you—maybe you more than anybody."

I saw Noelle for two more sessions. Then she told me she wanted to stop. After all, there was no need to keep coming. The thoughts that were bothering her had gone away.

A Moratorium for Noelle

Erik Erikson wrote about older adolescents taking a break from the hard work of forging their identity, putting their struggle on hold for a while. He called this break a moratorium. I have seen many adolescents struggling with issues of sexual identity take such a break. The going gets rough, and they bow out for a while. Such a break serves many purposes. It gives them time to get a little older. They acquire more self-confidence. Aspects of identity other than sexual are better understood before they decide to reenter the sexual area. Maggie Magie and Diana Miller, who spent a decade working on an exploration of lesbians and therapy, believe that many young people who are confused or frightened about same-sex attractions take a break and re-approach the topic at a later point. For many, the break gives them the courage they need to examine the sexual thoughts and feelings that are hidden from themselves. For others, the moratorium goes on too long, creating a pattern of repression that is difficult to end. Fortunately, Noelle returned to see me eighteen months later.

The field hockey uniform was gone, but that wasn't the only change. She was several inches taller. She seemed more at ease in my office, commenting on changes—my backyard seemed smaller because a room extension had been built, one neighborhood cat who had hung out there was absent, a bookshelf had been added. She was extremely polite, chatting with me, but not until the end of our session did she broach the subject of sex.

"Say a girl has sex with this guy. Does it mean she's straight?" She was watching me closely as she asked the question.

"Noelle, this is real important to you. I can't give you a quick answer to it. Knowing whether you're gay, straight, or bisexual is complicated."

"So you won't answer it?"

"I can't answer it for you."

"Then I'll go. Thanks, thanks a lot."

"Thanks for what?"

"Seeing me again. You listened."

"You haven't told me much."

"You really can't answer my question?" she asked again.

"No. We could talk about it, though."

"I don't think it would help."

"You can try it."

Noelle did come back, and the story of the past eighteen months of her life came out. She had had sex with not one guy, but two. Her first partner was a sixteen-year-old boy she had grown up with. They liked each other but, as she put it, they didn't *like* each other. She described their first and only sexual experience as if it were an anatomy lesson. "The penis was enlarged . . . the vagina was penetrated . . . he ejaculated." She did not believe she had an orgasm, but she wasn't totally sure, exactly. How many seconds of arousal were needed for orgasm?

I inquired gently about the feelings she had related to this experience. The best feelings were centered around the two of them going to a drive-in for hamburgers after they had "done it," and laughing so hysterically that they couldn't tell the waitress what they wanted to eat.

"What was so funny?" I asked.

Noelle answered, "Probably just getting through it."

Her second sexual experience had been very different from the first. After trying sex with her childhood friend, she decided to have sex with her boyfriend, the soccer player. She "*liked* him liked him." He was totally hot, at least all the girls at school thought so, but Noelle and he were not friends. The experience started out okay. She wanted to try it again after what had happened with her best friend, see if it was better her second time. It was different, but not better, she said. The sex with her boyfriend felt rough. She wanted to tell him to stop but couldn't, she could say the words in her head, but they wouldn't come out. Instead, her mind filled with images of Torie—the long runs she would make down the field at Kezar Stadium, her ready smile, and the dare-me tone in her voice when she lifted her T-shirt, whipped cream running down her breast, and said, "Hey, Noelle, wanna taste it?"

Noelle and the soccer player did not go for hamburgers after they had sex. She asked him to take her home. She wrapped herself up in blankets on her bed and sat by the telephone, wanting to call Torie, but she didn't.

After telling me the two stories, she asked again. Was she straight? I again told her that she was going to have to discover this for herself. It wasn't something I or anyone else could answer. Then I added that knowing the answer to this question seemed to be very important to her.

She nodded and gave me a pained look. "Dr. Ponton, I don't want to be a freak."

"What do you mean?"

"Do you remember that kid that I was talking to, that one time I saw you up in the clinic? He had these pink streaks in his hair? Wearing lots of earrings? He told me that he thought he was really meant to be a girl, and when he got old enough, he might have some kind of operation to actually become a girl. He was a trans-something."

"And you thought he was a freak?"

"God, this whole thing is so embarrassing. He was really nice. He asked me a lot about field hockey 'cause I was wearing my uniform." She turned red and paused before she added, "He started telling me about how he felt trapped in a boy's body. It was so sad. It wasn't like he was a freak when I was talking to him, but I've thought about it a lot. I don't know. What's going on with him?"

"Noelle, a lot of kids strongly feel that they are or ought to be the opposite sex. The body that they are born with doesn't fit their mental image of who they think they are, or should be. Some people live with the body they're born with, but adopt the identity of the opposite sex. They're called 'transgendered.' If they have the surgery, they're 'transsexuals.'"

"God, it's so complicated."

"Noelle, it's hard. There are a lot of kids, a lot of people, who struggle with their sexuality. Only some of that involves struggles with sexual orientation, you know, whether you are attracted to people of the same sex or the opposite sex. But you're right. It's pretty complicated stuff." I paused and then said, "I haven't heard anything about Torie. You and she still friends?"

"Yeah, good friends." She looked at my clock. "Time's up, huh? Gotta go."

"I'll see you next week."

"Yeah."

At our next session, Noelle also didn't bring up Torie right away. She covered almost everything else, though—school, friends, soccer. I waited and then brought it up myself.

"I thought you weren't going to ask."

"You were waiting for me to ask?"

"Yeah."

"Do you know why you waited?"

"The scared part, I guess, that I'm a freak."

"Noelle, struggling with your sexuality doesn't make you a freak."

She looked at me, smiled, and them mimicked me. "In fact, it makes you normal!" We both laughed at her close imitation, my singsong voice and optimistic attitude. Imitating me seemed to relax her, though, and she began her story.

"Okay, so I didn't call her the night after soccer boy, but I, like, think about her a lot, and when we do stuff together, it can be amazing."

"What kind of stuff?"

"Anything. Last Saturday we went to Nordstrom, and Torie wanted to try on swimsuits. 'It'll be so much fun!' *I* think trying on bathing suits is torture. I order my suits through the catalog. And I never go to dressing rooms in department stores—it's like a panic zone for me. Anyway, she's grabbing these suits off the racks and dragging me into the dressing room."

"And it wasn't torture this time?"

"Dr. Ponton, come on. She tries on this great-looking white two-piece, and I'm trying not to stare at her. She still has all that red-brown hair, but she wears it twisted into a bun at the back of her neck. Well, she pulled out her barrette, and it fell down her back. It was still wet from the shower that morning. I swear I had to sit on my hands to keep from touching it. Anyway, she gets me to try on this green two-piece just like her white one. She tells me I look ravishing in it, that it's the exact color of my eyes. What's really weird is that I believe her. I mean, when I'm in that dressing room with Torie, I feel great about my body."

"How do you feel about Torie, Noelle?"

"I don't know. I'm not sure that I love her. I just know that I feel really good about her and about myself when we're together. I'm okay with myself."

"That sounds like a big thing."

"Yeah, it's really something."

My sessions with Noelle left me thinking. From the first, she had been able to ask her questions, even if she, like most teens, wanted the quickest answer. Her persistent curiosity played an important role in the development of her sexuality. She also was willing to try things. She had powerful feelings and allowed herself to experience them and see where they might lead her. She felt uncomfortable with the thought that her strong feelings for Torie indicated that she might be bisexual or a lesbian, but she continued to acknowledge and explore the feelings. With Torie, Noelle felt better than she did with anyone else. Unlike many of her friends, Torie was extremely comfortable with her own body, and Noelle became more comfortable with hers when they were together. Noelle also recognized that with Torie, she felt extremely excited, feelings she had not experienced with either boy.

She and I had several discussions about my work with transgendered youth. We even talked about how sometimes people who thought they might be or want to be transgendered would discover otherwise, and go on to live happily, whether they were gay, straight, or bisexual. Our discussions helped Noelle to recognize that other teens were struggling with their sexuality, and that they were not freaks. Such struggles were normal parts of growing up.

Noelle's efforts to better understand her sexuality had already extended over years. A better definition of her sexual orientation was a vital part of that struggle. Fears that she was a freak or that others would call her a lesbian weighed on her, but she allowed her feelings to guide her. By the time she finally stopped seeing me, it was still unclear whether she was homo-, hetero-, or bisexual, but she was more comfortable with either or all of the possibilities.

Several years later, I received a phone call from Noelle after she had seen an article I had written in a magazine. Then a junior in college, she told me that her sexual relationship with Torie had developed, although they never had sexual intercourse. She told me that she had experienced another sexual relationship and was currently sexually intimate with a woman. At the time of the call, she identified herself as bisexual.

Working with Ian, Noelle, and others has helped me to understand that sexual orientation is not a choice for most teens. During an often drawn-out process they struggle to understand their own complex feelings that have already existed for a long time. In any case, they need help and support because they are not able to give this to themselves. Sexual orientation in adolescence is influenced by many factors. When it changes—in any direction—it is most often not at the hands of a therapist, but as the result of a young person's own growth and development.

8

A Tale of Two Pregnancies

. . . You can believe in something in theory, but then when it happens . . . you need to make the other choice. —Maria

I don't want to have this baby just because of some struggle I have going with my mother. —Naomi

On a foggy Thursday morning in early September, the high school taxi service that I operate several days a week is off and running. First my two daughters and me, then the friends, Bret and Jennifer. Finally, the usual question—should we stop to get hot chocolate for them, coffee for me? On this particular morning I decide that I really need it, so we pull over to Lava Java. Three of them get out and I am left in the car, trying to get the heat to work—it is cold—and discussing the music we will listen to with my older daughter, who has stayed behind. The tape from the musical *Rent* is booming. I have heard it a thousand times. She votes for Madonna ("It Revs Me"), or should it be the Sarah and Vinnie morning show on Radio Alice? I tell her I can handle anything but Alice this morning. We compromise with Elvis Presley's greatest hits. The three runners return with our drinks, and we're off. Preoccupied, I miss my turn and come to a sharp halt.

"Mom, the hot chocolate is spilling over the car! Get a grip," says the younger daughter. She's unable to find napkins, so I pull over, car still running, and hand her the morning newspaper; the spill is mopped up. Then another voice from the backseat: "I wouldn't go there—just look at their faces, full of hate."

"Go where?" I ask. I look up and see what she is talking about—twenty chanting picketers holding signs and marching. They are looking at my car angrily. Why? A car with three teenage girls, a lone boy, and me? The demonstrators start walking over to the car, and I drive on quickly. "What was that?" I ask.

"Mom, you should know. That's the abortion clinic."

Silence in the car. Then Bret speaks up. "A girl I know went there, and they had to sneak her out the back. Her mom thought they were going to kill her."

"If you go at night, it's easier. There's not so many of them."

Another voice says, "It's hard enough. They think kids *want* to do it?"

I drive away, remembering the image of those angry faces—and then it comes to me. The people on the street thought I was delivering a teen to have an abortion. I struggle with what to say to the kids, realizing that this is one of those conversations for which I am painfully unprepared. Finally, I tell them how surprised I was. Just my saying this starts them talking again, and I hear a lot about what they think about teen pregnancy before I drop them off.

Driving back to the university to see my first patient, I can't get those angry faces out of my mind. Thirteen-year-old Maria is sitting on the floor outside my office, an overloaded backpack lying next to her. Three weeks ago Maria came to see me for the first time, struggling with the recent news that she was pregnant. She had an abortion last week. Today she looks relieved when she sees me in the waiting room. She jumps up, pulling her heavy pack off the floor and putting one arm through a strap. I grab the other strap, and together we walk back to my office, awkwardly managing her load together.

"Maria, how did you ever carry this up the hill?"

A crooked smile lights up her slender, slightly wan face. Maria will be getting braces next week. It had been postponed after she discovered she was pregnant. She glances at my now lukewarm latte with more than mild interest, and I ask her if she has had breakfast. She shakes her head, and I offer her a jar of breakfast bars to choose from. She grabs an apricot-nut bar and takes a large bite.

"Oh, I brought you these." She reaches into her backpack and removes a paper bag, then takes out several items wrapped in waxed paper tied with dark string. "*Lumpia*—Filipino egg rolls. My mom made 'em for you." The words are garbled as she munches on the last of the breakfast bar. The room is filled with the sweet scent of the rolls' delicately perfumed vegetables.

"Oh, Maria, thank you. I can't resist—should we try them now?"

"You go ahead, I eat them all the time at home."

"How's home going?"

Her lip trembles. "It's been so hard. I think my mom's trying to make it up to me, even with the *lumpia* for you. She's talking to me now, at least." Tears start running slowly down Maria's face, but there is no sound. "Ever since she found out I was pregnant, she hasn't been able to talk to me. She hugged me today when I left, though."

I think back to the first call about Maria from her pediatrician: "Lynn, it's Anne. Can you see a girl this afternoon? She's just found out she's pregnant, a thirteen-year-old from a large Filipino family. They're all here now in my office, screaming at her. She's sitting on the floor with her hands over her face and won't say anything."

Out of the jumble of voices in the background, I heard a high-pitched woman's voice screaming, "Tell us who did this to you! Tell us!"

I felt like I had to scream to be heard over the noise on the other end of the line. "Are you in the clinic, Anne? I'll come over there."

Twenty minutes later, outside Anne's office door, I still heard the high-pitched voice coming from the other side. I knocked, and Anne, frazzled, opened the door. "You let him touch you! You are a whore!" is the translation, I later learn, for what I then heard in Tagalog. I put my hand on Anne's shoulder and asked her what might work best at this point. I sensed that she would like everyone to be gone from her usually calm office.

"I think you should get her out of here," she said, pointing at the slender child who was shaking on the floor. "I can handle the family."

"Are you sure?"

She flashed me a grin and said, "Why don't you bring her back in a half hour?"

I extended a hand to the quivering Maria, who grabbed on tightly and followed me. In the hallway, I asked, "Do you want to sit outside? There's a small garden near here." She was still holding my hand and indicated yes with a nod. We started to walk, and I asked, "Where do you go to school?"

She named a large academic high school in the city.

"You're young for high school, aren't you? Just thirteen?"

"I skipped a year," she offered.

We arrived at a small Japanese-style garden and sat down on a bench. It was quiet, especially after the din in Anne's office.

"What happened in there, Maria?"

"Did Dr. Joseph tell you?"

"She told me that you were pregnant."

There was a long silence. She covered her face again, but I knew she was watching me through her fingers. The idea was that she could look at me, but I couldn't see her. I waited before asking, "How did it happen?"

"A boy at school, a sophomore. He would help me with my homework. We went to the library together every day after school. My parents were working in their store every day until seven o'clock. They didn't know. They thought I was studying."

"What was he like?"

Her hands dropped from her face, and a pale rose spread across her face. "He talked to me, told me wonderful things about myself. He was the first person who had ever done that. Then it changed a little, he would hold me. I could sit in his lap." At this point she glanced at me, checking, I thought, whether I understood why.

"That felt good?"

"So good. My dad used to hold me on his lap when I was little."

"You wish he still did it?"

"Yeah. He works all the time now since they bought that store. And he's so tired, he falls asleep with his clothes on. I don't think my mom wants him to hold me, either."

"Why?"

"She thinks I'm too big. I am too big."

"You're too big to be held?"

"Yeah. Raffi didn't care, though." She smiled again and wrapped her hands around her knees, rocking herself forward. I didn't acknowledge that she had just told me her boyfriend's name. I could see that she was beginning to feel more comfortable with me, but I remembered her mother's screams.

"Maria, how are you feeling about this news you just heard?"

"Scared. We only had sex once. I'm worried my mom is gonna kill Raffi. He didn't want to. I pushed him into it."

"You forced him?"

"Well, not exactly, but I went with it. I wasn't forced. My mom screams, 'Who did this to you?' She doesn't know."

"You're pretty worried about your parents' reactions to this?"

"My dad, no. My mom—"

"But it's different with your dad?"

"He doesn't like it, but he's not gonna call me a whore."

"Maria, I know you've just found out about this, but have you thought about what you might want to do?"

"I have thought about it, but I don't know. Will you be there with me when I talk with my parents?"

"I will."

"I need to talk with Raffi, too."

"That seems like a good idea. There's a lot to talk about." A breeze passed and she shivered. "Okay, Maria, you ready to go back?"

"Not really, but no one would want to face my mom after this."

Face her mom we did, just a few minutes later. Carol, Maria's mother, said nothing during the entire family meeting. Her eyes were closed and she was holding onto a rosary, praying. Maria's father spoke instead.

"We'll get her help. I'm not happy about this"—he looked his daughter in the eye—"but we love you very much and we know that you need us now." Then to me he said, "Her older sister works at a doctor's office. She will help us."

Grateful, Maria looked up at him and the session ended quietly.

The next weeks were hard work. I saw Maria three times—alone, with Raffi, and with her mother. Fortunately, Maria's older sister, Lianne, was supportive and fairly sophisticated about the choices for a girl in Maria's position. "We'll find her the best people to talk to, Dr. Ponton. I want her to understand the options. I have a close friend who counsels about abortion. Maria can talk to her. I also have worked in an adoption clinic where they do counseling. Do you know any girls who kept their babies?"

"I do. She can visit St. Elizabeth's Home and talk to some girls there. How's it going with your family?"

"Hard. My mom still doesn't accept it. We don't know what she thinks about it. She still isn't saying anything."

"Maria is her baby, Lianne. It seems like this is pretty hard for her."

"She only mentioned sex to me once. 'Don't do anything, ever, until you get married, Lianne.' That's all she said. I was eighteen when she told me that."

"And your sister is a lot younger now than you were then." Remembering the rosary beads, I asked, "Has your mom ever said anything about how she feels about teenage pregnancy?"

"No, I have no idea how she feels about pregnancy, abortion, adoption, teen marriage—she never says anything. It worries me because Maria really needs her support."

"Well," I said, "at least she has you and your dad."

I thought about Lianne's words when I met with Maria and her mother together. It was a very difficult session.

"You let me down, Maria. I never thought this would happen with you."

Carol did not give her opinion about Maria's pregnancy or the options—abortion, adoption, keeping the baby—but she did say, "What matters now is what happens with my daughter." After she said that, I thanked her for coming, and she started to cry.

"I worry that I have been a terrible mother for my daughter. I have not talked with her about sex, and I call her a whore when I find out she is pregnant."

"Carol, blaming yourself or your daughter isn't going to help now. It takes courage to face this, and you and Maria have that." I said it, but I wasn't sure I believed it. At least not about Carol.

The session ended with Maria and Carol hugging, but Carol's anger at herself and her daughter did not disappear. It would diminish, then rise up again, seeming stronger than ever to her daughter. "Maria, how could you do this to me?" And then, "Dr. Ponton, she was named after the virgin. How could she get pregnant?"

I thought of her mother's question three weeks later as Maria and I sat there eating the *lumpia*. Looking back, I could see that Carol's reactions to her daughter's pregnancy had overshadowed her concern about her daughter's feelings. The more we talked, the more I realized that Carol had believed that her children would be protected from things like pregnancy because her faith was so strong. She didn't have to talk to her children about sexual matters, because they were guarded from risk. Maria's pregnancy was a shock to her. Carol's inability to believe that it had actually happened paralyzed her. She could not help her daughter, she was lost in her own struggle. Once her anger at Maria diminished, she was angry with the Virgin for failing in her protection. I suggested that Maria's father contact the parish priest, who met and counseled Carol.

Maria had also been reluctant to discuss her feelings about what had happened to her. She was worried about her parents and did not want to hurt them any more than she felt she already had.

This morning she and I sit and watch the fog roll in over the bridge as we drink our tea and eat her mother's food.

"How are you feeling?"

"It's hard. You know, I was always opposed to abortion. I don't believe in it, but I knew I couldn't be a mother—at least not right now."

"This has been very hard for you."

Slowly she begins to cry, looking away from me so that I can't see her. "It's funny how you can believe in something in theory, but then when it happens in your life, you need to make the other choice."

"What helped you make that choice?" I have been part of this process, and so know at least some of the answer to this already, but I want Maria to be able to think about what she has just been through.

Maria stands and looks out the window at the fog rolling past in waves. "I'm a lot older than I was a month ago, but I watched those girls at St. Elizabeth's with their babies. I couldn't do what they're doing. I thought a lot about adoption, but Lianne thought my mom would make my life hell. Raffi and Dad said they would stand by me no matter what I did. In the end, I made the decision."

"Not easy for you, Maria."

"I feel thirteen going on twenty-three."

Working with girls in situations like Maria's, I struggle to let them make their own choice, making sure that they consider all the possibilities. For many, sadly, this is the first opportunity that they have to participate in a decision-making process about any area of sexuality. In one jump, they're far beyond kissing or condoms.

Most Americans are convinced that teenage pregnancy is "epidemic" in the United States. In truth, two-thirds of unmarried women having babies are older than eighteen, yet it is the teenagers that are stigmatized by it. So why is so much energy and anger directed at this "problem" and the teenagers? Kristen Luker believes that teenage girls are bearing the brunt of anxieties about larger economic and social changes—the rising divorce rate, the growing number of single moms.

Although the problems of teenage pregnancy are more extreme, they are not so different from what happens to all adolescents with their sexuality. Adolescents are scapegoated for being sexual, girls more so than boys. Increasingly, adult women are choosing to become pregnant and raise their children as single parents. This is part of the changing social fabric in the United States, yet it does not receive the widespread negative attention that teens do.

Teenage pregnancy is also not well understood. Not all girls become pregnant for the same reason. There is no one "cause." Usually several different factors are involved for each girl. Maria was lonely. She was attending a difficult high school, and she found comfort in studying with an older boy after school.

Further comfort was found when he held her. Both her parents worked long hours, resulting in their having less time to give attention to Maria. Being held and kissed by her boyfriend reminded Maria of how good it felt when her father had allowed her to sit on his lap. The memory of how good this had felt fueled her desire to have more of the same. Maria also felt sexual desire, awakened by Raffi's touch. She was not a passive partner: "I pushed him . . . I went with it. I wasn't forced." It is a struggle for girls to discover what ignites their passion, so Maria's discovery was a vital one. The anger expressed by her mother after she discovered that her daughter was pregnant aimed and fired at that desire—"You let him touch you! You're a whore!" Fortunately, Maria's father and sister expressed being upset about Maria having unprotected sex at a very young age, but they also told her that they loved her very much. Maria, like most teens, had failed to use condoms the first—and only—time she had sexual intercourse.

Following the news of her pregnancy, Maria went through some very painful growth. She was opposed to abortion, but decided that she was too young to undergo a pregnancy or have a baby. Like Maria, many young girls have strong negative feelings about abortion. In their own minds, they are often struggling with basic questions about the meaning of life. Early adolescence is a period when many girls may be asking these questions for the first time. Little more than children themselves, they are also fearful about any medical procedure, and may connect it with a recent painful operation such as having their tonsils out. In thinking about pregnancy itself, and not the prospect of abortion, Maria listened closely to her pediatrician, who told her that her pelvis was not yet fully developed and explained the possible complications of carrying a baby to term. Maria and I also talked about how she was emotionally not yet ready to parent. She had a rocky relationship with her mother, evident long before she became pregnant, and had many things to work out before she made a choice to be a mother.

At thirteen, wanting to be held more than anything else, she was still very much in need of mothering herself.

Girls who struggle with their mothers are more likely to become pregnant as teens. Her mother was afraid to touch and hold her children, and Maria was searching for the physical comfort that she had recently lost with her father. In her sexual activity with Raffi, she discovered a similar comfort. Many teen girls believe that a baby will also provide that physical comfort—someone to love and hold them. Maria and I did not get to do a lot of work on this issue—her mother was generous with *lumpia,* but reluctant to come with Maria to sessions with me, and Maria was only able to make limited progress with insights related to her mother.

In so many cases, the role of the mother is crucial for adolescents who become pregnant, as the next story continues to show.

Naomi's Journey

Seventeen-year-old Naomi was referred to me by her mother, Cecily, who was a university professor. Her mother had conducted a computerized literature search after Naomi had told her that she was pregnant. Cecily discovered that I had written an article on risk assessment with adolescent girls, and called me, I believe expecting that I would advise her daughter to have an abortion. From the very first, she had her agenda.

"Dr. Ponton, I know that you are very busy, but you must see my daughter this afternoon. She has only a limited amount of time to make this decision."

"What decision is that?"

"Uh, well, she's pregnant. In fact, she's almost four months pregnant. She is saying that she wants this baby. I am hoping that you will convince her to have an . . . open mind."

Did this mother have an open mind? Did she have any idea what she was asking me to do? Or how impossible it was likely to be?

"Is your daughter willing to see me?"

"Yes. That much I did get her to agree to." I had no openings that day. This mother was going to have to tolerate a two-day wait.

I hung up the phone wondering how willing this woman's daughter really was. Not very, was my bet.

Two days later, I met Naomi for the first time. I noticed her sharply defined profile even as I walked into the waiting room. She had a beautiful arch in her nose and skin the color of café au lait. She had earphones on, her legs crossed underneath her, eyes closed. My normally noisy waiting room felt strangely peaceful.

"Naomi?"

No answer. She seemed to be in some sort of trance state. I later found out she was listening to a meditation tape. I repeated her name more loudly. Her eyes opened, and a strong gaze met my own.

"Dr. Ponton, it's a pleasure to meet you. This room has a powerful aura. I forgot where I was. It's very peaceful here."

As Naomi picked up her CD player and entered my office, I could see that she brought some of that peace with her. She sat down in one of my big leather chairs and pulled up her long legs beneath her, again sitting cross-legged. She began talking before I could start. Immediately, I was being interviewed instead of the other way around. "Cecily called you, I know. I don't care what you told her, but I am curious about what she told you."

I answered her straight on. "She told me that you are almost four months pregnant. Why did you come if you don't care what I have to say?"

She paused. "I care, but I have to be very careful this time."

I caught the words "this time," but decided to ask instead, "Why so careful, Naomi?"

"Cecily tries to control me, control everyone in the family. She's been pretty successful up until now." Naomi's jaw tightened, and I began to understand at least part of the need for caution. She was terrified that I, too, was involved as an extended arm of her mother's control. I sensed that battle lines had been drawn.

Control struggles are not unusual between mothers and daughters. They perform an important role in helping daughters to separate and understand who they are apart from their mothers. As one of my patients once succinctly remarked, "I know myself best, Mom, when I'm fighting with you." These struggles are a normal and expected part of growing up. There was one important difference here, however—Naomi was almost four months pregnant. The stakes were high.

"How has your mother been successful at controlling you, Naomi?"

"She's brilliant. She thinks of everything, analyzes it, that is, and then convinces you to do it because, see, you actually want to do it. You see that her way is the best way, that there is no other way. You see, don't you? She fucks with your mind."

Not only did I see, I felt as if I'd gotten a taste of it over the phone. I knew that Naomi suspected she was going to have similar struggles with me.

"So most of the time you end up going along with your mother's decisions, then you end up feeling taken advantage of."

"Yeah, that's part of it. She wants this abortion. She wants to kill this child inside of me."

"How do you feel about this pregnancy?"

She was ready to answer, but then looked at me curiously—I, too, must have an agenda. Slowly, she asked, "Okay, what's your deal? Proabortion like Cecily, or do you work for the Christian Right and want me to give up this baby for adoption—a black baby that will be placed in a horrible foster home? Or just maybe you think I should get married if I'm going to raise this baby." Naomi's last words were a near screech.

"The deal is you—what you want, not what I want," I said quietly. I could easily imagine Cecily and Naomi getting into explosive arguments. Where was the meditative pose I'd found Naomi in just minutes before?

"So you're supposed to help me figure that out?"

"If I can. You have to work with me, though."

"What if I don't know what I want?"

"It would surprise me if you did know. You're in a difficult spot."

"I know that. Have you ever seen the way people look at pregnant girls? Like they're—we're—dirt. Or stupid."

"Who looks at you that way?"

"When I go for my checkups at the university hospital and get off on the obstetrics floor. Everyone looks down at their feet, another 'fallen' teen girl. And it's worse, of course, because I'm black. They write you off completely, then. That's what my mother sees, what she thinks she needs to protect me from. That's why she wants me to get an abortion."

"I don't think your mother wants you to be written off."

"I think she believes it, too, though. She'd never admit it, that's all. But when she starts in on this, I know she's thinking I am in danger of writing myself off if I have this baby. And she's good, too. I even start to believe it myself." She paused. "But not all the time."

I remained silent, sensing Naomi had more to say. She did.

"I wanted to get pregnant. Does that surprise you? I tried to get pregnant for five months."

"Why, Naomi?"

"I want to have a baby. I want to be a mother."

"What do you imagine it will be like?"

"Oh, you know, I'll have the baby in a snuggly. We'll be walking down the street together—we'll always be together—and those people will be looking at us, but I don't care because I have my baby. I'll have something. Do you see that?"

"You don't feel like you have anything now?"

Naomi's elegant jaw started to move ever so slightly, and I thought I saw tears. Instead, she reached into a large black bag and pulled out a book. She handed it to me. It was a volume of poetry.

"Cecily wrote that, you know. She dedicated it to me—'To My Daughter, Naomi.'"

The volume was well-worn, the cover frayed. I wondered if Naomi carried it with her everywhere she went. It seemed like a heavy burden for a girl to carry—a baby, a book—even if loved.

"That book was my mother's passion."

"And this baby is yours?"

"Yes. I was pregnant before, Dr. Ponton."

"Is that what you meant by saying that you have to be 'more careful this time'?"

"Yes. I want this baby."

"Naomi, I believe that. But a few minutes ago you said you didn't know."

Here she narrowed her eyes angrily. "You need to ask that—at least I hope you need to ask that. Because if you don't, it's a harsh question."

"I need to ask, Naomi."

"You see, I'm like my mother, too. I told you I see how they look at me, another pregnant black girl. My mother thinks I don't see that, but she's wrong. I see it all. She says, 'Get your degree, Naomi, then they will treat you well.' After that it will probably be, 'Write a book, Naomi, then they will treat you well. Become a professor, then they will treat you well.'"

"And the baby?"

"Maybe the baby is my way of saying I don't care about all that other stuff, I don't care what people say."

"How did you decide to have an abortion when you were pregnant the first time?"

"I thought like my mother then. I was only fifteen. I'm going to be eighteen next month."

"Who went with you back then?"

"My boyfriend. Same boyfriend I have now. He wanted me to have the abortion then, said we were too young. He'll go along with whatever I decide this time, though."

"Do you want to come back and meet with me and your mother together?"

"No, I don't."

"Would you like me to talk with her?"

"Maybe. You won't change her mind, though. You know that, don't you?"

"I didn't change yours."

"No, you didn't." Naomi's last smile for me showed some triumph and a lot of relief.

Cecily's Hour

Mothers and daughters sometimes know each other too well. As Cecily knew that Naomi wasn't going to change her mind about having an abortion, Naomi understood that her mother wasn't going to change her mind, either, at least not for now.

Cecily, coming straight from teaching a class, was early for our next appointment. In her mid-forties, she sat in my waiting room, her laptop plugged into an available outlet. She looked up when I entered and started firing questions at me before we'd even moved into my office and sat down.

"What choice do I have if she doesn't want this abortion?"

"It's not your choice, Cecily, but there are different ways you can handle it."

"I don't want to 'handle' it. My sister 'handles' it. Two of her daughters are living at her house with their babies. She handles it all right. . . ."

"I didn't mean that you have to take care of this, Cecily. I was talking about handling your feelings about it."

"You mean I don't have to run a maternity home? That's what they expect."

"Who's 'they,' Cecily?"

"I don't know. I don't want this life. I worked too hard for my education, for everything. And I wanted something different for my daughter."

Remembering that her daughter had handed me a book of her mother's poems, I said to Cecily that I thought her daughter's life was already different. More than skeptical, she asked why, if it was so different, did Naomi want this baby so much?

"She told me the baby is her passion."

"Once the baby gets here, she'll change her mind about all that."

"Maybe. I don't think so, though. She's thought a lot about this."

"My nieces' lives are hell, pure hell. They dropped out of school, and they haven't gone back. Their babies are crying constantly."

"Is that the way you see it going with Naomi?"

"No, absolutely not. First, I am not my sister. Naomi will graduate from high school in two months. She's already looked into the day care at the junior college, but, Dr. Ponton, she could have gone to Barnard or Wellesley—with a scholarship! I don't understand why she would give all that up."

"I don't understand it completely, either, Cecily. You and I both waited years to have our children. Your daughter doesn't seem to want to do that."

"I suppose I'll have to help her financially."

"Do you want to do that, Cecily? You have choices here, too."

"Well, I'm not my sister. I'm not going to have a house full of screaming babies. I think she actually likes it that way—my sister, I mean." Cecily smiled. "Maybe Naomi's baby won't scream. She keeps meditating all the time, telling me it will calm the baby."

"Would you want Naomi and her baby to live with you?"

"Would she want to? I guess she might. At first I thought she wanted to live with her boyfriend, but they're on again, off again. I've heard he might accept an athletic scholarship that he's been offered."

"Naomi knows this?"

"She's the one who told me. It just doesn't make any sense to me. But no, I'm not going to kick her out. I can't do that."

Even though Naomi didn't want sessions with her mom, I was sure they would be helpful. Without them, I could imagine Cecily feeling manipulated into her sister's life, or Naomi packing up her baby and their belongings and storming out. I decided to give them some time to work things out, and waited. I didn't have to wait long.

Two weeks later, I received a phone call from Naomi. "Dr. Ponton, do you make house calls?"

"Not usually, Naomi. What's up?"

"Not much, I'm . . . down, lying in bed. The doctors are worried I might lose my baby. I'm on bed rest for four weeks."

"That's a long time. How're you feeling?"

"Not good." There was a long pause when I thought I heard her crying. Then, angrily, "My mother is driving me crazy."

"How?"

"I don't even know. That's what's so crazy. She's being so nice . . . why am I so angry with her being nice? What's wrong with me?"

"Maybe nothing is wrong with you, Naomi. Total bed rest would probably make anyone anxious. You described a happy picture of you taking care of your little baby in a snuggly. You, lying in bed, with your mother taking care of you, turns that picture around."

"You mean I wanted to be the mother, not the one being mothered? Well, I think you're right, but we still need you here."

"I'll think about it, Naomi, but I'm going to need to talk to Cecily about it."

Several days later, I was sitting in Naomi's and Cecily's living room, a meditation tape with sounds from the sea playing softly. Naomi was sitting on a pile of pillows on the couch, looking even younger than her almost eighteen years, and more than a little bit nervous. Cecily, on the other hand, seemed in complete control of the situation. She had brewed a large pot of herbal tea, which she was pouring into mugs, and nodding toward framed photos on the mantel.

"That's Naomi's dad. He teaches economics at State. We've been divorced for years, but he visits a lot more now that he's teaching in the area again. Those on the right are my sister and her girls with their babies—"

"Mom, stop it."

"I'm sorry, Naomi. I just thought it was important for the doctor to see our fam—"

"You're right, but I just can't stand this."

"Can't stand what, Naomi?" I asked.

Naomi looked angry, then sad. "I don't know, it's like she"—she motioned toward Cecily—"always has it all together—her job, her book. Now she's turning into this perfect grandmother. Meanwhile I can't do anything right, even have a baby."

Cecily had stopped pouring tea and was looking at her daughter. "Is that the way you feel?"

"What do you think? What do you think it's like to be your daughter? You're so perfect all the time."

"Perfect—that's the way you see me?"

Naomi was shifting around on the couch with the antsy movements of someone who wanted to stand but had been told to sit still. She finally leaned back, resigned. "No, it's not like that. Well, maybe. You just do everything so well."

"And you feel like you don't?"

"Yes. No. I don't know. God, I felt like I was doing fine with the pregnancy until this happened," she said, thumping the stack of pillows she was resting on.

I asked, "And now you don't feel like you're doing fine?"

"What do you think? Just look at me."

"I am looking at you. You're resting in bed, taking care of yourself and your baby."

"Well, it feels like I screwed up somehow. For a while I felt like I had it together, too. I liked being pregnant until this happened."

"What's changed?" I asked.

"Maybe it's what you said on the phone—I'm lying in bed; she's taking care of me. It isn't what I expected. I feel so stupid talking about this."

"Does it feel like your mom never screws up?" I asked.

This time Naomi looked right at her mother. "Yes. It feels like that most of the time."

"Most of the time, Naomi?" asked Cecily.

Naomi turned to Cecily. "You're a great mom. You're just driving me crazy."

"I make you feel small. That's not so great."

"Mom, it's not all you." I could already see that Naomi was looking at her mother differently. Cecily had acknowledged something. Now Naomi could do the same.

We all continued to talk quietly, and after I finished my tea, Cecily walked me to the door of their apartment and then came outside with me. Her body was so close to mine that I could feel her warmth. She whispered, "Dr. Ponton, if she's having this baby because of stuff she hasn't worked out with me, maybe she shouldn't be having this baby. Should I even talk with her about it?"

"You were doing just fine in there with her, Cecily. She's thinking a lot about everything, I know that. Keep listening. I really don't know what else to say."

It was nearly eight o'clock. I was exhausted, and sat for several minutes after I got into my car. I hadn't made a house call in years. It was hard work, and at the end, I hadn't really known the answer to Cecily's question.

What should parents say to teenage girls who are pregnant? And when? Cecily was struggling, wanting to tell her daughter, "Don't have this baby, especially don't have this baby if it's mainly about working stuff out with me. There are better ways to do it." She wanted to make her daughter's life better than hers had been. If Cecily interfered now, would she cause even more problems in their relationship? She had just heard Naomi say that it always felt as if her mother had all the answers, that she was perfect. Could Cecily really recognize that Naomi was struggling to find her own answers, and that in doing this, she might make some mistakes?

When I finally drove away from Cecily's and Naomi's apartment, I recognized that there was no single, definitive answer to Cecily's question. There is no one thing that you can say to pregnant teenagers, but as in other circumstances, parents and other adults still have to be there, and be open enough to listen to the teens talk about their choices—some of which we think might ruin their lives.

Two weeks later, I was back in Cecily's and Naomi's living room, sitting next to Naomi, who was still on bed rest, leaning back on a huge mound of pillows. She had telephoned, asking for a solo session. "I have things that I need to figure out. Cecily's still driving me crazy, but she's okay, really, it's me."

It takes a lot for anyone to recognize that it is her, her struggle. Even most adults don't, but then again, Naomi was different. She was strong. Once I was there, she did not waste time.

"Dr. Ponton, I don't want to have this baby just because of some struggle I have going with my mother."

"Is that what you believe I think is happening, Naomi?"

"Maybe in the beginning it was like that. I wanted to show her"—she laughed—"maybe show everyone that I, too, could do something well, make something good. But now I feel different. Cecily really is a great mother. She's given me a lot, even if she is too perfect. She's loved me a lot, and she's always made sure I knew that. I feel like I can be an okay mother, too." Here she paused and corrected herself. "No. A great mother. I won't be exactly like her, but I will be great, too."

"You've done a lot of thinking."

"Haven't had much choice, stuck here."

"You did have a choice, Naomi."

"Yeah, but I didn't see it that way."

"Have you and your mom talked?" I had already guessed the answer.

"All the time. . . . She's told me a lot of stories. Turns out when she was my age, she wasn't so perfect, either."

Delivery and Beyond

Cecily called me the night of that session with Naomi and let me know that she, too, was coming to terms with her daughter's decision. It wouldn't have been hers, but she could live with it and, more important, support her daughter with it. Cecily's support was vital. Less than two months later, Naomi delivered a three-pound baby boy, Toby, prematurely. Toby spent weeks in the intensive care nursery, struggling to stay alive. Either Naomi or Cecily stayed with Toby all the time, and finally he went home to their apartment.

Naomi did not go to college that year, or the one after. She worked part-time in a nursery for high-risk infants, the same nursery where Toby had stayed. She began college two years later, when Toby was transferred to a "normal preschool," his medical problems mostly resolved.

Cecily and Naomi continued seeing me during this period, coming once or twice a month. The toughest time occurred just after Toby's birth, when they were told by his pediatrician that there was a better than 50 percent chance that he could die. I visited mother and daughter sitting at his bedside.

At first, I tried to reassure them, pulling out knowledge long forgotten from my own days as a pediatric resident—"if the oxygen was adjusted . . ."—then I realized that I, too, was trying to be too perfect, and save a situation that was on its own course.

That evening, Naomi was berating herself as she pored over a large pediatric volume that she had pulled from the library shelves in the unit. "I caused this, Dr. Ponton. Teen girls have more preemies, with all kinds of problems."

She looked over at her tiny son, who was engaged in a heroic struggle to keep breathing. She also looked at Cecily, who was fast asleep in a rocking chair that was still moving. Naomi's appreciative glance at her dozing mother told me more than anything she could have said about their relationship. Naomi had matured during this pregnancy, but equally important, her relationship with her mother had changed. They were a team, a formidable one.

Demystifying the Decisions

Although many outspoken policy makers in Washington, D.C., suggest that teenage girls have babies because they can qualify for welfare checks and live independently, or because they don't know any better, the common reasons for adolescent pregnancy are far removed from those. The pregnancy seldom "just happens." Even though it doesn't always appear to be the wisest choice, usually it comes out of a complex process of decision-making.

One of the most recent and comprehensive studies of teenage pregnancy was conducted by Anne Dean, professor emeritus of developmental psychology at the University of New Orleans, in the river parishes north of the city. She studied teenage girls and their mothers, and found that girls who had not been able to negotiate a successful separation from their mothers were ninety times more likely to become pregnant as teens. Many of the girls in Dr. Dean's study were poor, most African-American. For many of these girls, having a baby ensured a continuing tie to an important kinship network in which their mother was a vital part. For many girls all over the United States who make a conscious choice to become pregnant, it may be their best opportunity in a world that offers them only poverty and limited—to say the least—career choices.

In contrast to the popular myth that most teen sexual activity happens impulsively, owing to out-of-control hormones, much of such activity is a largely conscious decision, thought about rationally. The choices made following a pregnancy are no less complex, and many factors play a role; often significant are the social expectations in the girl's environment. How a teen perceives the wishes of parents, sexual partners, and physicians is key, as Maria's and Naomi's stories reveal.

Like a growing number of young women, Naomi made a choice to remain unmarried and raise her child alone, albeit in her case with the assistance of her mother. Again, this was not an impulsive choice. Although Toby's father took the athletic scholarship that he had been offered and left for college, two years later he returned in order to attend a college nearby, and he and Naomi shared the care for Toby while Naomi started college. And though Naomi struggled, she did not apply for welfare; and she chose not to marry Toby's father.

Naomi represents a growing number of women—young and old—who are making a choice not to marry. In 1991, almost 30 percent of births were to unmarried women; by 2004, it is predicted this figure will be close to half. There are complex reasons for this trend. In Naomi's case, when I asked her whether she had considered marrying Toby's father, she said that she had thought a lot about it. One reason to marry lay in her hopes that it would end the painful comments she frequently heard aimed at herself and Toby, and protect him from any stigma he might encounter as he grew up as the child of an unwed mother. However, a big reason not to marry was that she didn't feel very committed to his father. She also said, "I've got to admit something else—I like being in charge." (This changed when Toby's father was able to return to the Bay Area and start to participate in Toby's care. He developed a close relationship with his son, and Naomi had to learn to share both the responsibilities and the authority in her son's life.)

In this chapter I have focused on two stories of adolescent girls who became pregnant. In some ways, Maria's and Naomi's stories are very different: one thirteen, the other eighteen; one Filipino, the other African-American; one who finds herself pregnant after her first experience with sexual intercourse, the other trying for five months to become pregnant; one who did not want to have an abortion but knew she could not raise a baby or go through a pregnancy to give the baby up for adoption, the other determined to have a child in the face of her mother's protests.

Yet Maria's and Naomi's stories have several things in common. Neither girl made her choices lightly or impulsively. They both struggled through difficult decision-making processes. During this intense effort they both learned about their bodies—Maria listening to her pediatrician, Naomi reading books. They also each experienced some aspect of the strong punishment that our society metes out to teenage girls who are sexual. Maria was called a whore by her mother, and Naomi was made painfully aware of the judgments she received as a pregnant black teenager. And both of them had the support of at least one significant adult in their lives.

Nearly four in ten teen pregnancies end in abortion. Since 1980, abortion rates among teens have declined steadily because—despite media hype to the contrary—*fewer teens are becoming pregnant, and even fewer still decide to have abortions.* When they do, one of the major reasons is that they don't believe they are physically or emotionally mature enough to be a parent. It is noteworthy that more than 60 percent of teens who do have an abortion do so with the consent of at least one parent.

I drove by the abortion clinic again one morning recently. The angry faces were there again, though I couldn't be sure if they were the same ones. Although I remember the statistics when I look at the angry faces, it is the stories of girls I have worked with—stories that explain how and why teenage pregnancies really happen—that help me understand the multiple sides of this painful issue. I picture Maria, at thirteen, being driven to this clinic, or one like it, with her mother in the car, fueled by the anger on the faces of those outside the car, feeling ever freer, or more compelled, to fling more names at her daughter. I picture Naomi, walking the halls of the obstetrics clinic alone, facing down the insulting stares she receives. Two pregnant adolescents, two different choices, both punished. Adults in our country back away from these girls at a time when they most need our support. This needs to change. Socially, we could, for example, develop comprehensive decision-making programs— in or out of school—that help train young minds to assess risk and consequence, and recognize key points during the course of any decision, including the one to become pregnant. If an adolescent becomes pregnant, she would have those skills in place to help guide her in the subsequent choices she must make. In the end, though, nothing can replace a supportive adult in an adolescent's life. And nothing should. So individually, we can, and ought to, step up and meet the challenge when young people need us.

9

Lara's Theme
Sex, Stigma, and STDs

*I already felt like I was damned . . . for even
thinking about sex, which I did all the time.*
                                    —Lara

Lara, a soft-spoken teenager born and raised in Baton Rouge, Louisiana, came to see me six months after she discovered that she was infected with HIV. She was not the first young person to come to my office facing this problem. Over the past fifteen years, I have worked with more than one hundred and fifty adolescents living and dying with HIV. But Lara was different. From the beginning, I felt an especially strong connection to her. The first time we met was one of the rare hot days that sometimes occur in a San Francisco spring. I had opened the windows, and I was looking out when I saw her walk down the path, carrying a handful of blue and white flowers. She handed them to me, explaining that she had picked them while climbing along the steep hill leading to my office. She immediately said she was grateful that I had agreed to see her, that it wasn't easy to find a therapist even in San Francisco. I know most women therapists who work with teenagers in San Francisco are usually closed to new patients. My practice, too, was overly full, but I try to find room for adolescents who are struggling with HIV. Lara quickly sat down, squeezing herself into one of the tight corners in my Victorian office. I got the feeling that she didn't want to take up too much space.

As she reached down to pick up a flower that had dropped on the carpet, I could smell her perfume, a faint odor of violets. Most often I am overwhelmed by the colognes that teens, both boys and girls, wear in to my office, a blast of synthetic scent—Tommy Girl, Calvin Klein. But Lara's was different, quietly sensual. From the beginning she and I worked well together. We found a paper cup to hold the wildflowers, and set them on a small table between us. Lara didn't speak for several minutes. I sat with her quietly, waiting. The sunlight pouring into the room reflected off Lara's hair, highlighting golden streaks shot through a darker ash-blond.

She was wearing a pale yellow halter dress, which she self-consciously smoothed as she struggled to find words to start. I didn't want to make her uncomfortable by staring, so I looked out the window until she finally spoke. "I got your name several months ago—when I found out." Her eyes clouded over, and again several moments went by as she fumbled in her purse for a white linen handkerchief. After years of watching teenage girls rifle through patched backpacks for crumpled Kleenex, I was surprised to see this, and reminded of my own background—old-style French aunts with lace handkerchiefs stuffed in their bosom. Finally, Lara's silent crying stopped—polite behavior before me, a stranger. She filled her handkerchief and reached for my Kleenex box.

"I didn't call sooner because I knew what you would say."

"You knew?"

"Yes . . . I knew you would think I was a . . ." And here her voice shook with judgment, self-judgment. She struggled to find the words. "A wh—a terrible person."

"Why would I think that about you?"

"You do know, don't you?" She looked at me like I lived on an alien planet.

"Lara, I don't know. I do know that there are many reasons that make it hard to see or talk to a psychiatrist. I know it took courage to come see me."

She turned her face away, starting to cry again. I could see it in the slight movements of her shoulders. Again, a long pause where I sat and waited, and then some carefully chosen words.

"Ponton. You are Cajun, too?"

"French Canadian," I said.

"Like my mother. You look like my mother." Lara wasn't the first adolescent to tell me that I looked like her, or his, mother. She'd already asked if I was Cajun, like her family, and I had already thought of my aunt with the delicate handkerchief, and myself with the wildflowers. We would have to see how all these connections each of us was feeling would develop. I wondered if she, too, was feeling this connection, so early in our work together.

Taking a deep breath, I asked, "Would your mother think you were a terrible person?"

"If she heard what I'm going to tell you, she would. Then again, you will, too. I know you will!" She bent over, her shoulders visible in the backless dress, now heaving.

I wanted to shout back, *No, I won't, and your mother won't either,* but I didn't. Instead, I waited patiently for Lara to stop crying and made her a cup of tea—ginger peach. When I handed it to her, she smiled, although she was still crying. "Even your teacups are like my mother's."

Watching Lara drink the tea, I thought, Still the focus on her mother, but I could now see that she was starting to tease herself and me about it. A little too much mother. I decided to go with it.

"I suppose she serves you peach tea, too."

With an even bigger smile, she joked, "Yes, but it's iced, Dr. Ponton. It's the South."

"No ice here, Lara. Sorry."

"It's okay, really."

That "okay" signaled that I had passed a test, and she was ready to begin talking. And talk she did. An hour later, when I ended our session, she was still talking. Her story had spilled out, at times overwhelming her and me.

Lara grew up as the youngest of five children in a Catholic family in Baton Rouge. She attended the same series of Catholic schools as her brother and sisters. She described herself as an early developer in terms of her interest in sex. By this she was not referring to her physical development but to what she believed was a preoccupation with sexual ideas. She told me that she had begun masturbating when she was seven or eight years old. Lara believed that her "heightened" interest in sexual matters was fueled in part by the Catholic educational approach at her elementary school, which repeatedly reminded her of how important it was to avoid not only premarital sexual intercourse but the entire range of sexual thoughts and activities. Yet even as these strictures piqued her interest in sexuality, they slowly worked to convince her that she was a bad person, a whore, for being interested at all. Indeed, her masturbation made her already damned, at least by the nuns in her school.

By the time Lara entered her Catholic high school, birth control was reluctantly taught, presented as something that might be needed in the far-off future, when she was in a proper, i.e., married, relationship. There was minimal HIV education, since students who waited until after they were married had only a small risk of contracting HIV. Condoms were mentioned but never shown, and certainly not provided. Lara tuned this program out, believing that it wasn't relevant to her, a girl who was already sexually active at this time. She told me that the nuns didn't understand her sexuality. How could they? she asked.

At the age of sixteen, Lara had begun to experiment sexually with boys, eventually having intercourse at seventeen. She did not use condoms or any other type of birth control. She already regarded herself as damned for being sexually active in the first place, so why should she bother with protection? This attitude about herself was also shown in her choice of sexual partners—in her words, "bad guys"—with, she could see now, looking back, profiles of significant risk behavior.

For all individuals, but especially youth, it is important to make general education about HIV and AIDS broad-based: that is, tolerant of different perspectives, but also personally relevant. A sex education program that excludes a comprehensive discussion of realistic situations in which real teens might find themselves, and appropriate options for those situations, can be harmful. In high school, Lara did not receive HIV education that directly related to her life. In fact, the school's program made her feel even more isolated about her sexuality, reinforcing her view that she was already damned for having sexual thoughts and behaviors in the first place.

Lara's life turned upside down on the day when one sexual partner, a young man in his early twenties, asked her why she was not protecting herself. He recommended that she go to a local birth control clinic, and offered to accompany her. He also told her that he had not used condoms during his adolescence, and that he now believed that he had been testing himself and his fate, drawn into taking a risk each time he had sex and then proving himself invulnerable after he survived without contracting HIV. Only gradually had he come to recognize what he was doing and begun to see how unhealthy it was for him. With his support, she agreed to an HIV test. She received the positive result two weeks later, the day after she turned nineteen.

Lara very quickly became aware of the stigma attached to being HIV-positive. This "boyfriend," whose own test had come back negative, disappeared rapidly, apologetic but very fearful. She told me how much that hurt. Although she understood why he no longer wanted to have sex with her, she had been relying on his support.

For several months, Lara reacted by hiding away. She holed up in her apartment, sleeping, often not answering the door or the telephone. She saw her HIV status as punishment, a validation of the fact that she was a bad person *because* of her sexuality. Friends, fearful that she might kill herself, finally brought her to the clinic that referred her to me.

Lara came back willingly after our first session together. She was an engaging storyteller and entertained me with stories of her Southern family—brothers, sisters, uncles, and even the family dog, Southern characters that she brought to life. I loved listening to her, and looked forward to our hours. I like my work and enjoy many of the hours with my patients, but I had to admit I was somewhat puzzled by my reaction to her. Just what was it about the sessions with Lara that made her so appealing to me? Finally I realized that Lara reminded me of my grandmother—beautiful Angeline, a classic storyteller with a French accent and a show-stopping laugh, the laugh I now heard in my office several times each week. With Lara, I again had someone with whom to enjoy that special laughter.

For her part, Lara told me I reminded her of her older sister, Claire. Like her, my eyes crinkled at the corners when I laughed, and I had a way of mixing French verbs and English nouns that was also like Claire. Lara and I talk about her sister a lot. We did not talk about her mother, although I felt her presence grow in the room with us. Lara still had not told her mother, Claire, or anyone else in her family about her HIV status, although she was slowly sharing that information with her friends. She was trying to decide whether to tell Claire, a first step that she and I were working toward one afternoon as we drank a strong tea, Lapsong Souchong, appropriate to the serious subject matter that we were working on in this session.

"Okay, pretend I'm Claire. Lay it on me, Lara."

"That's so right. She would say, 'Lay it on me' just like that. You and she are both so old." She started giggling.

I could see she was anxious, afraid to begin. "Ancient, Lara, but try it out."

"Here goes. 'Oye, Claire, remember the nuns at Sainte Jeanne d'Arc's? How could you forget them? They were so strict. Did you know that when they started telling us about sex, they terrified me? I actually felt like I was going to become like them, turn into them, that they could turn me into them, that I would dry up if I listened to what they had to say. So, well, I didn't listen. In fact, I did the exact opposite. I had sex with guys and did not protect myself. You see, when they started talking, I already felt like I was damned, damned for even thinking about sex, which I did all the time. Well, I don't know if I'm damned, but I do have HIV." She cut to the last line, and the words spilled out so quickly I barely heard it. The room became strangely quiet, and our role-play seemed real, very real.

I struggled for words, trying to think what Lara's sister Claire might say, but I was also at this moment acutely aware of what Lara was feeling here with me. I could see that she was terrified by what she had just said.

"Lara, thank you for telling me." Then I reached out my hand to her. When our hands touched, Lara linked her fingers with mine and locked them tightly.

We stayed that way while tears streamed down her face for several minutes. She was shaking, as was I, but our locked hands held.

That night, Lara told Claire over the telephone. They talked for hours, and Lara was comforted by her sister's warmth and kind words. "You are brave, Lara. I am proud of you." Claire encouraged Lara to tell their mother. She even volunteered to be there with Lara when she did it. Buoyed by her sister's support, Lara returned to Baton Rouge.

I was worried. I have worked with other teens who have told their parents that they are HIV positive. Sometimes the parents are supportive, and find the right words to say. But sometimes they are not. In their shock, anger, and fear, they cut off communication, sometimes irreparably harming the relationship. I did not want this to happen to Lara, but I wasn't in a position to control it, either.

When she traveled to Baton Rouge, I both worried and wondered about my own thoughts and feelings about Lara. Admittedly, she hadn't talked much about her mother with me, but Lara knew her mother, and even more important, she was learning to know herself. She believed she was ready to tell. I had to support her. So why was I so worried about her? Yes, there was HIV, but I knew better than many that kids were living, not dying, with HIV, at least here in the United States, where we have medicine, nutrition, and knowledge. Still, although I recognized that HIV was part of my worry, I knew that it had to be more than that. I was still wondering about it when Lara returned.

She was wearing an oversize gray sweatshirt and baggy jeans on the first day she came to see me after her trip home. She began coughing as soon as she started to talk and could not stop. I got up to get her water, and sat, quietly worried, while she worked to stop coughing. Years before, when the medicines had not existed, I had sat with other kids who could not stop coughing and then later died of AIDS. I could not forget the slow, hacking coughs of those kids while I was listening to Lara. I struggled to put them out of my mind.

"Lara, what happened?"

"I don't know if I can talk about it, Dr. Ponton."

It was the first time that she had called me Dr. Ponton. It reminded me that she needed me to be her doctor at this moment. I needed to pay closer attention to the bonds we had already forged.

Strong identifications with patients can be important clues for anyone practicing psychotherapy. They often help me to understand a patient's reactions, for example, or allow me to feel a patient's pain more easily. These ties can also be problematic. With Lara, I was worried that all these connections I had been enjoying so much might prevent me from helping her. Was I worrying that she was going to die, like Greg or Brendon, kids I have worked with who did die? Were our Catholic educations too alike? Was I missing what she was saying, blinded by my own thoughts and feelings? I certainly hoped not. Almost lost in these thoughts, I was pulled back to the moment by Lara, who tugged at my sweater.

"I'm going to throw up!"

I grabbed her hand and guided her into the bathroom. We sat on the white-tiled floor of my bathroom for several minutes. Lara did not throw up, but continued to cough quietly, sweat pouring down her face. I got a blanket for her, and we moved to the carpeted floor of my office, in front of the heater. She slowly started looking better; her face was now a grayish white, and she stopped sweating.

"It was a hard visit?" I asked.

"You can say that again. It was impossible. She started screaming as soon as we told her." I didn't have to ask who the "she" was. "She wouldn't talk to me for two days. . . . I felt like killing myself. Then she agreed to see me right before I came home. She was so controlled, Dr. Ponton. She said, 'Lara, I am sorry that this happened. Your family will try to help you.' Not her, my 'family.' Then she didn't want to talk about it, never again, no more." Lara had stopped coughing but had pulled the blanket around herself tightly, and I could see that she was still shivering. "Dr. Ponton, I should have let it go then, oh, I should have let it go, but I didn't. I started begging her to talk to me, 'Mama, please!' All she said was, 'God will take care of you. I am not going to talk about it.' I screamed at her, 'God never talks to me. I need you, please, Mama.' She just looked away and started praying in Latin. I felt like I was going crazy. Claire took me to her apartment. I stayed there until I flew back. Claire was wonderful."

Slowly I asked, "And your mother?"

"I felt like I did when I shut myself in my room after I found out, all locked up, planning to kill myself. This time I kept telling Claire I was going to kill myself. She was great. 'Not here, Lara, you know how I feel about the sight of blood.' It sounds so stupid, but we both started giggling. We couldn't stop holding onto each other and laughing. I love her so much." Then, reminded of my question she added, "My mother sent me a get-well card. Can you believe it? I get back here, and this card is

waiting. I'm not sick!" Then she looked down at the blanket wrapped
around her. "Well, okay, maybe I have a flu or something now."

"You looked pretty sick a few minutes ago, but you seem better. How
are you feeling?"

"Better. How could she send a get-well card?"

"Lara, I don't know. I know that some parents know very little about
HIV. From what you said, it sounds like she was in a state of shock."

"Claire said that too, but, Dr. Ponton, that is the way she always was.
If I ever told her anything, she'd pull back. The Virgin Mary—smiling,
but frozen, a statue. When she doesn't talk, I feel so bad. I already feel
terrible. I gave myself HIV."

"Well, you got HIV, Lara, you didn't give it to yourself."

"But I was so careless. No condoms. You have signs in your waiting
room—'Use Condoms'! I know you think I was stupid."

So this was another part of my connection with her mother. I, too,
would blame her.

I knew that I had to choose my words carefully here, but I also knew
that I had to be honest with her. "Lara, you had sex without protecting
yourself. Condoms would have made it safer. There would still have been
risks, however, physical and psychological. Sex is risky. You weren't stupid, but you did use poor judgment. I know it doesn't take the HIV away,
but you also are not the first person to have made this mistake. You are
very hard on yourself."

"I really screwed up. My mother's right."

"I'm not sure we really know how your mother feels, but we do know
that you are blaming yourself."

"Well, who do I blame?" She had thrown off the blanket and was
shaking again, this time with anger. It was filling my office. I did not answer her because I did not have a good answer to her question. There
were people to blame—the boy who gave her the virus, her mother who
would not talk about it, the boyfriend who dumped her when he found
out, the nuns who added to her feeling that her sexuality was bad, and
yes, even her own refusal to protect herself. Would it help her now?

I knew that Lara had to experience her anger about having HIV. Many
teens I have worked with feel sad, but many are also infuriated for

months after they are told the news. I knew that at this point I could not stop her from blaming herself, not yet. Her feelings were overwhelming to her, and at least blaming herself gave her a place to put them. I could also see that she was deeply wounded by her mother's reaction. Lara already believed that her sexual feelings were bad and the HIV status was her punishment. She saw her mother's reactions to the news—first the screaming, then the icy, polite withdrawal—as further punishment. I had no idea what her mother really felt, but I could see that Lara was filled with pain. I suggested that she wait in my waiting room until she felt well enough to drive home. Then I promised to telephone her and check in later that evening.

Several hours after that, I was sitting in my office, trying to do paperwork but feeling unusually exhausted, spending most of my time staring at the electric fire in my heater, when the phone rang.

"Dr. Ponton? Dr. Lynn Ponton?"

"Yes, it is."

There was a long silence interrupted by rapid breathing.

"This is Anne Beaucoeur, Lara's mother. Claire told me that you probably can't talk to me, but I am so worried about Lara. When she told me that she had HIV, I was truly terrified. I did not know what to tell her. I am so sorry—sorry about the HIV, sorry about the way I acted, too. Did she tell you what happened? What should I do?"

"Your other daughter was right, Anne. I cannot talk with you without Lara's permission." Once again in my work with Lara, I felt a struggle. I wanted to say to Anne, "Tell Lara yourself. Call her and share this." What if that made things even worse? I did not know this mother at all. Still, it had taken courage to call me. I told her this and hung up the phone wondering whether or not I had done the right thing. Usually, I think there is a whole range of possible ways I could act. With Lara, I could see that I was hesitant. I worried about making a mistake. The phrase "fatal error" stuck in my mind. I knew that I didn't blame Lara, but I also knew she had made an error, maybe a fatal error.

As I sat there looking at my fire, it hit me. I was scared—scared for Lara and even a little scared for myself. I had been trying so hard to be brave, too, to help her find her courage, that I had failed to see that I was afraid—for her. What I hadn't realized until this moment was that I was also afraid for myself.

I had begun seeing Lara at the time when HIV cocktails were experimental. None of the teenagers that I had worked with had yet tried them. Two years later, that would change. Even so, most of the HIV-positive teens that I worked with had been healthy—most of them. Sitting there alone in my office that late at night, I realized how afraid I had been working with many of them, not just Lara.

Shortly after, the phone rang again. This time I figured it would be Lara, and wondered if her mother had called her—maybe Anne had sensed my unspoken message—*share this with your daughter.* It was Lara, and she was crying. But Anne hadn't called her.

"I'm frightened, Dr. Ponton."

"What do you think is going on?"

"I feel really bad."

"So bad that you might feel like hurting yourself?" I asked, although I really didn't want to. No matter how I ask that question, it always seems clumsy to me.

Sarcastically she answered, "Good one. You're doing your job, Dr. Ponton, but I'm not going to commit suicide tonight, if that's what you need to know."

"It is my job to ask that, Lara, but I'm very sorry if my question upset you. I'm glad that you seem a little more energetic, even if it's anger at me. What's happening?"

"I'm afraid to go to sleep."

"Any ideas?"

"I'm worried I'm gonna die. . . ." Here her voice trailed off.

"You're worried that the virus will kill you."

"I guess. It's a stupid idea."

"No, it's not, Lara."

"Some nights I drink—a lot—to make myself fall asleep, I guess."

"Does it help?"

"With sleeping, yes, maybe, but I am getting more depressed. Dr. Ponton, why did this happen to me?"

"Lara, I don't know. There are many things we don't know answers to."

She seemed somewhat comforted by that, and a teasing edge slipped back into her voice. "At least you didn't say that stuff about condoms."

"Lara, you know that stuff."

"Yeah. I called that group."

"What group?"

"The one listed on the sign in your office—for HIV-positive teens. You told me about it."

"I'm glad you did."

"Thanks for letting me talk to you tonight. I feel better."

When she said that, I remembered my other phone call that I had received this evening. I needed to let Lara know about Anne's call.

"Lara, your mother called here tonight."

"She did?"

"Yes. I can't talk with her without your permission, but I want you to know she called me."

She was silent.

"Are you okay with that?"

"I don't know. Why's she calling you?"

"I'm not sure why she's calling, Lara. What she said was that she is worried about you, and she is sorry about the way she acted when you told her about being HIV-positive. She said she acted that way because she was terrified."

There was a long silence, then Lara said, "God, I'm glad she's terrified—that makes two of us, then."

I didn't add "three of us," but I thought it long after I hung up the phone.

Wherefore Art Thou, Romeo?

Weeks went by, and Lara and I continued to meet. Things got better. She talked with her mother on the telephone for hours and told her how sad and scared she had been when her mother shut her out after hearing about her HIV. Her mother apologized, listened, cried, and apologized again. Anne was able to tell Lara that she had been overwhelmed with fear when Lara told her, and yes, she had blamed Lara, but she had also blamed herself. They promised to support each other, and talked about what Lara's HIV status might mean for the future. They did not talk about how Lara got the virus. She also did not talk about this with me.

"I want to tell her, Dr. Ponton, but I can hardly talk about it here."

"Why do you think that is, Lara?"

On this particular afternoon, fog was rolling in in waves outside my window. The sun that had shone during our early sessions had disappeared months ago. Lara looked out the window. I asked if she wanted me to turn on the heater.

"You think that's going to make it better, Dr. Ponton? Nothing can make this better."

"Nothing that I know of can make you HIV-negative, Lara, but there are things that you can and are doing. You are taking care of your health. You've got your roommates eating all that organic food." I paused. "Sometimes it also helps to talk about it. You don't say very much about how you think you got it. Any ideas?"

"I like talking with you—it's not that. Most of the time I come here and I think, 'I'm gonna tell her that I was a sex nympho, that I was so stupid, that now I'm screwed up, celibate for life . . .'" Here Lara stopped abruptly. Once she had started, she had surprised herself.

"Keep going."

"I can't. Something stops me. I feel so awful."

"Are you worried about what I might think?"

She gave me a bitter smile. "It's not only you, Dr. Ponton. I can't even hear my own story. It would kill me to listen . . ." She was suddenly gasping for air again, reminiscent of the time she almost threw up in my office. She slid off her chair onto the floor and sat there for several minutes, taking slow, deep breaths. This was anxiety, not the flu. She pulled herself back into the chair. I could see that she was getting ready, preparing to tell me.

"Dr. Ponton, I damned myself. It wasn't the nuns, or even God. I knew about the condoms, but I didn't use them."

"Why, Lara?"

"I felt so bad about having sex, even though I was so angry with the nuns for telling me not to do it. I felt like I deserved the HIV. I was already damned for being sexual. So I deserved to be punished." Then she stopped and looked at me. "This is it, the punishment."

"HIV is a hard thing, Lara. It must feel like a punishment to you."

"It is. For one thing, I can't have sex."

"People with HIV have sex, responsibly."

"Realistically, Dr. Ponton, who would want to have sex with me?"

"Lara, there aren't any guarantees about this, but I work with a lot of people with HIV and they find some wonderful partners."

"You make it sound so easy." A sarcastic edge had entered her voice.

"Then, I'm sorry, Lara—it is not easy. But you are very hard on yourself."

"You mean, I wouldn't have sex with anyone with HIV, so why do I think someone would have sex with me?"

"Do you feel that way?"

"Some of the time. That's what I thought my boyfriend felt."

I took a deep breath. This was the first time she had mentioned her boyfriend after that first day with the wildflowers. "What was it like when you split up?"

"Bad. I felt like he felt sorry for me. He was trying to be so nice about it—'Lara, I love you.' If he had just said, 'Lara, I need to dump you because you have HIV and . . .'" Lara couldn't finish her sentence.

"Try to finish it, Lara."

"And I'm so afraid that I can't stick with you." She bit her lip.

"That's what he didn't say, and what you didn't let yourself think."

"How could I? He was so nice, Dr. Ponton; but he was a coward. And me thinking that is not very nice. Truthful, though. When he dumped me, I panicked. Maybe that's why I couldn't see that he was just scared, too. I just felt like I was the one who had the reason to be afraid, not him."

"It is scary, Lara."

Looking relieved that we had even begun to talk about her boyfriend, she continued to open up. "It changed how I felt about myself—the sexual me. The sex had been great with him, not like it was with the other guys. I would do all kinds of things, and he liked it. I liked it. More than liked it. He wanted to know all about my past. I would tell him, and he liked me anyway. He even got off on it. Dr. Ponton, it was fantastic. I had started to feel so different, like it was okay to be that sexual, like I wasn't some kind of weirdo; in fact, I thought it might be kinda great. Then, when he dumped me, it was like he was telling me that what we had done wasn't okay, like I was a whore after all."

"All the old feelings came back."

"Worse than ever. I felt like what happened with him, the feeling good part, was also wrong."

"Do you still feel that way?"

"Kinda, but it's changing." Here she smiled as if she was going to let me in on a secret she had been keeping from me.

"Well, I went to that group. The one that you kept telling me about."

"What was it like?"

"Okay. They had us do a play, an updated version of Shakespeare, only one thing's different—everybody's got HIV."

"How was it?"

"I was Juliet."

"As in *Romeo and Juliet?*"

"The same. *'Romeo, Romeo, I've got HIV.'* What do you think?"

"What did *you* think?"

"It went okay for the practice. We might do improv and take it to the streets, high schools, you know."

The image of Lara portraying an HIV-positive Juliet stayed with me. I knew that taking the role of a self-identifying Juliet had required, and would continue to require, tremendous courage on her part. Even though she wasn't talking with me about how exactly she had contracted the virus, she was at least telling people that she had it. I could see that she was making progress.

"What will Juliet tell the high school girls?"

"Besides the usual stuff, that Romeo has claimed my heart—*Ah, Romeo*—" Lara's sense of humor ran right beneath the surface. "I'll tell them that it is okay to have sex or not have it. They choose. And that if they do it, they are not bad. But they need to be doing it for themselves. And they need to be safe."

"Were you doing it for yourself?"

"I don't think so. I don't think I even knew who I was, Dr. Ponton. I used sex—let guys use me, is more like it—to find out who I was."

"Did it work?"

"Yeah, but not the way I thought it would. You have no idea how sick I was of people saying I looked like a little angel, a little golden-haired angel. They thought they knew me just because of the way I looked! They had no idea. I didn't even know myself. They thought I wasn't having sex because of the way I looked so sweet. When they said that kind of stuff, it made me want to do it more."

"It really bothered you when they acted like they knew you."

"It made me furious! It still does." She grimaced at me.

"Lara, do you feel like I try to tell you who you are?"

"No, but it's hard. You ask me all these questions that make me feel like I want to puke. It isn't easy."

"No, Lara, it isn't."

Talking about their own sexuality is hard for many teens. Add the newly discovered fact that one is HIV-positive, and it becomes nearly impossible. Lara was struggling to become more aware of herself and her sexual identity at the same time she was coming to terms with being HIV-positive. She was recognizing that not only did she have sexual desire, but that it was okay. She was exploring many issues that could have been discussed when she was in school.

Lara's school was not alone in providing a truncated, and possibly harmful, prevention program. Dr. Alayne Yates, a child and adolescent psychiatrist and a well-known sex educator, believes that the United States has a schizophrenic attitude toward adolescent sexuality. The culture exposes adolescents through various popular media—music videos, television, film, and so forth—to daily doses of teens like themselves being sexually exploited or practicing irresponsible sex. At the same time, it gives them the message that they should not be participating in sexual intercourse at all.

Dr. Yates highlights unconscious factors that she believes play a role in the inability to provide more effective general sex education and specific HIV education for adolescents. First among them is *an inability to acknowledge that adolescents, "children" in the minds of many Americans, are sexually active.* In Lara's case, she was perceived as "a little angel." Statistics showing that teens are having sex at an increasingly early age are often ignored. When I speak with parents about adolescent sexual activity, even here in the sophisticated and progressive Bay Area, they frequently believe that it is someone else's children, in some far-off city, who are the ones having sex.

A second unconscious factor is the idea that was so prevalent in Lara's community, that people *deserve to be punished for sexual activity.* Underlying this notion is the very basic and simplistic idea that sexual activity in and of itself is bad, so those individuals who engage in it are also bad. Effective sexual education would only get in the way of the "natural law" of punishing the bad people for bad deeds.

Lara believed that her sexuality had already made her a bad person, that she was irredeemable. Some of these ideas were conscious, but much did not emerge into Lara's awareness until several years later during her therapy with me.

HIV education especially, often provided in the context of traditional sexual education, carries with it a message that sexuality is both hurtful and should be punished.

To look at how we portray sexuality to children, one has only to examine the programs that enlighten children about sexual abuse. Often their first introduction to sex education portrays sexual behavior as a scary thing, where children can be and are victimized. How different these first programs would be if they focused on normal sexual development, encouraging self-exploration and sexual curiosity. Programs that begin with children in elementary school should mature into comprehensive programs as children's needs change.

Lara's story raises the question of what type of sex education works best. Abstinence programs such as the one at Lara's school exclusively emphasize values, attitudes, and skills for postponing sexual intercourse. In 1998, the United States Congress allocated 250 million dollars for abstinence programs, specifically programs that teach abstinence from sex until marriage. But the problem is, there is very limited evidence that abstinence interventions work. Even the most well-planned and well-researched abstinence programs do not show the long-term benefits of carefully developed safer-sex programs, where behavioral change was noted even months later. Safer-sex approaches, by contrast, address abstinence but emphasize information and training in skills and behaviors.

Safer-sex programs are especially important for teens who are already sexually active because they have shown longer-lasting effects, successfully reducing risky behaviors.

As exemplified by Lara's story, the unconscious plays a role in a teen's struggle with HIV. But it also plays a role in a country's struggle with it. In the United States, we still regard HIV as a taboo subject. In 1913, in *Totem and Taboo,* Sigmund Freud wrote, "Once again I will take a single fact as my starting point. It is feared among primitive peoples that the violation of a taboo will be followed by a punishment, as a rule by some serious illness or by death. The punishment threatens to fall on whoever was responsible for violating the taboo." In the eyes of Lara and many others, individuals with HIV have violated a taboo. Yet how can an effective prevention plan be put in place when AIDS is seen as the deserved punishment for bad behavior?

HIV rates are falling in the United States, but they are not falling for young people. The Centers for Disease Control (CDC) estimates that half of the forty thousand people being infected with HIV in the United States are twenty-four years old or younger. And Lara is not alone. It's easier for girls to become infected from boys than vice versa. Also, the adolescent girl's cervix and vagina are in the process of developing, and are different in important ways than those of the fully mature woman.

Heterosexual sex, including vaginal, anal, and oral contact, is also the most common route of infection for girls. Over and over again, girls tell me that they want to use protection but that they weaken in their resolve when their partners protest. Teaching girls to be strong and protect themselves is vital. Having a better understanding of the types of struggles that go on between girls and boys about using condoms is important. Dr. Gina Wingood, at Emory University, has talked to girls from all cultural backgrounds about the struggles they have getting their partners to use condoms. She says that many teenage girls find it easier to say no to sex than to communicate to their partners that they must use condoms. Negotiation is an important part of sexual communication, one that many adolescent girls find difficult. There are many reasons for this. Most girls are having sex with older partners, often three or four years older, and this fact alone shifts the balance of power, giving the older partner more social and often physical power. Dr. Wingood also notes that many girls having sex are doing so to confirm their physical or sexual attractiveness. This is not a position of strength and makes them more vulnerable to their partners' demands. If a girl is confident, she will more easily navigate the challenging task of negotiating with her partner. Sexual and physical abuse also plays an important role. Girls who have been abused are more likely to be intimidated, less likely to speak out. Preparing girls for negotiation is an important part of sexual readiness.

Lara and I talked about what she remembered about her discussions—or, in her situation, lack thereof—with her partners or anyone else during her teen years. She told me that most of them had been older and they had told her they were "safe." Finally, she admitted to me that she hadn't cared—having sex was enough. Insisting that a guy use condoms was too hard.

Lara continues to have sex, although she uses condoms and has told her partners that she is HIV-positive. She is fighting the stigma of her HIV status. Perhaps most important, she has stopped beating herself up. Barring medical miracles, she will remain HIV-positive, but she is working hard to change parts of that legacy for herself and other teens.

10

The Dark Side
When Violence and Force Join Sexuality

*I still wonder why I didn't scream, why I didn't
do anything. I was totally frozen.*
                                        —Garth

*It shocks me, too, Mom . . . It wasn't like they
asked my permission.*   —Angie

"I'm here for one reason only. I don't want this to happen to anyone else. Do you understand me?" asked eighteen-year-old Garth. He stood waiting in the entryway of my office for my answer. Intuitively I knew that he wasn't going to stay if I didn't let him know that I understood. I told him I did, and asked him to sit down.

Garth sat down and painstakingly began to untie a stained brown leather legal folder that he removed from a Northface backpack. From my chair, I could see a stack of depositions and police reports, and some yellow-edged newspaper clippings. Garth carefully lined them up next to his chair and then searched my face again.

"How many cases like mine have you seen?"

"You're the twenty-fifth, Garth."

"The twenty-fifth! My attorney told me you had seen a lot, but twenty-five—twenty-five boys abused by priests?"

"Yes."

"So I'm not alone," he said.

"No, you're not alone."

"Why so many?"

"I ask myself that question a lot, Garth. It went unchecked for many years. The boys who spoke out were not listened to, and many waited years before telling their stories. It takes a lot of courage."

"Yes. It has taken me five years. I wanted to talk about it sooner." Motioning to the articles, he added, "I saved these, the stories of the others."

"Did they help you?"

"Yes."

"And you want to prevent this from happening to others."

"I do, but twenty-five, my God. It seems hopeless." He swallowed. "And no one talks about it."

"You're talking about it."

"Well, I *want* to talk about it. . . ."

"You're here. That's a start."

"Did the others talk right away?"

"No, they didn't. Some waited more than ten years."

"I still don't want to talk about it, but I think about those other kids. God, if this guy is still doing this, I'll kill myself."

Like many other teens I had seen who had been sexually abused, Garth was taking too much of a burden on his shoulders. The abusing priest, not Garth, was responsible for what he had done with other children. Garth had to believe that he could change something, though. He had not been able to prevent his own abuse. He had a strong need to stop it from happening to other kids. *I'm here for one reason only.*

"Garth, it is important what happens to other kids, but you are not responsible for it."

He looked down at the newspaper articles in his lap. "If they had said something—"

"If they had said something, it might not have happened to you."

"Yeah. I guess that's what I'm thinking. Feels stupid being mad at them. After all, like you said, the priest did it, not them." Expressing anger at the other boys, the silent ones, wasn't easy for Garth. After finally saying it aloud, he couldn't meet my eyes for the rest of our session. It was okay. We sat on the floor and he read me part of his collection of articles. He couldn't talk about what happened to him yet, but at least he could read the stories of priest abuse and I could listen. Among the stories were those of two boys who had been molested in a summer camp.

They had both been thirteen, an age when many boys are making their way through puberty, development beginning, but not fully there, an age at which, I have discovered, many boys are molested. Garth read the first boy's story without visible emotion. I could see that it took much effort; even the "neutral" journalistic lingo could not disguise what had happened—sodomy, physical force, the humiliation of the priest blessing one of the boys afterward. These stories were hard to read, and hard to listen to. I felt my body tensing as Garth read. When he put the first article down and began the second, I asked him if he wanted to take a break. He shook his head and kept reading. Not long into the second story, I realized that what had happened to these two boys, at least the crude words used to describe the brutal actions, were similar. It was the same priest. Garth's voice was very flat. He continued to read, and then I heard it, the word "Fucker," in a deep, low voice. Garth read the stories of the other boys and left my office without comment.

After he left, I wondered whether I had actually heard what I thought I did. I wasn't sure. I noticed a brown manila envelope on my assistant's desk in the waiting room. Scrawled across the front was the plea, "Keep it, please." Inside were only those first two stories, about the boys at summer camp.

Garth was late for his second visit. I waited, thinking about what he had left me. I was pretty sure that the stories in the envelope were close to his own, that he was a "camp boy." I reminded myself, though, that although the stories might be similar—same age, same priest, same type of abuse—the victim's feelings and reactions were always different. What had it been like for Garth? And how did he feel knowing that the same man had done similar things to other kids?

Twenty minutes late, Garth arrived and began to talk quickly, but not about the abuse. Did I know that the 43 bus line didn't always stop at Willard, the stop for my office? Well, if you don't get off there, you end up at the medical center, and it takes you twenty minutes longer. As Garth and I talked about the misdirected bus line, I wondered about redirecting him back to his case. I had been hired by attorneys to obtain the details of his case, to figure out what would help him recover, if he could recover, and to estimate, if possible, how damaged he had been by the molestation. Then I saw the envelope I had left on my desk.

"You left me something last time, Garth."

"Did you read 'em?" This time his eyes met mine.

"You had already read them to me."

"Yeah."

"Any reason you left those stories and not the others?"

"I figured it would be easier."

"For you or me?"

"Both of us, if I didn't have to tell you."

"You think the stories are the same? That if I've read theirs, I know yours?"

"The details are the same," he said. "But the feelings . . ."

"Have you been able to talk with anyone about the feelings?"

"I gave the attorney a statement, if that's what you mean. I wrote it out. Do you want a copy?"

"Do you want to give me a copy?"

"It's better than talking about it."

"Easier."

"A lot easier. I don't know if I can talk."

"It's hard."

"I want to help other boys. I want to stop this kind of thing."

"What about helping yourself?"

"Of course you believe it would help me to talk about it!" He flashed me a smile. "All you shrinks think that."

"Actually, I don't always think it will help to talk about it."

"You don't?" I had surprised him.

"Sometimes it's too painful, and sometimes kids aren't ready."

"Dr. Ponton, I've already waited for five years."

"Yes, you have. That's a long time."

"How do I start if I'm gonna do it?"

"Garth, you've already started."

"Next time I'll bring my statement."

"Okay."

Next time Garth did bring his statement, and began reading.

"I was thirteen for my first time at camp, away from home. It was the summer that my parents divorced; they wanted me to have a good experience away from their struggles. The priest stayed at the camp, and each night he joined the campsite with a different group of boys. Usually he stayed two nights, with each group, and chose two boys, one each night. It started when he put his sleeping bag next to the boy's. Then he might suggest back massages for everyone, and then, when it got dark, most of the kids went to sleep. He slept next to me on the last night of the trip. I remember him pulling his sleeping bag next to mine and then, when the other boys had fallen asleep, I remember the priest unzipping his bag on the side nearest to where I was lying. I remember a purring noise that his zipper made when he unzipped my bag. Lying on my stomach, I turned around and saw his face framed by the light from the fire, what was left of the fire. He smiled at me. 'Don't worry, Garth, now it's my turn to give you a back rub. It's okay because you are such a wonderful boy.' I wanted to say something. I felt my mouth moving, I wanted to talk, but then he began to rub the lower part of my back, saying, 'Now it's your turn, wonderful boy, just lie still, it'll be great.' His massage continued with his hand moving lower and lower until he was fondling the cheeks of my butt. I was still lying on my stomach, trying to hold my legs together, holding my breath. He continued to touch me, eventually sticking one finger in my butt, moving it very slowly, in and out. After doing this, he moved out of his own sleeping bag and climbed in, on top of me. I was frozen. I could feel him moving on top of me, I could hear him grunting. I felt a sharp pain when his penis went in me. He kept saying 'wonderful boy' over and over in this soft voice while he tore me up inside, moving back and forth, going deeper and deeper until I felt him shake and shudder. Then he stopped. He was heavy, all I wanted was for him to get off of me. I felt so ashamed of what had happened. I was sure it hadn't happened with the other boys. I didn't sleep all night."

Garth had stopped reading earlier, telling me his story instead. He had it memorized.

"You're talking about it now, Garth."

"Yeah, I'm telling you, at least. I keep thinking of him doing this to bunches of little kids. It's so scary."

"What's the scariest part for you?"

"I guess that I want to kill this guy, feeling like that all the time. He makes me feel like a killer. I hate him so much. I keep thinking, How do these fuckers get away with it?"

"Well, he was a big guy and he lay on top of you, for one thing. It would have been hard to get away from him with all those sleeping boys around you."

"Yeah, I know, but I still wonder why I didn't scream, why I didn't do anything. I was totally frozen."

"You were terrified, Garth."

"I know that, but I still expected, still expect, more from myself."

"What would you like to have done?"

He laughed. It was a sharp laugh, painful to hear. "That's the thing, Dr. Ponton, there you asked the right question. I would have liked to have raped the bastard. Now I've said it. I'm not much better than him."

"But you didn't do that, Garth."

"Yeah, not yet, anyway."

When Garth left my office that day, I sat quietly by myself. I could see that he had a collection of feelings about this priest—paralysis combined with fear, a desire to kill him, to rape him—that had been raging inside him for years. But at least it was a beginning that he was starting to talk about them.

I ended up taking my time over the next few weeks. Interviewing him and preparing his legal report took much longer than either I or his attorneys had anticipated, and I had to ask for more time. Our work together went at a certain pace, and there was little I could do to make it go any faster. If I pushed too hard, Garth would clam up.

As our work developed, one area Garth avoided was that of his sexual fantasies. At some point we would need to talk about this. From my experience with other molested boys, I knew that is a very sensitive area where a molester leaves a mark. I remembered my work with Jim, a young set designer in his early twenties who had come to see me because he had difficulties completing his designs on the computer screen. What had emerged were daydreams, visions of men and boys engaged in violent fights that dissolved into erotic scenes. These were both sexually stimulating and very disturbing to Jim. Our work together revealed a painful story in which a young Jim had been confronted by a group of older, popular boys when he was a freshman in high school. He had hoped that they wanted to hang out with him, but instead all three jumped on top of him, delivering a steady rain of blows as they laughed loudly. One of these older boys whom Jim had thought was actually more friendly than the others ended up ripping Jim's underwear. Jim never remembered exactly what happened next except that he ran as fast as he could and got away.

He got away that afternoon, but memories of the event followed him long afterward. Just weeks after the attack, he found himself increasingly fascinated with men and boys beating each other up. He began to day-dream about these scenes, later drawing pictures and attending movies that showed such violent sequences. He was embarrassed, but also powerfully drawn to these images. They haunted him. When he talked with me about them, he noted that the person in the scenes with whom he identified could easily shift—he could be the victim or the attacker.

Jim had never spoken with anyone about these events until he came to my office. He was surprised at the strength of his feelings years after the event. He felt betrayed by the other boys, especially his so-called friend, but the overwhelming memory was the pounding of fists on his weak body and his sense of overwhelming powerlessness. He replayed those feelings over and over again in his fantasies.

The twenty-five boys I had interviewed before Garth had usually been molested between the ages of eleven and fifteen, before they had experienced any sexual activity of their own except masturbation, when they had felt their own erections but had never penetrated anyone else. Interviewing these boys and, in many cases, the men they became, I observed other patterns. Each priest had followed his own pattern no matter how many boys he molested, his own bizarre dance of "seduction." Force was almost always an integral part of the dance—a large physical size, forcing apart closed legs, anuses, mouths; sometimes threats whispered, *Don't tell . . . you'll pay . . . no one would believe you anyway, you're just a boy. . . .*

Presumably safe places were often the settings for these molestations—the sacristy, the priest's library, the church summer camp. Individual priests used the same words, settings, and actions with all the boys they abused.

Besides the mark left on their sexual fantasies, almost all of the boys drank to excess or used drugs to control their feelings and limit their pain, at least during the rest of their adolescent years. Hussey and colleagues report that male victims of sexual abuse use drugs and alcohol more frequently, have more frequent depressions, have lower self-esteem, have a sense of hopelessness about the future, have concerns about controlling their sexual feelings, and are more concerned with their appearance than boys who are not abused. Many of those with whom I met suffered from depression. All had lower self-esteem than their non-abused peers, and felt somewhat hopeless about their future. Most lost their close relationship with the church. Their molestation made them distrust other priests, and ate away at their spirituality. Researchers have noted that clergy often have special access to boys by virtue of their trusted position in the church and community, and that this deep respect makes detection of the abuse very difficult. If others discovered what had happened, their life was even more of a nightmare—boys at school called them "priest boys" and made obscene gestures. Many withdrew socially, unable to share what had happened to them.

The marks left on their sexuality were even more devastating. Many live in fear that they, too, would abuse, although only one of the twenty-five did. Some came to see me at the time that their wives were pregnant, worried that they might abuse their own children or that others would accuse them of it. All were struggling with their sexual fantasies, marked by looming figures holding them down, forcing apart their legs or forcing open their mouths, evoking strong feelings—hateful and erotic fantasies that they did not want to have, and would often pretend did not exist.

Robert Stoller, a psychoanalyst and former teacher at the University of California in Los Angeles, devoted much of his life to studying the darker side of sexual behavior and fantasies associated with reenactments of childhood sexual abuse. In an essay entitled, "Sex and Sin," he writes about abusers compressing powerful memories of their own mistreatment into sexual scenarios that they forcibly live out with others. Their scripts are delivered with force, infused by trauma, and packaged in a dangerous but exciting way. The abused often feels that strong energy. Most of the boys I have worked with recognize that they are being pulled into a priest's own dark struggle. Working with them, I have been able to tell that their own stories are horribly painful, but at the same time they can be powerfully exciting. It is a nightmarish legacy of this type of childhood abuse.

Not all boys or men who have been abused are able to discuss this legacy. For many it is forever hidden and will not be revealed to anyone. Keeping it hidden often protects them. I respect this, and thought about it often during my work with Garth.

We had agreed to meet for the final time when he was able to raise this issue. He was reading the final report that I had prepared, and he paused when he got to the campfire scene.

"His face is fading," he said to me, "you know?"

"I didn't know."

"Yeah, it's just—a shadow or something now, and the light from the fire. That's all I see."

"How often do you see it?" I hadn't asked this until now.

"Still every day."

"That's a lot."

"Yeah, but it's better."

Although Garth talked only briefly about his fantasies, I did discover more. He "needed" this fantasy of the priest in order to masturbate. This disturbed him deeply. He felt as if the priest had robbed him of his few former fantasies, and whatever fantasies would have later developed for him, and replaced them with the assault. Every time he masturbated, he felt humiliated.

I recommended four years of therapy to help Garth deal with the consequences of the rape. He called me after he had completed almost three years of therapy. Without my asking, he told me that the priest's image was gone; now it was just a feeling that spread over his entire body. Better? Yes, he was better, but the shadow on his life was still there.

The Hidden Tales of Sexually Abused Boys

Both physical and sexual abuse are underreported by boys. Our culture does not look kindly upon "victims," whether male or female, but boys who have been victimized may be even more prone to feelings of intense shame because our culture places such a premium on male strength and self-sufficiency.

Boys remaining silent are only part of the story. Many parents fail to believe their sons. Often the boys try to tell their parents the story, but before they can finish they are told that the priest is too nice, they must have imagined it. Garth's parents were in this category. He told them only that he "thought" the priest had "touched him," and they told him that he certainly must be mistaken. Many priests and other members of the Catholic Church in Northern California remained silent for a long time. When "episodes" with priests were discovered, the men were shifted to other parishes only to abuse again. In the book *Bless Me Father for I Have Sinned: Perspectives on Sexual Abuse Committed by Roman Catholic Priests,* various authors write about this often ignored problem, highlighting what can be done. The editor, Thomas Plante, cautions that the problem will not change until the Catholic Church is willing to openly discuss sexuality. He also says that there is no evidence that gay clergy engage in higher rates of child and teen molestation than heterosexual clergy.

Priests are not the only perpetrators. Boys and girls are abused by ministers, rabbis, teachers, coaches, Big Brothers, Boy Scout leaders, and other trusted adults charged with the care of children and teens. Sex is a part of this story, but the overriding legacy is one of violence, both physical and emotional, woven into memories and fantasies, and sometimes, unfortunately, into patterns of abuse. No one wants this legacy for his or her child.

Although men and boys don't talk about abuse, it shows up in other ways. Boys who have been sexually abused are more likely to be involved in coercive sex, either as the aggressor—forcing someone else to have sex—or as the victim—being forced by someone else to have sex.

In my first interview with Garth, I told him that he had courage to speak out about what had happened to him. The boys and men who spoke up before him had helped him to find the strength he needed. And then his story, once he shared it, helped other boys. This kind of truth telling is not always viewed as courageous. Male abuse survivors can also be seen as weak for letting it happen—real men don't get abused—

which is, of course, yet another version of blaming the victim. They may also be seen as complainers—real men would put up with it. Recognizing and commending the tremendous strength it takes to come forward with these experiences can help us develop a better definition of manhood.

It is important to understand, especially in the current climate of acknowledging sexual abuse, that the response of parents and family to the abuse plays a vital role. If the family denies or ignores it, the struggle becomes much larger for the child or teen, and the whole story may never be told. For incest survivors, the ongoing family dynamic in which the abuse occurred is often just as significant as the abuse itself. When the abuser has been a trusted adult, often the case for children abused by adult relatives, the sense of betrayal is tremendous, and usually results in a lack of trust in all or most adults, at least for a while.

Night Terrors

Thirteen-year-old Angie stopped to push up her eyebrows at my hallway mirror before she walked into my office for her first session. Walking right behind her, I saw the eye that she was working on—lavender shadow. She was wearing a lot of makeup. Some girls this age aspire to be cosmetic consultants. Then I looked closer. She was applying cover-up under her eyes. It looked like she'd been crying.

At that moment we both saw her mother open my office door. Angie gave her a drop-dead look. She needn't have bothered. Her mother, Jean, already looked beaten down, as if the weight of the world was on her shoulders. That didn't surprise me. I knew from an earlier phone call that she had been through a lot in the past few days. She was exhausted. I extended my hand to her, and she grabbed on and did not let go. I said that I would meet with Angie first; then the three of us could meet together. She said nothing but finally nodded.

I knew from the phone call that she hadn't slept for the past two days. The police had called her Saturday night. Thirteen-year-old Angie and a girlfriend had been picked up at a party—undressed, drunk, reportedly having had oral sex with several boys. No chaperoning parents were present at this party. The boys involved were all underage, mostly ninth graders. Angie and her friend, Rebecca, were both in the eighth grade. The police had been called by neighbors who complained about noise. Angie and Rebecca spent most of Sunday vomiting in the pediatric emergency room at the university hospital. Angie and Jean were interviewed by the police, who wanted to know if Jean wanted to prosecute the boys.

Angie, who looked at least sixteen, acted like she had spent half her life in a psychiatrist's office. She skillfully flipped my office chair so that she was lying back at a comfortable angle. Many teens don't manage to do this until their last session. After asking me, she plugged in my electric teapot and carefully chose an herbal tea—Tension Tamer. I sensed that she was prepared for almost anything, but probably not ready for what we were supposed to talk about. She poured tea for me, too, and I thanked her, commenting that she was wearing an attractive bracelet on her wrist.

"It's for serenity."

"Serenity?"

"Yeah, the bracelet, all the kids in my group wear them. There's one for creativity, another for love, power—different things."

"And you chose serenity."

"Weird choice, huh?"

"Weird?"

"Well, yeah, considering my situation."

I had been thinking the same thing, but knew that it was better for her to say it. "Do you want to talk about it?" I asked.

"No, but my mom says I have to. The police want to know stuff."

"You talked with the police?"

"Yeah, but I don't remember anything about it. I was still puking my guts out."

"What do you remember?"

"Anything?"

"Yeah. For instance, do you remember how you and Rebecca got to the party?"

At the mention of the party, Angie's eye began to twitch, and she rubbed it hard, but not before a stream of eyeliner made its way down her cheek. She began to bite her fingernails and hold her stomach, eventually doubling over in her chair. She was breathing deeply, struggling for air. She couldn't talk. I took a box of Kleenex and set it at her feet. She sat for several minutes, holding herself, eventually beginning to breathe more regularly.

"Angie, we can take it slow."

"No, it's okay." She pulled out a compact and adeptly removed the smear of eyeliner. "I'm fine."

She didn't look fine. She was holding her body stiffly, as if she was still nauseous, though she had stopped rocking. I noticed that the makeup and form-fitting adult women's clothing, designed to make her look older, weren't working that way now. She looked about ten years old, a girl dressed up in her mother's clothing.

"Angie, we can take our time here. I know the police are in a rush, but we don't have to be."

"It's okay. I got myself into this. I'll handle it. The party. Well, it was Rebecca's idea. See, I was sleeping over at her house when Trevor called. He said there was a group of guys at his house, all the popular guys. He said he liked Rebecca, and told me this really hot guy, D.J., a ninth grader, had a crush on me. Trevor lives about two blocks from Rebecca. So we snuck out and went over there. Her parents thought we were watching videos in the family room. We get to his house, and he was right—there are a bunch of guys, the most popular guys at our school."

"Are you one of the popular kids, Angie?"

"Kind of. It's hard for girls. Becca is, though."

"It can take a lot of work to be popular."

She looked relieved—at least I understood some things. "Yeah, you gotta get along with everyone, the girls and the boys. It's a lot of work."

"So you and Rebecca are at his house?"

"Yeah. The guys are all drinking—a lot. Becca starts drinking right away—vodka, lots of it. The guys have this funnel. They're pouring the stuff into it fast, really fast. It's so they can drink fast."

"Did they use the funnel with Rebecca?"

"Yeah. She was choking a little, but Trevor just kept pouring it."

"Are you drinking at this point?"

"Yeah, I have a drink, but I'm not drinking like that."

"Had you ever drunk before?"

"No. I'm just sipping it. It doesn't taste very good. They say you can't taste it? But you can. Anyway, this is when D.J. comes over. He starts telling me I'm the cutest girl at school. We're talking—it's kinda okay. Then—" She started gasping again. "Then I look over, and Becca is giving this guy head. It's, like, crazy. I don't want to look."

"What happens then, Angie?"

"I keep talking to D.J., and I'm sweating. I think I faint or something."

"You think?"

"Dr. Ponton, I don't know. I don't know what happened after that."

"You don't remember?"

"No! The next thing I'm in the E.R., puking." Angie wasn't puking in my office, but she was sweating and shaking, and the rocking had started again. "I am so stupid."

"What do you think might have happened?"

"Becca is saying that she remembers I was giving this guy a blow job, not even D.J., some other guy. She kinda remembers the police coming."

"And you don't?"

She shook her head.

I stared at Angie, thinking, *She's only thirteen*. The whole thing had happened so quickly . . . alcohol by funnel, I knew about the technique. Kids used it to get drunk quickly, but the combination of alcohol and oral sex, both first-time experiences with Angie, who had had more to drink than she realized, was particularly hard to listen to.

"Have you thought about what you might want to do, Angie?"

"No. I just wish it hadn't happened."

"Did you go to school today?"

"Yeah, my mom made me. The principal met with us, and with Becca and her parents."

"Was that helpful."

"Kinda. Mom wants to talk with you about what she—the principal—said. She has some ideas, I guess, about what might help at school—damage control, I guess, that kind of thing."

"How are you with that?"

"I was so mad at my mom. First this whole thing—God, I feel terrible about it—then the principal is involved, then I'm dragged here to see a shrink, no offense or anything."

"None taken, Angie. Any other thoughts about what happened Saturday night?"

"Like how I'm never going to do it again?"

"Well, if you feel you've learned that, how would you prevent it? I'm curious about how you think it was able to happen."

"Because I was stupid."

"How were you stupid?"

"I drank too much."

"What about the sex?"

She looked down. "When I looked over and saw Becca getting on this guy, I was shocked. She is the most popular girl at school. She was drunk, but . . ."

"But it was a pretty risky situation."

"Yeah, and the guys—I thought that Trevor really liked her."

"It didn't look to you like he was treating her that way."

"Nope. She got on two guys, though."

"By 'got on' you mean oral sex?"

"Yeah. What was she thinking?"

"Well, she was pretty drunk, and so were you. Alcohol changes the way you look at things."

"I don't remember anything. The principal says neither me nor Becca agreed to have sex with those guys, so we didn't consent. But we were drunk."

"What about the guys?"

"It makes me sick, thinking about this guy jerking off in my mouth when I'm passed out. What if I had choked and died?"

"Angie, it was wrong of those guys to have sex with you in that situation. I am very sorry about it."

"But?"

"No buts. You were drunk, but that doesn't mean that you agreed to oral sex or any other type of sex."

"You really think that?"

"I do. This is a tough situation, though, and the best choice for you here isn't completely obvious."

"You don't think I'm a slut?" Angie made eye contact with me and held it for the first time.

"No. I think you made a poor choice."

"Yeah, you're right there."

"Do you want to be here when I talk with your mom?"

"Okay."

Looking at Jean's face in my waiting room, I could see that she had been crying. Unlike her daughter, she hadn't carefully applied any makeup to try to hide it. I invited her into my office.

"Dr. Ponton, Angie's principal is going to call you today."

"That's fine, Jean. It's important. I'll be sure to call her right back if she doesn't get me directly and has to leave a message. Your daughter has been doing a good job talking about what happened. She recognizes that she placed herself in a high-risk situation."

"She does?" Jean seemed surprised and looked over at Angie. "She hasn't said that to me."

"Mom, God, I feel so dumb. It's embarrassing."

Jean sat quietly, struggling to take in what her daughter was saying.

"Jean, the past two days have been really difficult for you, too," I said softly.

She nodded. After a long pause, she spoke in a cracked voice, worn with tears. "Angie feels like she messed up. Well, I feel that way, too. Meeting with her principal, I just kept thinking, *How did I let this happen?*"

"How do you think you let this happen, Jean?"

She shook her head and whispered, "I must be a bad mother. I should have supervised her better. The sex—it shocks me."

"It shocks me, too, Mom," said Angie, her voice rising and strained with the tears that were filling her eyes. "It wasn't like they asked my permission."

"I know that, Angie, but you snuck out to go to that party, you got drunk . . ."

Angie's tears streamed down her cheeks as her mother spoke. "I feel so bad about this, please don't make me feel worse. I already feel dirty— like I'm a slut. Is that what you think, too?"

At the mention of the word "slut," Jean's mouth opened. "Angie—"

Shouting and crying at the same time, Angie spat out the words. "What do you think, Mom, the principal saying, 'We have reputations to protect here'? She didn't mean the guys, Mom. It's Becca and me. We're the sluts, we're the ones who're gonna have reputations now."

"Angie," said Jean. "You listen to me. You are not a slut."

"Well, I feel like one."

"That's something we've all got to work on," I said. "It may take some time."

"I think everyone thinks I'm a slut now."

"Angie," I said, "do you remember what we said about having made some bad choices?"

"And you're certainly not alone there," said Jean.

"What're you talking about?" cried Angie. "Becca? You think Becca's a slut?"

"No, Angie," said Jean. "I meant me. I made a bad choice here, too. Maybe more than one."

"So now I'm grounded forever?" said Angie.

I said, "Let's slow down a minute here. Angie, I think your mother is just saying that as a parent, she has some regrets about her decisions here, too. Let's see if we can talk about what the choices are now."

Jean spoke first. "The police want to know if Angie and Becca, or Becca's parents and I, I guess, want to prosecute the boys."

"Do you know what that means, Jean?"

"Well, I'm not completely sure. They said that Angie was"—Jean took a deep breath—"Angie was too drunk to stand up, and shouldn't have been expected to resist physically, or protest, that she couldn't have been a willing partner."

"Do you agree with that?"

"Yes."

"What about you, Angie?"

"I agree."

"Angie," said Jean, "they also said it could get nasty. That the boy might fight it, and say you did agree to sex before you drank." She was watching her daughter's face very carefully. "I'm not sure if you could handle that kind of pressure. I'm not sure I'd want you to."

At this point, the makeup was totally gone from Angie's face. She looked older, though, stronger.

"Mom, I know I could. It's what people would say about me, Becca, you. I just don't know about all that."

Angie, Jean, and I weren't able to work out a solution during the rest of our meeting, but we agreed on a couple of things. They would consult with an attorney who specialized in juvenile law, and try to get a sense of what might happen with prosecution of the boys. I would talk with the principal, who had, in fact, called while we were still in session. Jean would talk with Angie's father, who lived in another state, and tell him what had happened. They both wanted his input.

After walking Angie and Jean out, I called the principal back. The school Angie attended was one where I had often spoken at parent-teacher events, so the principal and I knew each other pretty well. She really was worried about reputations, she told me, Angie's and Becca's, yes, but also the school's. Did I know that this whole thing was ready to blow up?

I asked her what she thought should be done.

"If this thing goes, it will be terrible for those girls. The boys involved are serious players, though, and they won't tell the truth."

"So what do you suggest?"

"The girls are only thirteen—it'll ruin their lives."

"How do you think it should be handled with the boys, then?"

"Well, I can't do anything. It didn't happen on school grounds."

"Have you met with the boys and their families?"

"No. The girls and their parents came willingly. I mean, it was the parents' idea."

"You don't think the boys' parents would come if you asked them to?"

"I don't know."

After we talked a bit more, she decided to try to arrange a meeting with the boys and their families, and we agreed to stay in contact. Over the next few days I spoke with Jean and Angie a number of times. They were a team, trying to make the best decision. Eventually, a decision was made to file charges solely against the boy who had had oral sex with Angie. One of the other boys agreed that a boy had had oral sex with her while she was nearly passed out. The district attorney agreed to prosecute, but he would be filing a misdemeanor charge, not a felony rape. After much discussion with the police and everyone else, Angie and Jean agreed to this. With Rebecca, the situation was quite different. The boy said that Becca had agreed to have sex with his friends before she was drunk. In effect, she had consented to what had happened. All of the kids involved were under fifteen.

After our early, and somewhat troubling, phone call, the principal tried hard. She did get the boys and their families in, and made referrals for treatment for all of them. She discussed the situation with counselors at her school, and they worked out a way to role-play a similar situation so that all of the kids could think about potential risks of alcohol and drugs. And I found out that the principal had accomplished her first goal after all. Rumors were quelled and reputations were saved—the school's and the girls'. At least temporarily. Word got out about Becca, fast. She was deemed a pro at oral sex—the school expert. Another incident happened before her parents finally arranged counseling. Her popularity hadn't suffered, but her self-esteem had.

Becca's story reminds us that many twelve-, thirteen-, and fourteen-year-olds are having oral and other types of sex voluntarily. Stories like Becca's lead me to believe that in many cases, popularity is more notoriety than anything else. And some teens would rather have some reputation than none at all. In some cases, girls feel that it elevates their status. This phenomenon tells us that girls need help in being able to negotiate better for themselves in this important area.

It wasn't all smooth sailing for Angie, either. Boys said things, so did girls. She defended Becca and herself, but she got tired of talking about it. She told me that she felt like she should wear a button: *I made a mistake, but I'm not the only one.* That sturdiness which I had observed after her makeup wore off continued, and she got through it. So did Jean. She learned things that she had never wanted to know—what constitutes the legal definition of rape, for example—but she also saw her daughter admit a mistake, stand up for herself, and move on with her life.

A Question of Consent

A better understanding of the concept and realistic parameters of sexual consent is important for teens and adults both. Even in the most progressive states, where freely given sexual consent to a sexual act is required, the law makes little effort to define consent itself. Coercion or physical force are needed to violate consent, but even coercion is not well-defined. As a result, many prosecutors fighting rape continue to insist on evidence of physical force, and a greater amount than that which is normally involved in sexual intercourse. This is a very narrow definition of force. Was Garth forced? Well, the priest lay on top of him. They had anal intercourse. Garth had not consented to this, but he did not scream or resist, other than pushing his legs together. As he told me, he was frozen in a state of shock. He was also thirteen years old. Technically, his situation is viewed as a child molestation based on age alone.

Angie was too drunk to protest. And, like Garth, she did not resist. Critics of the way we prosecute violent sexual acts suggest that our country's focus on rape as narrowly defined by force is wrong. Instead they recommend that we look at protection of sexual autonomy—in other words, whether a person's rights to make his or her own sexual choices are being ignored in a specific situation. Both Angie and Garth were coerced into sexual activity, and their consent was not obtained. Our society as a whole lacks knowledge about this important and frightening area.

Rape by and of adolescents is a significant problem. Studies vary slightly, but youths under the age of twenty are responsible for 18 percent of single-offender and 30 percent of multiple-offender rapes. Eleven percent of all female victims of rape are between the ages of twelve and fifteen, and 25 percent are between the ages of sixteen and nineteen. Statistics on males are more difficult to obtain. One study reported that 16 percent of all men were sexually abused as children. According to a 1997 report from the U.S. Department of Justice, an estimated 9 percent of rape victims are male.

Often the abuser victimizes many boys before the abuse is reported. It is important to understand that although rape is most frequently associated with sex, it primarily serves nonsexual needs of power, domination, and control. It occurs far more frequently in cultures that fail to respect the sexual rights of all citizens, in the United States, women and children. This violence is not inevitable, but much has to change. Teens are dramatically affected by a culture's attitudes in this area. Studies show that many adolescents believe forced sex is acceptable under certain circumstances. For example, many teens believe that if a girl is wearing provocative clothing, she is asking to be raped. Educational efforts need to address such grave misconceptions.

Wendy Shalit, author of a recent book on sexuality, advocates a return to modesty for girls. She believes that this would help protect against many things, rape among them. Yet her attitude again places responsibility on the victims. In a culture that is the most violent in the industrialized world, we do need to educate girls and boys about the real risks. The Angies and Beccas need to know about teen boys' attitudes about clothing, but we also have to work to change everyone's attitudes that violating the sexual rights of a person is unacceptable under any circumstances. *It is never acceptable.* This is an area where parents, school, and politicians need to be very informed and very proactive. Though initially she had not wanted to meet with the boys at all, Angie's principal eventually developed a program to work with all of the students about date and party rape.

I frequently think about Garth's first words to me: "I'm here for one reason only. I don't want this to happen to anyone else. Do you understand me?" I only hope that we can all understand, and help in this effort.

None of My Business
Parents and Sex

Am I, like, a pervert for listening? —Casey

I know I'm not my father, but it feels like I could be. —Derek

"**S**he should be the one here with you, not me. She's the one with the sex life!" shouted sixteen-year-old Casey a few minutes into her first session with me. She was referring to her mother, Nina, who had insisted that they come in for mother-daughter therapy after Nina's remarriage.

Casey continued. For someone who didn't need to see me, she was really quite a talker. "She leaves my dad after twenty years. That's one thing. They weren't getting along so great, so okay. Then she meets this hot guy, a dad, no less. Can dads be hot? I don't think so, but she does, obviously."

"How long ago did your mom remarry, Casey?"

"They *just* got married and they're having sex all the time. What is wrong with her?"

"Do you really think something is wrong?"

"Well, yeah. She is over fifty. They are like bunnies—so cute. So sick."

"How do you feel about it."

"I'm there, but not for long. That's one thing you can do for me, get me out of there."

"You don't want to live there?"

"The guy's okay. It's just being around them."

"What's that like?"

"I told you—sex, all the time."

"How do you and your mom get along?"

"We used to get along great." Casey's steady verbal stream paused. "She is a cool mom, except for this. She always listens to me. She can usually see both sides."

"Does she see both sides this time?"

"Probably she does. It's me. I can't stand it."

"Casey, the whole thing is pretty tough for you. Sounds like you are pretty close to your mom, and her remarriage hit you pretty hard, especially the sex."

"Yes." In the silence that followed, Casey played with her shagged brown hair, twisting it into a bun.

"Are you dating?"

"Not now. I had a boyfriend last year."

"Sounds like you've got enough to deal with—with this."

"That's the thing—it's like I should be the one dating, maybe not having sex. It's not fair."

"What's not fair about it?"

"Well, teens date. Parents are, like, settled."

"Is it that way for your friends' moms?"

"No, their lives are a mess, but mine, she was a good mom."

"So—good moms don't date, and they don't have sex."

We both started laughing here. "It sounds so funny when you say it," said Casey.

"But you think that way?"

"Yeah, I guess."

"What about your mom?"

"Yeah." Casey's eyes looked sad. "She told me she wasn't happy married to my dad. He had a lot of temper tantrums. He was always trying to control us."

"How did that go for you?"

"It was really hard. I love him, a lot, too. Mom would stand up for me."

"What's it been like since the divorce?"

"Not too bad. I can stand up to him myself. He's trying to change. The thing with my mom is so hard, and it used to be so great."

"Hard to understand it, Casey. You and your mother were—are—pretty close, but you've both been through a lot of changes."

"She says maybe I want her to be unhappy."

"What do you think?"

"I want her to be happy, but now I'm unhappy."

"What's the divorce been like for you?"

"Okay, I told you, they weren't great together. It's just—she's *so* happy now."

"That's hard for you?"

"Yeah. Maybe she's right. I liked her better unhappy."

"Maybe there was something easier about it for you."

"Huh?"

"Well, you were used to it. You and she were very close, with no one else there. Her sex life seems really to bother you, too."

"Yeah, but you can't change that."

"Bet you're right."

A couple of days later, Nina, Casey, and I met together for the first time. Nina, the principal of an elementary school, wore a relaxed gray pantsuit. She had the same thick, long dark hair as her daughter, although she had a silver streak on one side. They had stopped for ice cream and were eating it in my waiting room. I noticed that they both ate their cones the same way, working from the bottom up. Maybe they were trying to be polite—no ice cream on the office carpet—but I guessed that it pointed to a lot of other similarities. When I interrupted them, Casey, who helped out at her mom's school, was telling a story about one of the young teachers.

"So, Mom, she doesn't know I'm your daughter, and then she says, 'This principal is superstrict.' Then she really looks at me, and figures it out. She about faints. I tell her, 'Don't worry, you got it wrong, girl.'"

"So your mom wouldn't be a boss to worry about, Casey?"

"Nah, the teachers think she's great. Of course, principals are supposed to be scary, right, Mom?"

"Right, Casey."

"Nina and Casey, the two of you look like you deserve the mother-daughter award of the year, but you're sitting here in my office, so what would you like to talk about?"

After a short pause, Nina said, "We need to talk about sex."

"Oh, Mom, not that again—"

"Well, Casey, it's where we've run into trouble, so let's give it a try."

"I already told her everything," said Casey, nodding at me. "It's okay."

"So don't mess with it now?" I asked.

"Dr. Ponton, you know what I mean. I feel better after you and I talked. Mom's spending more time with me."

"So all is well. Have you and she talked much?"

"Kinda," Casey said. "Look, I told her it bugged me, all the sex. They toned it down. I try not to listen too hard."

"You were listening? Oh, Casey—"

"It kinda shocked me, Mom."

"What shocked you?" Nina asked directly.

"It wasn't only the noise. You were, are, so different, so—happy. Seeing you so worked up because of Bret—" Clearly words failed her here. She struggled on. "Mom, I'm glad you're happy. You deserve it."

I could see she was holding back. "But it leaves you feeling something, Casey."

"Left out, yeah, though you and Bret are always trying to include me. I feel sorry for Dad."

"Casey, the thing with Bret surprised me, too," said Nina. "After the divorce, I wasn't expecting to meet anyone. Bret and I were really good friends, and then this kind of—happened. I feel bad about parts of the marriage with your dad, too. He and I tried hard."

"I know you did, Mom. Maybe if I'd been in college—"

"It's hard for you to watch, Casey."

"You're so happy and you're so out there. One of my friends saw you hanging on Bret. She says, 'Is that your mom?' "

"Did she say anything else, Casey?" I asked, sensing she was leaving something out.

"Well, she was surprised you were so—sexy." Here she looked directly at her mother.

Nina said, "That isn't the word she used, I'll bet."

"Well, no . . . it wasn't, Mom, but it's okay . . . it's just a shock."

"That your mother has a sex life," I said.

"Yeah, and it's a big deal. That's the shock."

"Does your dad's sex life affect you the same way?" I asked.

"My dad—well, he dates, but I'm not as close to him."

"So it's not the same thing."

"Mom's probably right. Seeing Bret make her so happy bothers me. When I was the one who made her happy, it was different."

"Honey," said Nina, "you still make me happy."

Casey's face lit up. "Only one other thing—tone it down."

Here, Nina smiled. I could see that she was fighting not to burst into giggles. Casey smiled, too.

"Well," I said, "it is kind of funny. Usually the moms are in my office telling their kids they need to tone it down. It seems like there is more to it than that, Casey. I think your mom could hear it if you'd be willing to say it."

"Hmm. Well, it feels stupid, but, Mom, I have this thing about you and Bret and the sex."

Nina's ice cream cone was gone, and I could see that she was really listening to her daughter. "Try, Casey. It isn't stupid."

"It just doesn't feel right to me, like it's ethically or morally wrong for you to have sex."

"Because I'm a mom?"

"Maybe."

"Casey, I understand how you could feel that way. Your father and I waited a long time before we separated. We worked on our marriage that whole time. It wasn't easy. He and I both sacrificed a lot to keep the family going. Most of that time, I felt like my happiness was secondary to the family's."

"You did?"

"Yeah, for a lot of years, Casey."

"Well, that wasn't good, either, Mom." She reached over and touched Nina's hand.

"I know that, Casey. But there weren't any easy choices for me. You mentioned the moral-ethical thing. For me, it's about the people around me and how you treat them."

"The choices were tough, Nina," I said.

"Yes, they were. I guess I never talked about it with Casey. I was trying to protect her," Nina said to me.

"Mom, it's better when you do talk. I can take it."

"I see that you can now, Casey, but a few years ago—you were pretty young."

Nina and Casey continued to talk in this session, and the one that followed. Nina was a good mother. She told her daughter more about her choices, but I could see that she was still trying to gauge how much a sixteen-year-old could handle. More than Nina had thought, but maybe not as much as Casey was pressing for. When the session ended, I sensed that their relationship was better—still bumps, but they were able to talk with each other directly.

I had a last meeting with each of them alone. My session with Casey was enlightening, as much for what she couldn't say as for what she could. We continued to talk about her feelings about her mother's recent sexual awakening.

"Yeah, she's toning it down, but there's something about it I still don't like."

"So toning it down hasn't solved everything?"

"That thing you said about moms having sex? Well, that's there. . . ."

"Any ideas, Casey?"

"Uh, really, it's, like, all kinds of things, but they're so dumb."

"I doubt that; try to say 'em."

"Okay. They're still noisy, but, Dr. Ponton, I'm trying not to listen. And she is so happy, all the time. That bothers me. Crazy, huh? She's wearing different clothes. She looks better than I do. Then she leaves him all these little Post-its all over the house—sweet, huh? Why does this stuff bug me so much? I'm spoiled, huh?"

"What makes you think that, Casey?"

"I don't sound like I care about her. I used to not think about her a lot. She was the perfect mom."

"Well, it sounds like you were pretty used to the way it was. She was taking care of you, and you really didn't think about her very much. What do you think about her life now?"

After a long pause, Casey said sadly, "It's better for her." Then she paused again before adding, "I'm kinda going with this guy now. Yeah. He's really, um, easy to talk to. We hang out together, watch videos and stuff."

"So your mom isn't the only one with the life that is changing."

She blushed and I could see she was trying to hide something. I looked away, and when I turned back, she was even more red.

"Charlie and I were lying on the couch watching this video. It was sad, so we had our arms around each other, real huggy. Then Bret and Mom open the door. They don't say anything except, 'Oh. Hi.' and they close the door. Embarrassing."

"What would you have liked them to do?"

"Not open the door, I guess, or maybe act more normal, like come in and watch the video with us."

"But it felt weird when they just closed the door. Did you and your mom talk about it?"

"Yep. She brought it up, said she was respecting my privacy."

"Sounds believable. What did you think?"

Casey's face was pretty crimson, and I could see tiny drops of sweat on her forehead.

"Well, I didn't do that with her."

"What do you mean?"

"I mean, I spied on them. I would, like, *try* to listen to them."

"From everything you said, Casey, they were kind of loud. It sounds like it was hard to avoid hearing them."

"Yeah, but I would really listen, you know, at their door."

"What do you think about that?"

"I don't know. I guess I was curious, but the privacy thing . . ."

"You're saying you didn't respect your mother's privacy."

No words came from Casey, but a quick nod answered my question.

"You must have felt pretty bad when she was here and we were talking about her toning it down."

Another nod, and then slowly, "Am I, like, a pervert for listening?"

"What do you think?"

"I don't know."

"Sex can be pretty hard to hide when you live close to people. You see things, hear things. Everyone gets curious, and it is stimulating."

Until I said the word "stimulating," Casey was with me. After that, I felt as though I had said the wrong thing.

"'Stimulating' as in her sex gets me excited? Is that what you're saying? 'Cause no way!"

"Casey, I didn't put that very well. What I meant was that it's difficult to be around your mom when she is so sexual. Lots of feelings come up." Now I was sweating, too.

"Okay, but me being turned on by it—no way."

"Got it." I thought about asking her more, like why it had bothered her so much to think that was what I meant, but I decided to keep quiet. Casey already had enough to think about for one session. We had talked about a lot that day. She had admitted to me and herself that she had violated her mother's privacy. She had also been able to talk about her beginning relationship with Charlie, not an easy subject for Casey, a girl who valued privacy and was very hard on herself about the intrusions she had made into her mother's life. Casey's harsh critique of her own behavior is common in adolescents. They hold themselves and others, including their parents, to very high standards. There is often a certain rigidity to what they expect in terms of behavior of all types, not only sexual. Their thinking can be very black-and-white in this way, and they are not very comfortable in the gray zone. One thing parents and adults can model for them is a greater flexibility, and the ability to examine things from different perspectives.

My final session with Nina also gave me quite a bit to think about. Like her daughter, Nina was examining her own behavior.

"Dr. Ponton, Bret and I are 'toning it down,' but I know you said there's more than that going on with Casey, and I agree with you."

"Nina, even if you toned it down completely, Casey would be having strong feelings. You and her father divorced, and you're remarried now, and a lot happier."

"I am. I worry that I've messed up badly with Casey, but I'm not sure what I should have done differently. She probably told you that I walked in on her when she was lying on the couch with her friend Charlie. It was probably innocent, but she looked so guilty. I guess I worry that my sexuality could push her, somehow—" She stopped here.

"Push her into being sexually active?"

"Yes. Of course, before I met Bret, I was worried about how she would see marriage, if she would think all of them were like her father's and mine. And that stuff she brought up about morals—I want her to have good morals."

"Nina, is there any reason why you think she might not?"

"Well, I got divorced and I fell in love with someone else."

"And you worry that your choices might affect Casey's morals and values negatively?"

"All the time."

"How did you act immorally?"

There was a long silence. Finally Nina spoke. "As principal of an elementary school, I help my teachers to develop programs for teaching morals and values, so I think a lot about it. When you ask it that way, Dr. Ponton, I realize that no matter what I teach, or even think about moral development, nothing fits here. Rationally, I don't believe that children of divorced parents have weaker morals or values, but intuitively I fear it. So maybe I'm biased."

"Maybe, Nina. It is often more difficult for kids when the parents are divorced, but you seem to be blaming yourself a lot here. You're still the same parent, working to help her daughter develop her own values and morals."

"Probably working harder than ever now!"

Nina is only one of many mothers and fathers I have worked with who worry about the impact of divorce and their subsequent sexual lives on their children. During the past thirty years, American families have changed a great deal. David Elkind, who writes eloquently about these changes, describes the transition of families of the 1950s and '60s—the original "nuclear" families, to the families of the '90s and beyond, whom he terms "permeable" families. Nuclear families not only included the well-known members—working father, stay-at-home mother, and children—they included a set of beliefs centering on the importance of maternal love and devotion to the family, often at the expense of the mother's needs and development, and the belief that relationships within the family are more important than those outside. Each of these sentiments encouraged maternal sacrifice for what was viewed as the good of the family. Elkind describes the permeable families of the '90s quite differently. There are, first of all, many different forms—traditional, two working parents, single working parent, blended, and co-parenting divorced, among others. But the most important change he notes is that the family is not so sealed; it communicates with the world. The families of the '90s are very different for mothers. The majority are working outside the home. Responsibilities at home and work can be tremendous. Role strain from overwork, both physical and emotional, can be overwhelming. Nina, struggling with her job as school principal, managing a home, and co-parenting Casey with her former husband, was aware of this burden, but she had very high expectations for herself. She was trying to fulfill the role of the nuclear mother, 100 percent available all the time, and the mother of the '90s simultaneously. It was impossible. To stop blaming herself was an important first step.

Nina's and Casey's story also brings up the important question of how to share morals and values with teens, and most important, how to help teens develop the ability to define their own morals and values. Values are principles of quality that individuals or groups see as having intrinsic importance. Morals—part of values—are more specific and focus on principles of right and wrong. As a teen grows, his or her beliefs in general principles that have some ideological basis are increasingly founded in the adolescent's own values rather than values passed on from parents or authority figures. This is a complex process that occurs in late adolescence, often long after emotional and physical development have taken place. There are also important differences between boys and girls in the underlying principles that they rely on as they develop morals. Boys tend to rely on traditional ideas about morality which emphasize justice, whereas girls emphasize those that prioritize care for others.

What does all this mean for teens and parents struggling with sexual issues? Developing a sense of one's own morals and values in the sexual arena is vital for teens. They resent being told what their values should be. Internally, teens are struggling with this process. They are often harsh with themselves and others, choosing extremes, seeing black-and-white more often than gray. Complicating this further, society often labels teens as lacking values entirely, unfairly scapegoating and angering them.

Helping teens to develop values in the sexual area is a partnership wherein adults act as guides, not judges. Much like learning risk assessment, this is a process that also is not easy. Teens learn from conversations with adults, but they also learn by example. They watch parents and other adults closely. Nina was having conversations with Casey about her moral choices during the period of her divorce and remarriage. Nina herself shared some of society's traditional values—women should be in the home, sacrificing for children and family. But at the same time her behavior was quite different. She worked outside the home and proceeded with her divorce and remarriage. Like her mother, Casey also expressed the belief that her mother's remarriage and sexuality was immoral. Since this is an area where teens struggle developmentally, it is especially important that parents discuss it with them. After our session, Nina again talked with Casey, sharing some of her conflicts about her choices, but indicated that she did not think she had done anything immoral, although her choices might conflict with societal beliefs. This conversation gave Casey another opportunity to talk with her mother about what she found uncomfortable about her mother's choices.

Casey's and Nina's story also reminds us that there is a place for privacy in matters of sexuality. When I brought up the importance of privacy with her own boyfriend, Charlie, Casey was able to admit that she had been intruding on her mother's privacy. I learned from a later phone call with Nina that she and Casey continued to have conversations about privacy and sex long after they stopped their work with me. A dialogue had begun.

Front-Page News

Teens learn about sex not only from what adults say but, more important, from what they do. I observe this on a daily basis, but on one particular afternoon I was hearing about it from Mrs. Waters, a worried high school counselor. She was calling me about sixteen-year-old Derek, a good student and a member of the basketball team.

"Dr. Ponton, I don't know if you saw it, but the article about his father, a prominent businessman, was in this morning's paper. The poor kid hasn't left my office today. He doesn't want to go to classes. He's sure all the other kids know."

"Know what?"

"Well, the article says that his father has been accused of sexual harassment by an employee, a secretary. There are some details, but it's a short article. I think Derek is overreacting."

"But you still called me?"

"Well, he is refusing to leave my office."

"And you think he would be willing to come to mine?"

"He said he would. I spoke with his mother by telephone, and she thinks it's a good idea."

"What about Dad?"

"Derek doesn't want his father called."

"Doesn't surprise me." I paused, stalling for time. I had a cancellation that afternoon, but I was tired and experience told me that a session with Derek was going to be highly charged—a boy's father accused of sexual harassment, the story on the front page of the paper, was definitely not easy stuff.

Mrs. Waters pressed ahead, encouraging me to see Derek. "You would really like him. He writes for the school paper. He could take the 43 bus over right now."

"Okay, let's try it."

I sensed her broad smile on the other end of the phone line. Getting a teen who isn't suicidal seen by a psychiatrist in less than an hour is quite a coup. I told the counselor to have Derek's mother call me. After confirming her permission for me to see Derek, I called back and said Derek should try to get to my office by three. Derek showed up a half hour later. He was carrying a sports bag, unzipped, with a basketball uniform falling out, but his clothing was neat and casual—khakis, a crew neck sweater. He was carrying the front page of that day's paper. He threw it on my desk before he sat down. "Take a look," he said. "Hope it doesn't shock you."

"I will read it, Derek, but first I want to meet you. I'm glad you got here so fast. Mrs. Waters was pretty concerned."

"Yeah, she wanted me out of her office so she could go home."

"I think she was worried about you, Derek. She said you haven't gone to any classes today."

He shrugged and sat quietly while I read. It was a short article, only two paragraphs, but on the front page. Derek's father and his partner were being sued by three women who worked for them, charging that their office environment promoted disrespectful behavior toward women. The article noted sexual insults, jokes, and obscene language, which the three women said took place every day. One of the women suing believed that most of the senior partners and the company administration treated women employees as sexual objects toward whom it was acceptable to express hostility.

The article did not list any specific offensive actions on the part of Derek's father, but it was frankly critical and must have been extremely difficult for Derek to read. I read it twice, trying to think about how to respond. I gave the paper back to Derek, and we sat silently for a couple of minutes. Finally I said, "Derek, that wasn't easy for me to read. I can't imagine what it was like for you."

He bent over and put his head in his hands, and stayed that way. After several minutes had passed, I tried again. "Derek, it's tough. Is there something I can get you, some water maybe?"

He looked up. His eyes were red. His voice cracked when he spoke. "You sound like my mom. You can't make this nice."

"No, I can't make it nice, Derek. But it might help if we could talk about it. What is your relationship with your dad like?"

"I used to think it was fine, good, even. It's been weird for a while, though, I guess. At least for me."

"What's made it weird?"

"I—" He paused. "I saw things about him I didn't know were there. Now everyone knows they're there."

"Because of what's in the paper?"

"Yeah. Did you know my mom called me at school to tell me? She wanted to tell me before anyone said anything. She read it in the morning paper herself, right outside, when she picked it up off the steps. There it was—front page."

The image of Derek's mother standing on the steps to their house reading about her husband, and his father, was painful for Derek. He winced twice while describing it, and again could not speak.

"Derek, have you talked to your dad?"

"Nope."

"Did he call the school?"

He shook his head. "I wouldn't talk to him anyway."

"You wouldn't?"

Again, he shook his head.

"Did your mom say anything about your dad when you spoke with her?"

"Only that he said he was sorry he hadn't known it was going to be in the paper."

"But he hadn't told her what was going on?"

"He hadn't told her anything." Derek sat straight up in his chair and began rereading the article. I sensed he was looking for something that might help him understand how this thing had happened.

"You have any ideas about what's going on with your father?" I asked.

He looked up from the article and spoke slowly. "Yeah . . . Yeah, I think I do. . . . I worked there last summer. Didn't like his partner, the guy they mention here. He was, like, real mean, and . . ." A long pause followed.

"And what, Derek? Is it about your dad?"

He stood up and walked over to my bookshelves. His face was turned away from me when he finally spoke. "My dad was kind of like this guy when he was with him."

"Kind of?"

Another pause. "A lot. I told my dad I thought the guy was a jerk. He acted like it was no big deal. I kept at it and finally he sort of agreed, but said he and this guy go way back, and that the guy wasn't gonna change."

"What did you do then?"

"I quit. Only had two weeks before school started anyway."

"But you didn't want to work there anymore?"

"No. It wasn't even being with that guy. It was watching . . . him."

"Your dad?"

"Yeah. It was awful."

"So the stuff in the article—it doesn't surprise you?"

"Some. I felt really bad about the office stuff, but I didn't expect it to be in the newspaper. Mrs. Waters, she's real nice, says most teens don't read the paper."

"But you're worried about what the other kids will think."

"Yeah. It's stupid, but I am worried. About them and my mom."

"How did she sound to you when you spoke by phone this morning?"

"She's pretty strong." He looked at me again with some relief. "You know, I think I told her why I quit a couple of months ago—not the stuff about my dad, but about his partner."

"That must've taken some courage. How did she deal with it?"

"I don't remember. My mom, she's real nice. She's always been supportive of me."

"But you don't remember what she said?"

"No. Funny, huh?"

"Maybe not, Derek, but worth paying attention to. You've also said your mom is nice a couple of times here today."

He shook his head and said, "I keep thinking about her standing there reading that paper. She told me her mother called after reading it, too. Grandma was shocked."

"Do you think your mom was surprised?"

"You're saying she knew?" He was looking right at me.

"I wasn't saying that, but I do wonder, after hearing what you told her."

"Maybe she knew but couldn't see it. Do you still have some water?"

"Sure." I stood up to get it. "Derek, this is going to be a rough road for your family. There's your dad's work situation, your relationship with him, your concern about your mother, your parents' relationship—how can we work together to help you? You're right that nothing's going to make this nice."

He smiled. "Just don't want you shoving it under the rug."

Like your parents? I wondered, but didn't say. "I won't, but you'll need to get through it."

"Well, maybe if I took a couple days off from school."

"How many's a couple?"

"The semester maybe." He laughed. "You're gonna think I'm one of those high-risk kids now, huh?"

"I don't think that. After today you probably need a break."

He smiled again. While he was packing up his athletic bag to go, his mother, Marie, called. I scheduled a time to meet with Derek's father and her the next evening. When I hung up, I asked Derek if he wanted to be there for the family meeting.

"No way. Only, one piece of advice."

"What's that?"

"Don't be too nice."

"Is that advice or a request?"

"I'm not sure."

The next evening, as I sat there with Derek's parents, I was thinking about his instructions. At this point, Bob, Derek's father, was saying for the umpteenth time that he didn't get why the women were suing him. Derek had given me permission to talk about what he and I had discussed, so I asked Bob why Derek had stopped working at his office last summer.

"He had to go back to school."

"Bob," interjected Marie, "he quit a couple of weeks early and told you he didn't like the way Jack was treating the employees."

"Marie, the kid is too sensitive. That's this business world."

My turn. "Bob, what do you think the impact of this situation is likely to be on Derek?" I wondered how much he knew, or let himself know, about his son's reactions.

"Well, hard on him—the stuff in the paper. I tell him it will blow over soon. He's just got to ride it out, that's all."

"How do you think he sees your behavior?"

"What do you mean?" His loud, hale-and-hearty voice dropped a couple of decibels.

"He told you he was so bothered by how Jack treated the women employees that he had to quit. Do you think he felt the same way about your behavior at the office?"

"I don't know."

"Does it matter to you how he feels?"

"Of course it matters. Look, I'll have him talk to my attorney; he's got a whole strategy for dealing with this."

"I'm not talking about what was in the paper, Bob. I'm talking about how your son saw you act when he was working at your office, and how he felt about it, about you."

Marie had been quiet until now. "Bob, Derek told me that he was ashamed of the way you treated the women. It made him sick to watch you. That's why he quit. Jack was only part of it."

Bob was silent.

"Marie," I asked, "have you and Bob talked about this before tonight?"

"I've tried. Bob doesn't listen."

"You've tried?" Bob sounded incredulous.

"Yes, I have, but I've been weak, too. Bob, when I saw the paper yesterday morning, I thought maybe I could have prevented this if I had talked more honestly with you about what Derek had said to me, and how I felt about it, too. I didn't. I was scared."

"Scared of what?" Bob seemed genuinely bewildered by this.

"Marie," I said, "it's hard to admit mistakes and try to do things differently."

"You know, I was upset for Bob when I first saw the article, but I was also glad." Her gaze shifted from me to her husband. "I guess I hoped it would cause—change."

The three of us sat in silence for a while. I didn't say anything to make it easier. Finally, I drew the focus back to their son. "How do you think we could help Derek at this point?"

"He's not going to school," said Bob. "He's gotta go to school."

"Any ideas about how we can help him with that?"

"Help him? We just tell him to go, that's all."

Marie spoke. "I don't think it would work, Bob. You can't do it, and I'm not going to. Maybe if you and I talk with him together, tell him we understand that this is difficult. That might help."

Bob nodded.

"Bob, where are you with what Marie said about her own feelings and those of your son's?"

"I don't know."

"But you heard her, right?"

"Yes."

"It's just important for you to listen now. Even when you feel you're being attacked professionally, it's important to listen to your wife and son."

He nodded again.

Derek did go back to school the following week. He and I talked for several weeks. I also met with Marie, Bob, and Derek twice. Those sessions were hard for everyone. Bob would either shut down, saying nothing, or push ahead, ignoring what the others were saying. When confronted by everyone, he would listen, sometimes. In contrast, Marie continued to speak her mind, and began her own therapy.

At one point, in a session alone with me, Derek said, "I thought my dad would change the day he saw that article in the paper—no way. Not my dad."

"When do you think things started to shift?"

"When my mother stood up to him. She told him she knew how those women in his office felt because she felt that way all the time. Then she walked out. I was there. Dad was shocked. His face kind of dropped to the floor, but then he recovered. He treats her differently now—he's kind of afraid of her."

"What's that like for you?"

"I just think he sees things that way—you're either on top or on the bottom—nothing in between. When he was putting that woman down at work, it was like that."

Derek had never talked about what he saw that made him quit working at his father's office. I took this opportunity to ask him.

"Celia, his secretary, is really loyal. She likes Dad. They worked together for six years—before Dad became partners with Jack. So one day Dad was out of the office, and Jack was treating all the women like dirt, screaming at them in front of the other employees. 'Women are for shit in this company! You are brainless. Why'd I ever believe women could do this job?' So these two women, they're pretty young, around nineteen or twenty, I guess, are really crying. Dr. Ponton, everyone was watching this, the whole office, with Jack and these other two guys sort of smirking, not doing anything. Celia was working with me. She got up, walked over, and said, 'Stop it, Jack.' He screamed something at her, and then Dad walked in. He saw the women crying, talked to Jack for one second, and then yelled at Celia to get back in her office—'where you belong.' Then he says to the women who are crying, 'Come on, be the beautiful ladies I know you are and just try and do better next time, okay? Because if you don't get your acts together around here, you're gonna be a disgrace to all the women doing such a good job waiting tables at topless bars.' It was sick. It was like he thought it was funny, what he was saying."

"How did you feel, Derek?"

"I was watching. I was watching the whole thing."

"What had you been thinking might happen when your father walked in?"

"I thought it would be different. When I saw home he acted, though, I didn't want to be his son. I didn't want to be me."

"Watching your father then must have been extremely hard for you, Derek. It sounds like it was difficult for you to separate yourself from him somehow."

He nodded. "Yeah, and not just then. Now, too. When I'm with girls now, I feel like I am him. Like I'm some monster, and they're scared of me."

"What do you mean?"

"I always think they're scared. Of me. I'm not great with girls. Any little thing, and I'm out of there."

"Was it always this way for you with girls?"

"No! I mean, I haven't had tons of experience or anything, but I didn't used to worry I was gonna be an asshole."

"Seems like you're scared you're going to act like your father."

"I know I'm not my father, but it feels like I could be."

Adolescents, like adults, struggle with moral dilemmas. Derek is not the only teen I've worked with whose father was accused of sexual harassment. He is the only one who witnessed his father's behavior. Other teens have denied it or minimized it—*My dad wouldn't do that . . . They're lying. . . .* Not only did Derek see what his father was doing, he made a moral choice to stand apart from it. He was a thoughtful young man who cared a great deal about others, including his father, and I admired the way he made his choices. His sexuality, however, suffered a great deal. Derek feared he would be like his father, and because of this anxiety, he became extremely inhibited. It was easier to stay away from girls altogether. Unfortunately, Derek and I worked together for only a couple of months. I fear it wasn't long enough to help him overcome what he was struggling with. I wasn't even altogether certain how interwoven his own identity was with that of his father, and how that played itself out in his sexuality. Did Derek have his own fantasies of behaving abusively toward women? How had he perceived his parents' relationship before he saw his father behave badly at work? What was really at the heart of his almost paralyzing discomfort with girls?

Do What I Say

Teens learn by imitation, particularly imitating those with whom they identify. Teens learn more from what parents do than from what they say. Derek had worked with his father for a summer. He saw how his father and his father's partner treated women. He had his own feelings about it, and decided that he himself could not work there any longer. His father's behavior made him sick, but as his father's son, he also felt that he, too, was somehow responsible for the same behavior.

His father, who eventually had to pay a financial settlement, did not believe that his behavior was inappropriate or offensive to women. Like many men who sexually harass, he could not see anything wrong with his behavior. With his partner, he was in an environment where others were harassing; the behavior was acceptable. As members of a gang, his responsibility for the behavior seemed difficult to quantify and grasp, even if he was the boss.

When confronted by his son about what he had seen and felt, Bob started to listen. He had been proud of his son, and Derek let him know that he felt badly let down, ashamed of his father's behavior. Bob also eventually began to listen to Marie, but not at first. She had to fight back and speak out loudly about how she felt about Bob's harassing behavior toward women in the workplace. It wasn't easy for Marie, who ended up questioning her marriage in the process, and who, when we last spoke, was still unsure what she wanted to do.

Harmful patterns of sexual behavior are everywhere. And teenagers are watching closely. Because they usually haven't had enough time to consolidate their own sexual ideas and identities, the risks for them can be quite high. We are potentially their greatest teachers. We need to pay attention to what they're learning from us.

EPILOGUE
Ready or Not

Fifty percent of America's sixteen-year-olds are having sexual inter-course, a figure that is actually lower than those in many developed countries. The United States excels in one area, however, that of danger-ous sexual risk-taking—i.e., unprotected sexual intercourse resulting in unwanted pregnancy and sexually transmitted diseases. For generations, this country has struggled with adolescent risk-taking of all types. Amer-ican culture is defined by risk-taking—the successful pursuit of the American Dream virtually requires it, but we are not a society particu-larly adept at risk assessment.

The general attitude about risk-taking is only one factor that con-tributes to higher rates of sexual risk-taking, however. Attitudes about sexuality also play an important role. Our culture is plagued with conflict about how to handle sexuality. Parts of this country are extremely re-strictive, discouraging masturbation, homosexuality, and even adoles-cent sex, and labeling them as crimes, sins, or sickness. Adults try to discourage young people from becoming sexually active by lecturing them about the virtues of virginity, by not openly discussing sexual mat-ters, and by making it difficult for teens to obtain contraception. Yet as much as conservatives criticize teen sexuality, the United States is not by any means a sexually permissive culture, despite the idealized and very disturbed views of teenage sexuality in the media. If anything, the United States is a fairly restrictive sexual culture characterized by strong taboos, poor communication, and restrictive gender roles. We do not give a consistent message about sexuality.

As the stories in this book reveal, teens struggle to discover their sexuality in a culture that is giving them a highly conflicted message. It is a tribute to their energy and power that many are able to develop healthy sexual lives. Many, sadly, are not.

Sexual education efforts in this country are paralyzed by these same conflicts. Many states insist on abstinence-based sex education efforts and do not allow access to contraception. Teens' views of their sexuality, however, differ from those of adults. For teens, the ways of sex are fraught with struggle, but also filled with excitement and pleasure.

While working on this book, I had the opportunity to speak with hundreds of teens about what their sexuality means to them. Some answered that it made them feel lovable, or more adult. Some described intense physical pleasure. Some told how it nurtured intimacy with another person, or fulfilled a desire to become pregnant, or promoted status in his or her peer group, or allowed for a surrender to desire or to another person. For some it brought relief from boredom or escape from life's pressures or an opportunity to test out biological equipment. For others, it involved reenactments of a sexually traumatic event from the past, or was useful as a tool for barter in obtaining money or material goods. Some characterized it as an expected part of a current relationship, a representation of "true love," a useful weapon, or a personal expression of growth and spirituality. As the stories in this book reveal, there is not one meaning, but many.

The sexual culture of the United States is not only confused, alternating its messages between restrictive and permissive, but violent as well. Violent sexual images are often transmitted through the media, but teens experience this violence in other ways, too. Teens struggling with their sexual identity or orientation fear that violence will be directed at them if they deviate from the norm. This affects all teens at some point in their lives, because at some point every teen feels that he or she is sexually different and fears reprisal. The narrow gender and sexual orientation norms affect all teens, not only girls like Angie or Miriam, who were sexually active at early ages, or boys like Joel and Ian, who believe that they are gay. Narrow gender roles force a macho identity on boys like Jacob and Rory, who are striving to become men in a patriarchal culture. Boys feel the pressure to rapidly acquire experience and become sexual experts, to have penises that are powerful. The culture reinforces and rewards this. For girls, the message is more contradictory. On the one hand, they, too, are encouraged to become powerful with their sexuality, told explicitly and implicitly to use it as their main source of control. On the other hand, girls who do this are often cast out as sluts. The double standard continues. Teens of both sexes are fearful as they struggle to develop and understand their sexual orientation. Frightened of their own feelings and the culture's reaction, some scapegoat others. Many adults encourage this attitude. Tolerance and understanding of sexual diversity are too little discussed or understood.

Into this restrictive, confusing, and punitive picture came the Human Immunodeficiency Virus (HIV). The lethal risks associated with HIV has been frightening for parents and teens alike. One quarter of those infected with the virus acquire it as teenagers. The crisis has encouraged the United States to begin to examine its attitudes about sexuality. In a recent interview I did with Dr. Joycelyn Elders, the former U.S. Surgeon General, she said that she believes that HIV has done more to change attitudes toward sexuality and sex education than anything else in the past decade. It has forced the United States to look at an area of taboo. Conversations about teen sexuality started. However, Dr. Elders also said, "We need to know what our teens are doing in the backseats of cars, and we don't." She's right about that, and of course it's not just what's going on in cars. Teens are sexually active everywhere—most commonly in their homes. Before we find out where teens are doing what sexually, we need to be able to both listen and talk with them about sexuality.

HIV is one factor that is forcing our culture to reexamine teen sexuality, but there is another—the teens themselves. Gilbert Herdt, professor of sexuality at California State University at San Francisco, notes that young people questioning their sexuality aren't satisfied with the answers they have been given, and are struggling to define a better world, one that is more tolerant and understanding of sexual diversity. Many of these teens have joined support groups, have written about their struggles, and have spoken out on these subjects with peers.

This book has introduced the idea of sexual readiness for teens. I believe that teens need to ask themselves several important questions before they become sexually active, including: whether they are engaging in sexual activity for themselves; whether they feel rushed by a partner or the situation; whether their bodies feel ready; whether they trust their partners; and whether they would be comfortable saying no, even at the last minute. (Please see the Appendix for a complete list of readiness questions for teens.)

This book also introduces the concept of parental readiness. Sonia's struggle to prepare herself to guide her daughter Miriam into a healthy sexual life, and Peter's struggle to understand Ian's sexual orientation illustrate the importance of parental contributions. Many parents know that they should prepare themselves to guide their child through the teen years, but when they think about sex they shut down. Rather than letting embarrassment paralyze them, it should act as a clue, helping parents detect what they are afraid of. In talking with teens about sex, it is important to be direct, use simple language, and admit to your own embarrassment. In general, teens don't like jokes about sex unless they are telling them, so begin slowly in this area. The discussions need to start long before a child is a teenager. Some ideas for earlier discussions include biological information, identifying and exploring language a child may learn outside the home, and observing and discussing messages around sexuality in the media. It is preferable for parents to talk about feelings and lessons they've learned through experience without disclosing specific personal details. Exploring stories about other teens—real or fictional—can also promote discussion. Ask teens for their opinions, don't just give them yours. Educate yourself about the spectrum of adolescent sexual behaviors. Enforcing rigid gender roles or sexual orientation can be extremely damaging. The wise parent recognizes that adolescence is about taking risks, sexually and in other ways, and will want his or her teen to have safe, healthy options, even if this means engaging in activity that runs counter to parental values. (For a complete list of suggestions for talking with teens about sex, please see the Appendix.)

All teenagers have sexual lives, whether with others or through fantasies, and an important part of adolescence is thinking about and experimenting with aspects of sexuality. This helps adolescents to discover and develop their individual sexual identity, a vital part of one's overall identity. Parents need to educate themselves about sexual identity, which is more than sexual orientation. Encouraging your teen to talk with other trusted adults about sexuality is also important.

Parents communicate values and morals best by example, so be aware of how you speak and act concerning sexual and gender issues in front of your teens, who are watching, whether they acknowledge it or not. They respond best to suggestions rather than directives, highlighting the importance of the parent's role as guide during these crucial years.

The imperatives around knowing more about teen sexuality extend to the culture at large as well. Parents should find out what sexual education their children and teens are learning in school, and what they are not learning. Many teachers will welcome parental input. There are other sources of sexual education besides school. Many youth organizations for girls and boys offer programs. Health care providers such as pediatricians, specialists in adolescent medicine, child and adolescent psychiatrists, psychologists, or social workers are familiar with programs and are available for individual consultation also.

Helping society understand this taboo and complex subject may seem overwhelming. Educating yourself and your child is an important place to start, but it is largely uncharted territory. Conversations about these important subjects are unusual enough among adults, so it is not surprising that they are even more rare between adults and teens. Adults have to start these conversations.

If you listen openly to your teens' own stories to learn about their hopes for and struggles with sex, and offer them guidance without being authoritarian, you will have gone a long way toward helping them develop their own healthy outlook on their sexual lives, and fostering the risk-assessment skills they'll need along the way.

APPENDIX

Guidelines for Teens: Thinking about Sexuality & Sexual Activity

1. All teens have sexual lives, whether with others or through fantasies. An important part of adolescence is thinking about and experimenting with aspects of your sexuality. This will help you to grow and discover who you are.

2. An important part of your sexuality is the physical changes your body goes through, for example, puberty, which includes the onset of the first menstrual period for girls, and the first emission of semen for boys. Because of changes in nutrition, these changes in your bodies occur at earlier ages than they did for your parents.

3. Many teens are physically ready for sexual activity before they are emotionally ready. It is important to think, learn, and plan for sexual activity.

4. There are many risks connected with sexual activity, including healthy ones (for example, feeling close to another person, enjoying physical pleasure, and learning about yourself), and unhealthy ones (for example, becoming pregnant or getting someone else pregnant;

or catching a sexually transmitted disease such as herpes, venereal warts, or HIV, among others).

5. Sexual intercourse of any type—vaginal, anal, or even oral—can transmit disease. It is important to learn the rules for safer sex and to be able to talk and negotiate with your sex partner in order to protect yourself.

6. Some of the red flags which indicate that you are involved in dangerous sexual risk-taking include participating in unprotected intercourse or having sexual relationships in which you do not trust your partner, or feel victimized or abused, or feel that you are abusing or victimizing someone else. If you are in any of these situations, it is important to ask for help.

7. Try to speak directly with your parents or other adults about sex, using simple language to describe both your feelings and activities. Remember that most adults, including your parents, are often more embarrassed than you are.

8. Sexuality is confusing for children, teens, and adults alike. There are extremes in our culture, with some believing that teens should not be feeling or acting sexually, and others projecting images of teen sexuality in ways that make you think all teens are sexually active. It is important to think about sex carefully, and develop your own ideas.

9. Before you become sexually active, it is important to prepare by learning about your own body, committing to safer sex, and maybe even role-playing tough situations so that you are ready to protect yourself when the time comes. "Sexual readiness" means more than whether your body is physically ready or able to have sex. (Please see the questions about sexual readiness in this Appendix.)

10. Respect your body and the bodies of others. Do not force yourself or others into any sexual activity, no matter what you may already have experienced with that person. Learn about what it really means to give consent for sexual activity, and think about it both for yourself and for any potential partner. It is important to think carefully about how you treat yourself and others in any form of sexual activity.

Ten Tips for Parents:
Talking with Your Adolescent about Sex

1. Speak directly with teenagers about sex, using simple language to describe both feelings and activities.

2. The discussions need to start early. If you wait to address sex until your child is a teenager, and then frame it only in terms of fears and prohibitions (e.g., risk of pregnancy or disease), it will be nearly impossible to develop reasonable communication. The topics will shift as your child matures, of course, but it will be much easier to address personal choices for sexual activity when your child is older if you have already had direct talks. Some ideas for earlier discussions include biological information, inquiring about and exploring language your child may hear outside the home, and observing and discussing messages around sexuality in the media.

3. Remember that sexuality is confusing for teens. Talk with them about the extremes in our cultural attitudes toward sex, from Victorian embarrassment to sexual provocation and exploitation.

4. Talking with teens about sex doesn't mean you have to discuss your own sexual experiences. It is possible, and preferable, to talk about feelings and lessons you've learned through experience without describing specifics. Exploring stories about other teens—real or fictional—can also promote discussion. Remember to ask teens for their opinions and ideas, and not just give them yours.

5. It is not one talk that makes the difference, but an ongoing dialogue, and communicated morals, values, and examples. Addressing what teens encounter in the media, and whether it is accurate or not, is important; it can also be a great way to start a discussion.

6. All teenagers have sexual lives, whether with others or through fantasies, and an important part of adolescence is thinking about and experimenting with aspects of sexuality. This helps adolescents to discover and develop their individual sexual identity, a vital part of overall identity.

7. The wise parent recognizes that adolescence is about taking risks, sexually and in other ways, and will want his or her teen to have safe, healthy options, even if he or she is engaging in a behavior that

runs counter to parental values. Encouraging your teen to talk with other trusted adults about sexuality is important.

8. Red flags that may help identify dangerous sexual risk-taking can include unprotected intercourse, repeated exposure to victimization in unhealthy or dangerous sexual relationships, or a history of sexually abusing others. Other more general psychological problems such as depression, anxiety, low self-esteem, self-mutilation, and clusters of unhealthy risk-taking (shoplifting and driving recklessly; gang activity and substance abuse) might occur at the same time.

9. Educate yourself about the spectrum of adolescent sexual behaviors. Enforcing rigid gender roles or sexual orientation can be extremely damaging. Also, be attuned to the pressures on teens around sexuality (e.g., gender roles such as being a macho male or, as a female, having to have a boyfriend, etc.).

10. Parents communicate values and morals best by example; it's important to be aware of how you speak and act concerning sexual gender issues in front of your teens, who are watching, whether they acknowledge it or not. Adolescents respond best to suggestions rather than directives, highlighting the importance of the parent's role as guide during these crucial years.

Aspects of Sexual Identity in Adolescence

Sexual identity makes up a large part of the overall identity of some adolescents; for others, it represents a smaller part. Like most adults, most teens have both private and public sexual identities. Sexual identity in adolescence is not always fixed and stable, but can be more fluid, changing over the course of the teen years or over a lifetime. Vital aspects of sexual identity include the following:

1. Self-esteem.
2. Fantasy life.
3. Orientation (homosexuality, heterosexuality, bisexuality).
4. Biological aspects (including a capacity for physical pleasure/orgasm),

sexual drive, and the level of physical development (including menarche and semenarche).

5. Desire and desirability.
6. Style, including how one makes sexual decisions or takes risks (e.g., adventurers, exploiters).
7. Fertility and reproductive aspects of sexuality.
8. Relationships (e.g., with parents, with sexual partners).
9. Sex or gender roles. These are characteristics and behaviors defined by society and specific cultures as appropriate for members of each sex. Culture, especially popular culture, affects adolescent gender roles and sexual identity directly. Here again, the impact varies depending upon the adolescent and may change with development.
10. Life events (e.g., loss of parent or partner, trauma).
11. Sexual behaviors (e.g., masturbation, intercourse, and a whole range of activities).
12. Spirituality. Sexuality is a complex subject for all teens; it frequently provokes larger questions about the nature of existence, the meaning of life, etc.

Sexual Readiness: Questions to Ask

1. Are you doing this for yourself?
2. Do you feel rushed by your partner, the situation, or yourself?
3. Is your body ready? Do you feel physical arousal and desire?
4. Do you trust your partner? Can you talk freely with him/her?
5. Would you be comfortable saying no, even at the last minute?
6. Have you and your partner practiced with other sexual experiences prior to deciding to have intercourse (foreplay using hands, mouth, genital and hip pressing, etc.)?
7. Have you planned for protection from pregnancy and sexually transmitted disease?
8. Are you able to engage in sexual activity without getting drunk or high first?
9. Are you knowledgeable about sex? Do you know what oral, anal, manual, and vaginal intercourse are?

10. Have you thought about the impact of this event on your life, considering whether it matches your values?

Sexual Activity and Teens: Some Possible Meanings

Being sexually active may have multiple meanings to adolescents. Certainly these meanings are highly subjective, and vary among individual teens. From the teen's perspective, it may mean or represent . . .

that s/he is lovable
that s/he is now an adult
physical pleasure
intimacy with another person
desire to become pregnant or have a child
status in his/her peer group
surrender to desire or to another person
relief from boredom or escape from life's pressures
desire to test out biological equipment or fertility
reenactment of a sexually traumatic event from the past
a sex "trade," i.e., a way of obtaining money or material goods
an expected part of his/her current relationship
"true love"
personal expression of growth
spirituality
a weapon or conquest

Understanding Sexual Abuse: Guidelines for Parents

1. In the United States, childhood sexual abuse has been reported up to 160,000 times per year. Although this figure appears high, such abuse is dramatically underreported both because children are afraid to tell and because the legal process is difficult. Statistics vary,

but actual abuse, whether reported or not, may occur with as many as one-third of all girls and one-fourth of all boys.

2. Once sexual abuse has been identified, the child should receive professional help. The long-term psychological effects can be devastating for children who have been sexually abused (see following item).

3. "Red flags" or symptoms that may help identify children who have been sexually abused can include unusually increased or decreased interest in sexual matters, sleep problems, school avoidance, self-harming or aggressive behaviors, seductiveness, and enactments of molestations in play.

4. Children who have experienced repeated incest may become passive and seemingly accepting of these acts over time, a process known as "the accommodation syndrome." They usually have low self-esteem and an abnormal perspective on sexuality.

5. Children who care for their abuser are often trapped between feelings of loyalty to that person and the sense that the sexual activities are wrong. Incest also affects a child's relationship with all other family members.

6. Sexual abuse of boys is seriously underreported. Like girls, boys are more commonly abused by men; these boys may experience confusion about their sexual identity and fears of homosexuality at the time of the abuse or later.

7. Children and adolescents who have been sexually abused are more likely to engage in dangerous risk-taking behaviors during adolescence, including coercive sex (as either the aggressor or the victim), unprotected sexual activity, and self-harming behaviors such as cutting, driving while intoxicated, and even suicide attempts.

8. Parents need to educate themselves about both normative and unhealthy sexual behavior in childhood, and promote good communication with their children. As a part of this, parents need to alert their children to the potential of adults touching their bodies, and encourage the children to tell them if this happens.

9. Parents need to encourage professional prevention programs in schools.

10. Parents need to pay attention to their own attitudes and behaviors around sexuality, including participation in dangerous patterns, ne-

glect of sexuality as a healthy aspect of life, or forced sex. Children are watching and imitating, whether they acknowledge this or not.

Ten Tips for Parents: Understanding Your Adolescent's Behavior*

1. All teenagers take risks as a normal part of growing up. Risk-taking is the tool an adolescent uses to define and develop his or her identity, and healthy risk-taking is a valuable experience.
2. Healthy adolescent risk-taking behaviors that tend to have a positive impact on an adolescent's development can include participation in sports, the development of artistic and creative abilities, volunteer activities, travel, running for school office, making new friends, constructive contributions to the family or community, and others. Inherent in all of these activities is the possibility of failure. Parents must recognize and support their children with this.
3. Negative risk-taking behaviors that can be dangerous for adolescents include drinking, smoking, drug use, reckless driving, unsafe sexual activity, disordered eating, self-mutilation, running away, stealing, gang activity, and others.
4. Unhealthy adolescent risk-taking may appear to be "rebellion"—an angry gesture specifically directed at parents. However, risk-taking, whether healthy or unhealthy, is simply part of a teen's struggle to test out an identity by providing self-definition and separation from others, including parents.
5. Some adolescent behaviors are deceptive—a teen may genuinely try to take a healthy risk that evolves into more dangerous behavior. For example, many adolescent girls fail to recognize the trap of dieting and fall into a pattern of disordered eating, sometimes even developing a full eating disorder. Parents need to be well-informed in order to help their adolescents with such struggles.
6. Red flags that help identify dangerous adolescent risk-taking can include psychological problems such as persistent depression or anxi-

*From *The Romance of Risk: Why Teenagers Do the Things They Do,* Lynn E. Ponton, M.D., (Basic Books, 1997)

ety which goes beyond more typical adolescent "moodiness"; problems at school; engaging in illegal activities; and clusters of unhealthy risk-taking behaviors (e.g., smoking, drinking, and driving recklessly might be happening at the same time, as might disordered eating and self-mutilation, or running away and stealing).

7. Since adolescents need to take risks, parents need to help them find healthy opportunities to do so. Healthy risk-taking, not only important in itself, can help prevent unhealthy risk-taking.

8. Adolescents often offer subtle clues about their negative risk-taking behaviors through what they say about the behaviors of friends and family, including parents. Parents often stay silent about their own histories of risk-taking and experimenting, but it can be important to find ways to share this information with adolescents in order to serve as role models, to let teens know that mistakes are not fatal, and to encourage making healthier choices than those the parent may have made during his or her own adolescence.

9. Adolescents look to their parents for advice and modeling about how to assess positive and negative risks. Parents need to help their teens learn how to evaluate risks and anticipate the consequences of their choices, and develop strategies for diverting their energy into healthier activities when necessary.

10. Parents need to pay attention to their own current patterns of risk-taking as well. Teenagers are watching, and imitating, whether they acknowledge this or not.

ENDNOTES

Introduction: Forbidden Fruit

1. Steinberg, L. 1999. *Adolescence* (5th ed.) San Francisco: McGraw Hill, 335. For twenty-five years, Lawrence Steinberg has written and updated one of the finest texts on adolescence. His section, entitled "How Sexually Permissive Is Contemporary Society?" deserves close reading.

2. Yates, A. 2000. "Normal sexual development." In *Textbook of Adolescent Psychiatry*, ed., R. Rosner. Washington, D.C.: American Psychiatric Association Press. Alayne Yates, professor of psychiatry at the University of Hawaii, has also written about adolescents and sexuality for more than twenty-five years. She concurs with Steinberg: The culture in the United States is either sexually restrictive or semi-restrictive, at best. It is not permissive.

3. D'Emilio, J. and Friedman, E. B. 1997. *Intimate Matters: A History of Sexuality in America* (2nd ed.) Chicago: University of Chicago Press. An excellent history of sexuality in the United States. The section on the 1970s and 1980s chronicles the development of the "New Right" political movement and identifies its impact on how we look at adolescent sexuality, emphasizing the vital role played by politics.

4. Ponton, L. E. 1990. "Adolescent dreams: An examination of their sexuality." In *Dialogues: Journal of Psychoanalytic Perspectives* 8:49–56. Many teens will talk about their sexuality. Some will not, at least not directly. This paper discusses how adolescent sexuality is revealed in dreams.

Chapter 1: Studs and Sluts

1. Ponton, L. E. 1996. "Sexual harassment of children and adolescent girls." In *Sexual Harassment in the Workplace and Academia: Psychiatric Issues,* ed., D. Schreir. Washington, D.C.: American Psychiatric Press, 181–201. Sexual harassment of girls is still largely an unrecognized problem. This article discusses how it occurs and what therapists and parents can do when it does.
2. Tanenbaum, L. 1999. *Slut.* New York: Seven Stories Press. This easily readable book would appeal to teens and parents alike. Leona Tanenbaum wrote about a number of self-identified sluts, and offers practical advice.
3. Ponton, L. E. 1993. "Issues unique to psychotherapy with adolescent girls." In *American Journal of Psychotherapy* 47(3):353–372. Several books and articles have focused on the problems of teenage girls. This article outlines the major problems and strategies for helping girls address them.
4. Orr, D. and Ingersoll, G. 1995. "The contribution of level of cognitive complexity and pubertal timing to behavioral risk in young adolescents." In *Pediatrics* 95:528–533. This article focuses on pubertal timing and cognitive patterns to adolescent risk-taking.
5. Orr, D. and Ben-Eliahu, E. 1993. "Gender differences in idiosyncratic sex-typed self-images and self-esteem." In *Sex Roles* 29:271–296. Donald Orr, a specialist in adolescent medicine, has written a number of thoughtful articles on gender and the onset of puberty in teens.
6. Pleck, J., Sonnestein, F., and Ku, L. (1994). "Problem behaviors and masculinity ideology in adolescent males." In *Adolescent Problem Behaviors: Issues and Research,* eds., R. Ketterlinus and M. Lamb. Hillsdale, NJ: Lawrence Erlbaum, 165–186. The "macho" image is a tough one for teenage boys. Teens and parents alike need to understand the dark side of this stereotype.
7. Steinberg, L. 1999. *Adolescence* (5th ed.). San Francisco: McGraw Hill. Again, this is the most comprehensive text on adolescents that I have found. Lawrence Steinberg writes extensively about gender issues in the teen years.

Chapter 2: Here Comes Puberty

1. Schowalter, J. E. and Woolston, J. L. 1987. "Adolescence." In *Pediatrics* (18th ed.), ed., A. Rudolph. Los Altos, CA: Appleton-Lange, 44–50. This is an academic article that includes some well-hidden definitions, *tupura* among them.
2. Havens, B. B. and Swenson, I. 1988. "Imagery associated with menstruation in advertising targeted to adolescent women." In *Adolescence* 23(89):89–97. This article highlights how media portrays and influences girls' first experiences with tampons. The messages are subtle, but extremely effective.
3. Berg, D. H. and Coutts, L. B. 1993. "Virginity and tampons: The beginner myth as a case of alteration." In *Health Care for Women International* 14(1):27–38. A second article discussing media influence in this intimate area of girls' and women's lives.

4. Lupton, M. J. 1993. *Menstruation and Psychoanalysis.* Urbana and Chicago: University of Illinois Press. Menstruation, like many other areas of sexuality, is largely taboo. Ms. Lupton's book is an enjoyable read that informs us about this hidden topic.
5. Brooks-Gunn, J., Samelson, M., Warren, M. P., and Fox, R. 1986. "Physical similarity of and disclosure of menarche status to friends: Effects of age and pubertal status." In *Journal of Early Adolescence* 6(1):3–4. Peers play important roles during the teen years. Sharing news about the first period and those that follow is important, allowing girls to support each other.
6. Herring, L. 1992. *Celebration of the Maiden.* Spring Valley, CA: Chinaberry Press. In contrast to *The Period Book,* this is a more spiritual version of this milestone in a young girl's life. Some girls prefer this more narrative, yet entertaining book.
7. Gravelle, K. and Gravelle, J. 1996. *The Period Book.* New York: Walker and Co. This is a carefully written and well-illustrated book on periods for girls. The drawings are definitely not Walt Disney. I recommend it to all.
8. Schlegal, A. and Barry, H. 1991. *Adolescence: An Anthropological Inquiry.* New York: Free Press. This is a fascinating sociological reference work on adolescence.
9. Bataille, G. and Sands, K. 1984. *American Indian Women: Telling Their Lives.* Lincoln, NB: University of Nebraska Press, 35–37. Not all cultures have hidden this developmental milestone. This book reveals the stories of several Native American women.

Chapter 3: Alarming Arousal

1. Huhner, M. 1939. *Sexual Disorders.* Philadelphia: F. A. Davis Co., 179. This is a medical text with wide use in the 1940s and 1950s, revealing frightening but important ideas about sexuality that were believed and taught. Masturbation and homosexuality are two of the topics in this volume identifying "disorders."
2. Stekel, W. 1923. *Onanii und Homosexualitat.* Berlin. Masturbation—or onanism, as it was once called, mistakenly, for the sin of Onan in the Bible (which was withdrawal prior to perceived ejaculation, not self-stimulation)—was historically often linked with homosexuality, and both were conceptualized as sins or diseases. It is important to remember that these ideas are alive and well today. Teens are still affected by them, leading to self-doubt, self-hatred, and repression of their own sexuality.
3. Blos, P. 1962. *On Adolescence.* New York: The Free Press, 159–162. This is a classic volume on the topic of adolescence. Peter Blos highlights the importance of sexuality in teen development. Like Sigmund Freud, he emphasizes the resurgence of childhood feelings (both pre-Oedipal and Oedipal) in adolescence as part of the reworking of childhood issues before an adolescent enters adulthood.
4. Person, E. 1995. *By Force of Fantasy: How We Make Our Lives.* New York: Basic Books. Ethel Person understands the vital role that fantasies, both sexual and otherwise, play in teen and adult lives alike. Her work is well written and fascinating, and should be at least perused by anyone with an interest in this subject.

5. Smith, A. M., Rosenthal, D. A., and Reichler, H. 1996. "High schoolers' masturbatory practices: Their relationship to sexual intercourse and personal characteristics." In *Psychological Reports* 79(2):499–509. Masturbation foreshadows the patterns of intercourse that follows. Girls' hesitations in this area potentially have many implications, including an uneasiness with intercourse.

6. Leitenberg, H., Detzer, M. J., and Srebnik, D. April 1993. "Gender differences in masturbation and the relation of masturbation experience in preadolescence and/or early adolescence to sexual behavior and sexual adjustment in young adulthood." In *Archives of Sexual Behavior* (2):87–98. This is an academic article highlighting gender differences in fantasy and masturbation among teens.

7. Jones, J. C. and Barlow, D. H. 1990. "Self-reported frequency of sexual orgasm, fantasies, and masturbatory fantasies in heterosexual males and females." In *Archives of Sexual Behavior* 19(3):269–279. A similar article focusing on college students.

8. Benson, R. C., Jr. Jan. 25, 1985. "Vacuum cleaner injury to penis: A common urological problem?" In *Urology* (1):41–44. An academic article, but it underscores how frequently this actually happens.

9. Osca, J. M., Broseta, E., Server, G., Ruiz, J. L., Gallego, J., and Jimenez-Cruz, J. F. 1991. "Unusual bodies in the urethra and bladder." In *British Journal of Urology* 68(5):510–512. An academic article with similarities to Benson's classic article. It is quite revealing regarding the number and types of objects that can be inserted into the penis.

Chapter 4: Safety in Numbers

1. Elkins, G. R., Gamino, L. A., and Rynearson, R. R. 1988. "Mass psychogenic illness, trance states, and suggestion." In *American Journal of Clinical Hypnosis* 30:267–275. This academic article focuses on trance states, highlighting groups such as teens who are uniquely susceptible. Currently there is a type of teen music termed "trance," which acknowledges that it is trying to bring about an altered state of mind.

2. Nemzer, E. 1996. "Somatoform disorders." In *Child and Adolescent Psychiatry*, ed., M. Lewis, 693–702. Baltimore, MD: Williams and Wilkins. Professor Elaine Nemzer is almost as fascinated with tarantism—a medieval concept that suggested the nighttime bite of a spider sparked a teen's risky behavior—as I am. Teens repeatedly tell me that they are able to feel things while listening to music that they are not able to experience in other ways. Sexual feelings are only a part of this, but one that parents often ignore when they see teens moving to the beat of their headphones.

3. Ponton, L. E. 1997. *The Romance of Risk: Why Teenagers Do the Things They Do.* New York: Basic Books. The present chapter on moshing highlights how risk-taking and sexuality are interconnected. Adolescent risk-taking of all types is fully discussed in this book.

Chapter 5: Coming and Going Online

1. Magrid, L. 1994. *Child Safety on the Information Highway.* Arlington, VA: National Center for Missing and Exploited Children. See following note.
2. Magrid, L. 1998. *Adolescent Safety on the Information Highway.* Arlington, VA: National Center for Missing and Exploited Children. Each of these pamphlets can be obtained by contacting the National Center for Missing and Exploited Children in Arlington, VA. They can be reached at 877-466-2632.
3. Bremer, J. and Bauch, P. 1998. "Children and computers: Risks and benefits." In *Journal of the American Academy of Child and Adolescent Psychiatry* 37(5):559–560. This is an easily readable article on the pros and cons of computers for children and teens, highlighting both sides of the issue.
4. Siege, R. and Dietz, W. 1994. "Television viewing and violence in children: The pediatrician as agent for change." In *Pediatrics* 94:600–607. It is important to understand that television shows as many, if not more violent images, to children than Internet sites and video games.

Chapter 6: Unnatural Partners?

1. Bouris, K. 1994. *The First Time.* Berkeley, CA: Conari Press. Karen Bouris is a sensitive interviewer and writer. Her well-chosen words about girls' and women's first sexual experiences capture the pain and poetry.
2. Alan Guttmacher Institute. 1994. *Sex and America's Teenagers.* New York: Alan Guttmacher Institute. For years, the Alan Guttmacher Institute has devoted its resources to the study of teenage sex, conducting and publishing landmark studies. This glossy report is packed full of information.
3. Ponton, L. E. 1997. *The Romance of Risk: Why Teenagers Do the Things They Do.* New York: Basic Books. Again, this book describes how risk-taking is used to shape teens' identities.
4. Katchadourian, H. 1990. "Sexuality." In *At the Threshold*, eds., S. Feldman and G. Elliot. Cambridge, MA: Harvard University Press. A comprehensive article on sexuality in a well-written text on adolescence.
5. Wolf, N. 1996. *Promiscuities.* New York: Random House. Naomi Wolf writes about the development of her own and a close group of girls' sexuality. This is a well-written book that took considerable courage to write.
6. Moen, P., Erikson, M. A., Dempster-McClain, D. 1997. "Their mothers' daughters? The intergenerational transmission of gender attitudes in a world of changing roles." In *Journal of Marriage and the Family* 59:281–293. That mothers' attitudes about their own sexuality and gender affect their daughters' is certainly no surprise. This article, however, highlights the importance of change in this process.
7. Usmiani, S. and Daniluk, J. C. 1997. "Mothers and their adolescent daughters: Relationship between self-esteem, gender-role identity, and body image." In *Journal*

of Youth and Adolescence 26:45–55. Well-known authors in the area of female sexuality, their works are thoughtful and inspiring to others.

8. Grogan, S., Williams, Z., and Conner, M. 1996. "The effect of viewing same-gender photogenic body models on self-esteem." In *Psychology of Women Quarterly* 20:569–575. No surprise, girls' self-esteem spirals downward when they look at same-sex models in photos.

9. Sorenson, R. E. 1973. *Adolescent Sexuality in Contemporary America.* New York: World. This is a very early volume, but a classic. I only wish these studies could be repeated today.

10. Savin-Williams, R. 1994. "Verbal and physical abuse as stressors in the lives of gay male and bisexual youths: Association with school problems, running away, substance abuse, prostitution, and suicide." In *Journal of Clinical and Consulting Psychology* 62:261–269. This author is one of the most thoughtful writing on gay youth. Although often an academic writer, he has a very readable and well-researched book, *And Then I Became Gay* (1998, Routledge), another classic in this area. This article highlights the strong association between abuse of gay youth and unhealthy risk-taking.

11. Herdt, G. and Boxer, A. 1996. *Children of Horizons.* Boston, MA: Beacon Press. Gilbert Herdt is a well-known teacher and writer in the field of sexuality. This book, coauthored with Andrew Boxer, chronicles the lives of gay teens in Chicago. It includes an important historical perspective on how gay identity has evolved over the past decades. There are many interesting ideas here.

12. Pipher, M. 1994. *Reviving Ophelia.* New York: Ballantine Books. This popular book highlights the problems of adolescent girls. It reads easily and addresses some aspects of sexuality.

13. Pollack, J. 1998. *Real Boys.* New York: Random House. Written several years after *Reviving Ophelia,* this book highlights the problems of boys—teens and younger. Sexual matters are only a small part of this book.

14. Roberts, E. J. 1980. *Childhood Sexual Learning: The Unwritten Curriculum.* Cambridge, MA: Ballinger. A well-written early work on childhood sexuality.

15. Roberts, E. J., Kline, D., and Gagnon, J. 1978. *Family Life and Sexual Learning,* 10. Cambridge, MA: Population Education. Another well-written, early work on childhood sexuality.

16. Giovacchini, P. L. 1986. "Promiscuity in adolescents and young adults." In *Medical Aspects of Human Sexuality* 20(5):24–31. Giovacchini is an adolescent psychiatrist with a well-developed interest in sexuality. This article is both informative and easy to read, highlighting the differences between teens and adults.

17. Petchesky, R. 2000. "Sexual rights." In *Framing the Sexual Subject,* eds., R. Parker, R. M. Barbosa, and P. Aggleton. Berkeley, CA: University of California Press. A recent volume that highlights aspects of sexuality that have been ignored. Sexual rights is one such area. Just what are sexual rights? This author does not lay them out in stone, but suggests that the opportunity to develop a healthy sexual identity and not experience violation from others are crucial aspects. It is interesting to me

that there is little discussion about this subject in a country that values rights so highly; this underscores how strong the taboos are regarding anything sexual.

18. United Nations. September 1995. Platform for action of the Fourth World Conference. Beijing, China, 4–15. Even the United Nations struggles with saying "sexual rights," although it is clear that violations of sexual rights are worldwide problems. This Fourth World Conference on Women in Beijing did speak out, however, noting that rights need to be talked about and protected.

19. Joannides, P. 1999. *The Guide to Getting It On.* Hollywood, CA: Goofy Foot Press. An explicit and practical guide to sexual activity. Parents and teens alike can learn from this humorous text.

Chapter 7: Not My Child

1. LYRIC stands for the Lavender Youth Recreation and Information Center (415-703-6150). This is an important organization for teens in Northern California.

2. Puterbaugh, G., ed., 1990. *Twins and Homosexuality: A Casebook.* New York: Garland. Twin studies indicate that genetic contributors play a role in sexual orientation. How much of a role remains an open and much-discussed question.

3. Tyson, P. 1982. "A developmental line of gender identity, gender role, and choice of love object." In *Journal of the American Psychoanalytic Association* 31:61–86. In this thoughtfully written article, Phyllis Tyson, a psychoanalyst, discusses the development of different aspects of sexual identity.

4. Massad, C. 1981. "Sex-role identity and adjustment during adolescence." In *Child Development* 52:1290–1298. The first article to suggest that teenage girls might function better with a combination of masculine and feminine traits.

5. Orr, E. and Ben-Eliahu, E. 1993. "Gender differences in idiosyncratic self-images and self-esteem." In *Sex Roles* 29:271–296. Similar to Massad's article, the authors here conclude that more androgynous girls—those with a combination of masculine and feminine traits, function better. This refers to character and characteristics, not physical appearance.

6. Allgood-Merten, B. and Stockard, J. 1991. "Sex-role identity and self-esteem: A comparison of children and adolescents." In *Sex Roles* 24:129–140. One of the first studies to suggest that children, both boys and girls, with a combination of masculine and feminine traits function better.

7. Stein, J., Newcomb, M., and Bentler, P. 1992. "The effect of agency and communion on self-esteem: Gender differences in longitudinal data." In *Sex Roles* 26:465–484. This academic article describes the benefits of a combination of male and female traits for men and women.

8. Steinberg, L. 1999. *Adolescence.* New York: McGraw-Hill. Lawrence Steinberg devotes considerable space to the subject of gender role in adolescence.

9. Cohler, B. (Unpublished manuscript.) "Psychoanalysis and homosexuality." In *The Report from the Committee on Scientific Activities of the American Psychoanalytic Association.* I was fortunate to be able to read this manuscript in one of its later

drafts. The sections on adolescent sexuality are extremely well written, authored by Andrew Boxer and Bertram Cohler. This manuscript raises vital questions about sexual orientation and, more importantly, does not feel obliged to answer them.

10. Herdt, G. and Boxer, A. 1996. *Children of Horizons*. Boston: Beacon. An outstanding and easily readable work, focused on the lives of young gay men in Chicago, but touching on many important issues related to sexual identity.

11. Ponse, B. 1978. *Identities in the Lesbian World. The Social Construction of Self.* Westport, CT: The Greenwood Press. This author discusses the "coming out" process, identifying how it is different for women. Although in general there is a movement away from a step-by-step developmental structure to more fluid models of sexual identity staging, it is important to understand what these models include and how they might be different for boys and girls.

12. Troiden, R. 1989. "The formation of homosexual identities." In *Gay and Lesbian Youth,* ed., G. Herdt. New York: Harrington Park Press, 43–74. Troiden's staging of homosexual development is generally accepted, but has been critiqued for the reasons that other staging models have been—things don't always follow the expected format.

13. Savin-Williams, R. 1998. *And Then I Became Gay.* New York: Routledge. This book tells many stories about being gay, beginning with feelings in earliest childhood and ending in late adolescence.

14. Savin-Williams, R. 1990. *Gay and Lesbian Youth: Expression of Identity.* Washington, D.C.: Hemisphere Publications.

15. Remafidi, G. 1991. "Risk factors for attempted suicide in gay and bisexual youth." In *Pediatrics* 87:869–875. Gary Remafidi has conducted many studies on risk behaviors of gay youth. His work is considered controversial by some, too much of a focus on negative risk-taking, but he highlights how important it is to identify such behaviors in a culture that is not receptive to gay youth.

16. Erikson, E. 1958. *Young Man Luther: A Study in Psychoanalysis and History.* New York: Norton. This is one of Erikson's less familiar books that focuses on the life of young Martin Luther, using his story to highlight some of the developmental struggles young people go through.

17. Magie, M. and Miller, D. 1997. *Lesbian Lives: Psychoanalytic Narratives, Old and New.* Hillsdale, NJ: Analytic Press. Two psychoanalysts have written a well-researched volume discussing many aspects of lesbian lives. This book is more than psychoanalytic narrative; it identifies the vital struggles and developmental steps that many lesbians experience.

18. Brown, M. L. and Rounsley, C. A. 1996. *True Selves: Understanding Transsexualism.* San Francisco: Jossey-Bass. An outstanding volume on a hidden and distorted subject—transsexualism. It reads easily, explains what is known more than adequately, and asks the questions that need to be asked.

Chapter 8: A Tale of Two Pregnancies

1. Luker, K. 1996. *Dubious Conceptions: The Politics of Teenage Pregnancy.* Cambridge, MA: Harvard University Press. Kristen Luker dispels many myths in this well-written book about teen pregnancy.
2. Ludtke, M. 1997. *On Our Own: Unmarried Motherhood in America.* Berkeley, CA: University of California Press. More and more women are deciding to become mothers without marrying. The largest proportion, over two-thirds, are adults, not teenagers.
3. Dean, A. L. 1997. *Teenage Pregnancy: The Interaction of Psyche and Culture.* Hillsdale, NJ: The Analytic Press. This book is a sensitive and well-written volume telling the tales of many teen pregnancies. Seldom does it "just happen," and often it happens to the same person more than once. This author highlights how culture, family, and a girl's individual characteristics can all affect the risk of teen pregnancy.
4. Ponton, L. E. 1997. "Mothers and daughters: The slippery slope." In *The Romance of Risk: Why Teenagers Do the Things They Do.* New York: Basic Books. This is a story of mother-daughter conflict and closeness which illustrates the role that mothers play in helping their daughters learn to assess and take risks.
5. Adler, N., Kegales, S., Irwin, C., and Wibblesman, C. 1990. "Adolescent contraceptive behavior: An assessment of decision processes." In *Journal of Pediatrics* 116:463–471. Decision-making around risk-taking is itself a very complex process; this article, a complex but valuable read, examines it from several perspectives, highlighting the many factors involved in use or nonuse of contraception.
6. Alan Guttmacher Institute. 1994. *Sex and the American Teenager.* New York: Alan Guttmacher Institute. This institute has focused its work on America's teens. Understanding why a teen girl makes a decision to have an abortion is important. It's not an easy choice.

Chapter 9: Lara's Theme

1. Yates, A. 2000. "Normal sexual development." In *The Textbook of Adolescent Psychiatry,* ed., R. Rosner. Washington, D.C.: American Psychiatric Press. Alayne Yates, a professor of psychiatry in Hawaii, has devoted decades of her life to the study of child and adolescent sexuality. Her thoughtful conclusions about teen sexuality elucidate why this area is so difficult for teens and parents alike.
2. DiClemente, R. J. 1998. "Preventing sexually transmitted infections among adolescents: A clash of ideology and science." In *Journal of the American Medical Association* 279(19):1574–1575. This carefully written editorial alerts us to how we are exposing our teens to increased risk of sexually transmitted diseases when we choose an abstinence-based sex education intervention.
3. Jemmott, J. B., Jemmott, L. S., and Fong, G. T. 1998. "Abstinence and safer sex HIV risk-reduction for African-American adolescents: A randomized controlled

trial." In *Journal of the American Medical Association* 279(19):1529–1536. This article compares safer sex and abstinence-based education programs and indicates that safer-sex programs offer teens a full range of sexual choices and have much longer-lasting effects, such as safer behavior and more frequent use of condoms, especially among teens who are already sexually active. More than half of American teenagers are sexually active by the age of sixteen. Half of African-American boys are sexually active by the age of fourteen, African-American girls by sixteen.

4. Freud, S. 1955. *Totem and Taboo*. In The Standard Edition of the Complete Psychological Works of Sigmund Freud, J. Strachey, ed. and trans., 13:1–161. London: Hogarth Press. (Original work published 1913.) Freud was quite interested in how taboos develop among primitive people. This essay teaches us much about how we currently regard adolescent sexuality, even in our contemporary civilized society. A central idea in this work was that violation of a taboo would lead to punishment. Many teens, not just Lara, share in this thinking.

5. Bowler, S., Sheon, A. R., D'Angelo, L. J., and Vermund, S. H. 1992. "HIV and AIDS among adolescents in the United States: Increasing risk in the 1990s." In *Journal of Adolescence* 15(4):345–371. Special Issue on HIV/AIDS and adolescents. An extensive academic article that highlights and predicts risks related to adolescent occurrence of HIV infection.

6. Wingood, G. M. and DiClemente, R. J. 1998a. "Partner influences and gender-related factors associated with noncondom use among young adult African-American women." In *American Journal of Community Psychology* 26(1):29–51. See following.

7. Wingood, G. M. and DiClemente, R. J. 1998b. "Gender-related correlates and predictors of consistent condom use among young adult African-American women: A prospective analysis." In *International Journal of STD and AIDS* 9:139–145. Both of these articles focus on how young African-American women make decisions about condom use. The authors point out how important it is for girls to learn to negotiate with their partners. Although the focus is on African-American girls, this work has relevance for all girls.

8. Wingood, G. M. and DiClemente, R. J. 1997. "Child sexual abuse, HIV sexual risk, and gender relations of African-American Women." In *American Journal of Preventive Medicine* 13(5):380–384. This article highlights how sexual abuse limits girls' abilities to negotiate and protect themselves sexually—vital skills.

Chapter 10: The Dark Side

1. Ponton, L. E. 1997. "Fighting back." In *The Romance of Risk: Why Teenagers Do the Things They Do*. New York: Basic Books. This present chapter revisits themes I first wrote about in the story and discussion of Jim in *The Romance of Risk*. Jim was abused by a group of boys—scapegoated and assaulted—and suffered inescapable consequences that extended far into his adult life.

2. Hussey, D., et al. 1992. "Male victims of sexual abuse." In *Child and Adolescent Social Work Journal* 9(6):491–503. The consequences of sexual abuse for boys and

men are seldom addressed, but they are always felt. Even though a boy may not be experiencing overt symptoms after he has been abused, it is important to obtain a compassionate and thorough assessment, and treatment, if required.

3. Isley, P. and Isley, P. 1990. "The sexual abuse of male children by church personnel: Intervention and prevention." In *Pastoral Psychology* 39(2):85–99. Boys are sexually abused by church personnel from all religious backgrounds. Besides suffering the loss of an often trusted adult, the abuse is often complicated by a loss of spirituality and religious faith.

4. Stoller, R. J. 1975. *Perversion: The Erotic Form of Hatred.* New York: Pantheon. Robert Stoller was a well-respected teacher at UCLA who pursued the study of sexuality with passion. Although twenty-five years old, this book is a classic and helped me understand why there is such power, even in stories of perverse sex.

5. Plante, T. G., ed. 1999. *Bless Me Father, For I Have Sinned: Perspectives on Sexual Abuse Committed by Roman Catholic Priests.* New York: Praeger. A volume that comprehensively addresses the subject of sexual abuse by priests, this multiauthored book is extremely thoughtful and makes several sound suggestions regarding what the Catholic Church can do in the way of intervention and prevention. For anyone interested in abuse by religious personnel, this is a necessary resource.

6. Schulhofer, S. October 1998. "Unwanted sex." In *Atlantic Monthly* 55–66. This well-written article focuses on how the United States needs to develop a clearer definition of sexual consent. Several of the cases described here involve teens. Currently, many prosecutors require evidence of considerable physical force before they will prosecute for rape. What constitutes force? Are bruises and broken limbs necessary, or is lying on top of someone enough? The author suggests that we shift our emphasis to protection of rights, in this case, sexual autonomy.

7. Kerschner, R. 1996. "Attitudes about rape." In *Adolescence,* 31(21):29–34. This well-written article gives statistics, as well as attitudes, regarding adolescents and rape.

8. U.S. Department of Justice. 1985. "Crimes of rape." Washington, D.C.: U.S. Department of Justice Publication 96777.

9. Timnick, L. August 25, 1985. "22 percent in survey were victims of abuse." In *Los Angeles Times,* 1, 34.

10. Greensite, G. 1999. *Historical, Psychological, and Sociocultural Aspects of Sexual Assault.* Santa Cruz, CA: Rape Prevention Resource Center. This is a very well-written, historical analysis of rape, offering a wealth of clinical knowledge about both the abusers and the abused.

11. Cassidy, L. and Hurrell, R. M. 1995. "The influence of victims' attire on adolescents' judgments of date rape." In *Adolescence* 30(118):319–324. This study reveals that teens, like adults, believe that girls dressed in provocative clothing are asking to be raped. I believe that girls need to understand that this is a common attitude, whether they agree with it or not, and make wise choices in light of it. Both boys and girls, as well as society at large, need to be educated in order to change this misconception.

12. Goodchilds, J. D., Zellman, G., Johnson, P., and Giarrusso, R. 1988. "Adolescents and their perceptions of sexual interactions." In *Rape and Sexual Assault,* ed., A. W. Burgess, vol. II. New York: Garland. This article covers the question of how teens perceive sexual consent. There is, of course, a range of beliefs about this important matter, but going on a date or accompanying a boy to his residence or car can indicate consent to some. Studies like this indicate how important it is to educate teens about what constitutes consent, and to ensure that our laws define it adequately.

13. Shalit, W. 1999. *A Return to Modesty: Discovering the Lost Virtue.* New York: Free Press. Wendy Shalit's book argues for a return to modesty in dress, behavior, and attitudes as a solution to many of the problems in the sexual arena that females struggle with. This position places the responsibility on the shoulders of girls and women, and discounts both the double standard that is alive and well and the violent culture in which we are raising our sons and daughters. Yes, it is wise to counsel our children of both genders about the real and perceived implications of girls' attire, but at the same time, boys and girls need to understand issues of sexual rights and consent. Ms. Shalit is also opposed to much sexual education—too embarrassing. I say better embarrassed than infected.

14. Kindlon, D. and Thompson, M. 1999. *Raising Cain: Protecting the Emotional Lives of Boys.* New York: Ballantine Books. This book thoughtfully discusses boys who exploit others.

Chapter 11: None of My Business

1. Elkind, D. 1992. "Why kids have a lot to cry about." In *Psychology Today,* May–June, 38–41. David Elkind has written extensively about the evolution of the American family. He describes how it is evolving still, and most importantly, how this impacts on children and parents. Changing women's roles are only one of the factors noted here.

2. Ponton, L. E. 1997. "Career and parenting: Making it work." In *Dilemmas of a Double Life: Women Balancing Careers and Relationships,* ed., N. Kaltreider. Northvale, NJ: Jason Aronson, 141–165. This chapter is one of several in this volume that focus on women's multiple and changing roles.

3. Steinberg, L. 1999. *Adolescence,* 292–299. San Francisco: McGraw Hill. A fine discussion of the moral development of teens is included in this comprehensive text.

4. Gilligan, C. 1982. *In a Different Voice: Psychological Theory and Women's Development.* Cambridge, MA: Harvard University Press. This classic work on how girls develop and change in adolescence explains how girls and boys think differently not only about morals, but many aspects of life.

5. Gilligan, C., Lyons, N., and Hamner, T. 1990. *Making Connections: The Rational Worlds of Adolescent Girls at Emma Willard School.* Cambridge, MA: Harvard University Press. This book continues to expand upon issues related to girls' moral development. A well-written essay, "When is a moral problem not a moral problem,"

by Lyn Mikel Brown, suggests that what constitutes a moral imperative for girls is not always considered moral by the culture at large.

6. Kohlberg, L. and Gilligan, C. 1971. *The Adolescent As a Philosopher: The Discovery of the Self in a Post-Conventional World.* New York: Daedalus, 100, 1051–1086. It is interesting to note that Kohlberg and Gilligan worked together at an early point in their study of adolescent moral development. This thoughtful paper highlights the boys' perspective, but is an interesting read.

7. Bondurant, B. and White, J. W. 1996. "Men who sexually harass: An embedded perspective." In *Sexual Harassment in the Workplace and Academia,* ed., D. Schrier, 59–79. Washington, D.C.: American Psychiatric Press. An academic article, but one that is both readable and enlightening about the perspective of men who harass. The entire volume is valuable and includes various articles about harassment, including a discussion of sexual harassment of children and adolescents.

Epilogue: Ready or Not

1. Neinstein, L. and Nelson, A. 1996. "Contraception." In *Adolescent Health Care,* ed., L. Neinstein. New York: Williams and Wilkins. This adolescent health care guide offers clear, basic information about teen health.

2. Ponton, L. E. 1997. *The Romance of Risk: Why Teenagers Do the Things They Do.* New York: Basic Books. Included here is a discussion of American culture as one characterized by risk-taking, not risk assessment.

3. Former U.S. Surgeon General Dr. Joycelyn Elders kindly agreed to speak with me about contemporary American teens when I interviewed her on behalf of the American Academy of Child and Adolescent Psychiatry. A copy of that interview was published in the March 2000 *Academy Newsletter*.

4. Gilbert Herdt, professor of sexuality at the State University of California, San Francisco, and coauthor of *Children of Horizons,* has devoted much of his work to the study of adolescent sexuality. These comments are based on an in-person conversation we had in 1999.

Lynn Ponton, M.D., a professor of psychiatry at the University of California, San Francisco, and a psychoanalyst, is a leading figure in adolescent psychiatry who has spent more than twenty years working with teenagers and their parents. Dr. Ponton's work has been featured in leading newspapers and magazines, including *The New York Times* and *Newsweek,* and she has appeared on *60 Minutes* and *Dateline.* She has two teenage daughters and lives in San Francisco.

BOSTON PUBLIC LIBRARY

3 9999 03959 021 9

WITHDRAWN
No longer the property of the
Boston Public Library.
Sale of this material benefits the Library.

ALLSTON

GAYLORD S